The
Ancient
Tea Horse
Road

The Ancient Tea Horse Road

Travels with the Last of the Himalayan Muleteers

Jeff Fuchs

VIKING
CANADA

VIKING CANADA

Published by the Penguin Group

Penguin Group (Canada), 90 Eglinton Avenue East,
Suite 700, Toronto, Ontario, Canada
M4P 2Y3 (a division of Pearson Canada Inc.)

Penguin Group (USA) Inc., 375 Hudson Street,
New York, New York 10014, U.S.A.
Penguin Books Ltd, 80 Strand, London WC2R 0RL, England
Penguin Ireland, 25 St Stephen's Green,
Dublin 2, Ireland (a division of Penguin Books Ltd)
Penguin Group (Australia), 250 Camberwell Road, Camberwell,
Victoria 3124, Australia (a division of Pearson Australia Group Pty Ltd)
Penguin Books India Pvt Ltd, 11 Community Centre,
Panchsheel Park, New Delhi – 110 017, India
Penguin Group (NZ), 67 Apollo Drive, Rosedale, North Shore 0745,
Auckland, New Zealand (a division of Pearson New Zealand Ltd)
Penguin Books (South Africa) (Pty) Ltd, 24 Sturdee Avenue,
Rosebank, Johannesburg 2196, South Africa

Penguin Books Ltd, Registered Offices:
80 Strand, London WC2R 0RL, England

First published 2008

1 2 3 4 5 6 7 8 9 10   (RRD)

Text and photography copyright © Jeff Fuchs, 2008

Manufactured in the U.S.A.

Library and Archives Canada Cataloguing in Publication data available upon
request to the publisher.

Visit the Penguin Group (Canada) website at **www.penguin.ca**

Special and corporate bulk purchase rates available;
please see **www.penguin.ca/corporatesales** or call 1-800-810-3104, ext. 477 or 474

To those men of stone, the lados,
who "journeyed through the sky,"
and to a little woman from Batasek
who started it all.

An ancient tea set sits on a traditional burner in Weishan, Yunnan.

Contents

What started it all—a simple cup of tea.

I

Shangri-La, China: Curry, Tea, Horses, and Men

Maps are but pieces of paper.

—DORJE KANDRO

"BHASKAR'S CHICKEN CURRY, yes, and, of course, the dumplings, and the yak with local mushrooms and herbs ... and knowing you, you'll want some tea." Dakpa's accent was unusual to my ear, and his speech was littered with words from the five languages he had in his arsenal. His suggestions of what to eat were not suggestions but statements. This was what I would be eating. Dakpa's handsome, unshaven face gleamed as he trotted off to the kitchen of Arro Khampa, the restaurant he co-owned, to deliver the order to the chef, Bhaskar, himself. I was sitting in a Tibetan restaurant in a place called Shangri-La in southwestern China, ordering Indian food that would be prepared by a Nepali chef.

At that moment, the confluence seemed perfect, as all these regions were to play a role in my imminent journey along one of the most treacherous and lengthy trade routes on Earth. Two days had passed since my arrival at this eastern entrance to the Himalayas, and the realization that it was the culmination of a bold three-year plan to travel the mythical Tea Horse Road pulsed through me. Three years of dreaming, fretting, and planning can be as tortuous as it can be inspirational, but here I was in Shangri-La awaiting the beginning, a tracing of the route into the clouds. The earth still held signs of the winter freeze, and nearby mountaintops retained a white crust as a reminder of where we were. It was two days short of May.

Shangri-La had, at one time or another, been known variously as Zhongdian, Jiantang, and Gyalthang. At thirty-three hundred metres, it sits in a valley in the Hengduan Mountains, which marks the eastern edge of the rugged Tibetan Plateau. It would function as a regrouping and refuelling point, and a home of sorts for me: homes away from home were to become a recurring theme in my life in the coming months. Many disputes have arisen as to the origin of Shangri-La, as well as to who had territorial control of it, but the what and the where seemed unimportant now, as the name had become inducement enough to draw the masses. Shangri-La had at one time been part of Kham, the easternmost section of the old Tibetan empire, and in the hearts of Tibetans it still was. On modern maps, it sits in the northwest chunk of Yunnan Province, in southwestern China. While the old town has remained tiny, each year the number of gift shops selling identical wares grows and the idea of Shangri-La as a tranquil place of beauty seems more remote.

Here in the mountains, the senses were forced open, widened and sharpened, the air expelling the muddled sensations that come with airports and travel. The grey ambiguity of cities was erased by daily cleansings of sun and wind.

My last couple of days had been spent acclimatizing and letting the environment seep in, heaving in gulps of air and marvelling at the speed of change even here, at the edge of paradise. I had arrived in Shangri-La from the "big grey" of Beijing via Kunming, the capital of Yunnan, and any last-minute doubts about my upcoming travels had subsided as rubber touched the tarmac. Remnants of the harsh winter remained in the winds that blew recklessly through town, and the onslaught of tourists had thankfully not yet started. In recent years, the majority of travellers to Shangri-La had been Asian tourists who were content to walk, shop, and leave. It was the modern world's version of paradise, now accessible by plane. You could simply stroll in to the mountains, breathe in the sharp air, hop back on a plane, and take off. But if you were to remain and wander through the green, soothing hills to the monasteries, feel the winds and the unrelenting sun, you would glimpse nature's version of Shangri-La, and perhaps get just a sniff of the town's past. My reasons for coming here were to find neither the modern world's paradise nor nature's. I had come to find out about an ancient route—a route that had been known to Asians for centuries but that had successfully remained a mystery to outsiders.

In Shangri-La there was a time when the only outsiders who passed through came bearing goods on the backs of mules, and they came not in search of paradise but to set off on an ominous journey. They were intrepid voyagers with set destinations on brutal schedules, and their destination was the very heart of the Himalayas. Known as Gyalthang then, the town had played host to these travellers and their cargo as it now played host to me.

Leading caravans along mountain edges, into blizzards, and through bandit-ridden hills were the *lados,* the deliverymen (and they were all men) on the highest trade route on Earth, and for centuries leagues of the mighty muleteers led traders and mules loaded with cargo destined for Tibet, India, Nepal, and other points west. It was this route of a thousand forks, bends, subsidiary paths, and feeders crossing and re-crossing through the Himalayas that I had come to explore. But the muleteers whose livelihood had them trudging through the mountains had become a dying breed. In the corridors of stone, engines now ruled. Motorcycles, tractors, roaring trucks, and cars conveyed cargo now, the fearless duo of man and mule no longer considered practical. Men willing to battle dust and stone, and risk death daily, were no more. Tough and weathered, clad in leathers and skins, the muleteers spent most of their lives in perpetual motion, ferrying goods to and fro, winding their way in disciplined ranks through dozens of cultures and over dizzying peaks. Their exploits had rarely been heard of. A few of these men and women—the women having travelled the route in other capacities or with relatives who did—still lived but had never recorded their stories. Theirs was an oral history, the memories kept alive by the tongues of a handful of survivors.

In a little more than a week, I and five others would begin the first segment of a journey to trace what remained of the famed passage through the mountains that came to be called the Tea Horse Road. But before our own journey, and even before the journeys of the hardened traders, there had been another voyage, one that had prompted the

mythology of the Tea Horse Road, a voyage that had to do with politics, a fair maiden, and a vivid green leaf.

DURING CHINA'S TANG DYNASTY (618 to 907), borders were ever
changing, and the armies newly unified under King Songtsen Gambo,
of the Tibetan Tubo Dynasty, were considered a potential threat to the
East. In a shrewd ploy, the Chinese leaders came up with a simple but
effective plan of appeasement. In the fashion of the time, they would
offer the king of Tibet a bride in an attempt to forge a politically expe-
dient alliance. Marriages of necessity were not uncommon, and
throughout Asia borderlands had thus been secured, however briefly.

The mighty Tibetan king already had one wife, of Nepali blood,
which effectively secured the southern border of Tibet, and an offer
from the Tang Dynasty helped ensure a safe middle frontier between
the two expansionist empires. Wives were considered a commodity,
used as insurance and for political unions. A king having multiple
wives was a wise strategy, as it was through the women of royal families that the armies were linked. It was agreed that the beautiful
Princess Wencheng, a niece of the Tang emperor Taizong, was to be
the bride, and a magnificent dowry was prepared. All manner of gifts,
including silks, seeds, scriptures, and statues, were ornately prepared
in massive quantities to be transported in a bridal convoy to the
mountain kingdom of Tibet. One other item was added, an item that
initially seemed of little value: just a few hundred leaves, the importance of which would eventually overshadow all economic, political,
and marital negotiations for a thousand years. The leaves were known
as *cha* to the Chinese, *jia* to the Tibetans—tea. This contract of the
flesh would lead to centuries of contracts of "the leaf."

Escorted by a Tibetan envoy, the princess's kilometres-long caravan
left the Tang Dynasty's capital of Chang'an (modern-day Xian) and
began its withering journey, which according to historians took somewhere between a year and three years, to meet her betrothed. The
journey covered three thousand kilometres and took the princess
from the most populous city on Earth at the time to one of the most
remote. Through the fierce western hinterlands and deserts and into

the grey peaks of the Himalayas, it was a journey few other than the mountain peoples could, or would want to, make. Dust, bandits, and fleas were along for the journey, but the caravan did eventually arrive in Tibet, bride and dowry intact, in AD 641. Few of the orderlies, emissaries, eunuchs, soldiers, and mules could have conceived of the historic impact of their inconspicuous green, leafy cargo.

The union of the Tubo king and the Tang princess ushered in a brief period of peace and an unending period of tea. The princess's generous dowry was shared throughout the kingdom, the tea being the most well received of her gifts. Once a treat consumed only by royals in Tibet, tea quickly became widely used as both a tonic and a food of the masses. Before long, it was considered a necessity by the nation. Tea also became an essential part of tributes the Chinese courts gave to neighbours and allies, and particularly to the Tibetans. It became an invaluable political tool, and as such, its importance would only increase for the next thirteen hundred years.

Then came the tricky part for the Chinese imperial court. Tea was a success—such a success that it became a commodity like no other for the tribes of the Tibetan Plateau. As an offering for perceived slights or a bribe for oversights, it gradually became a bargaining chip without equal; it became, in social terms, the great panacea. While peace reigned, the attention of the Chinese was focused on how to get more tea to the Tibetans in the least amount of time.

Although the route the princess had taken was practical for politicians and dignitaries travelling from the Tang capital to Tibet, a more direct route was needed for the increasing amounts of tea being sent into the kingdom, a route that linked the tea sources—tea plantations in southern Yunnan Province—to the distant tea drinkers in the high, arid mountains of Tibet. And so, an ancient mountain path experienced a revival, a renaissance. Having long ago been used for trading salt, silks, and jewels, and favoured by marauders eager to rob passing traders, the forked path found new life with tea's ascension in value. Before long, it was humming with renewed activity as caravans of tea from the humid south of Yunnan made their way north and west, destined for the princess's new domain. The Tibetan tribes referred to the trail as Drelam (Mule Road), or more commonly as Gyalam (Wide Road).

Tea's rise to prominence occurred at a time when the Tang Dynasty was desperately trying to secure its fractious northern borders, and China's supplying of tea in vast amounts to Tibet was part of a wider strategy, one involving a much-valued four-legged animal. The importance of horses, never doubted in the Tibetan and nomadic regions farther west, suddenly grew for the Chinese: with cavalries, the Chinese's military force would be more mobile, and this could only help solidify their claims to lands. There were no horses, and indeed few animals, with as valued a pedigree as those from that desolate land to the west, where a Tang princess now resided: Tibet.

A convenient and mutually beneficial exchange began, and the tea trail became a tea and horse trail. Tea and horses became much-sought-after commodities, meeting briefly on their travels along the road as they passed each other travelling in opposite directions. Tea was strapped onto mules and moved west along the perilous cliffs, as nimble, raw-boned horses destined for military service moved east. In time, the road became Asia's predominant overland trade and migration route. Monks, maidens, armies, pilgrims, pillagers, and migrants all passed along its precarious paths, and it became so important that it was given the name "Eternal Road"—an eternal road that took lives, moved lives, and gave life. Linking dozens of isolated cultures, the road was also crucial in keeping alive cultural and economic exchange along its thousands of kilometres. Known from the jungles of Southeast Asia to India's great northern expanse, the passage had regained a purpose, and gained another name, Cha Ma Dao, the Tea Horse Road.

The fair princess would eventually pass away, as would dynasties, kingdoms, and treaties, but tea and its highway, the Tea Horse Road, would survive for more than a millennium. Market towns were born, and existing towns along the route became swollen with products, traders, buyers, and intermediaries. In southwestern China, the ancient tribes that harvested and grew tea now had markets leagues away spurring on their economies. India happily imported wool and tea, and exported textiles, dyes, and trinkets via the road. Year-round, the Tea Horse Road buzzed with traffic, couriering items of news and trade, including, of course, that most precious of commodities, tea. For many of the remote tribes it was the only link with the outside world, a vital information pipeline. Trade passed along the seemingly immortal, ancient highway until it reached a feverish pitch during the Second World War, when it once again proved indispensable, providing an alternative supply route for goods, contraband, and personalities. But this proved to be its swan song: activity gradually slowed to a trickle, a trickle that then slowed to a halt. The Cultural Revolution had brought the beginning of the end to the fabled route. By the mid-1960s, that omnipotent intruder, the paved road, cut both time and distance for traders, making the dirt paths, the unheralded mules, and the muleteers themselves obsolete.

MY OLD FRIEND DAKPA, with his lean figure and long hair, returned to the table with a steaming pot of *masala chai*, an Indian spiced milky tea. I often wondered if he didn't have some DNA from the subcontinent in him, lover of all things Indian that was he.

I had first encountered the charismatic Dakpa on a journey I had made a few years earlier to Shangri-La to satisfy a longing to visit the easternmost extension of the Tibetan Plateau. Dakpa's love of local lore and the obsession we shared with tea and Bollywood music bonded us, and it had been while listening to his life story that I learned of the Tea Horse Road. On one of our jaunts into the mountains, my view of a stunning peach-coloured sunset was interrupted by his long finger pointing at a faint line leading down the length of the valley. It seemed not much more than a wisp of dirt. Barely a path, it looked to be a herdsman's trail at most. In his deep voice, Dakpa told me of an ancient trade route that for centuries had been used to transport tea, horses, and other goods in and out of Tibet in mule caravans. Unknown to the rest of the world—no outsiders had travelled its length—this was a route for only the ambitious, and the desperate.

"My journey from India back here after my monkhood was along this Himalayan highway," Dakpa said, his voice softening.

As the wind blew dusk into the valley, my eyes traced what little there was of the path as it wound its way into the darkening hills, the sunset all but forgotten.

"Why don't we travel the entire route?" I ventured impulsively.

Dakpa smiled but said nothing as his eyes strayed into the distance. Then he nodded his head and said, "We should do it."

He hadn't ridiculed the idea! Our mutual wanderlust and the love of mountains were powerful forces in both of us. We shook hands on it, pledging before a Himalayan sunset that somehow, some way, at some point, we would do it. That point came three years later.

"Drink while it's hot." Dakpa poured a cup of the chai and shoved it at me. Its sweetness sent quivers through my jaw. Food came a short time later in the hands of the chef, Bhaskar. A bull of a man and wearing a chef's hat that added two feet to his short stature, he set the dishes down on the table with quick movements. The introductions made, he insisted we eat while the food was hot. As we ate, he hovered about us, his eyes boring into our plates and then our faces. It soon became clear that he would hover until he was satisfied that the meal was adequate. We mumbled compliments to him through mouthfuls, and he strutted off, content.

Minutes later, dull thuds on the restaurant's stairs signalled an arrival. "Yaaa," said the figure coming toward us, and Dakpa welcomed Dorje Kandro, a rugged-looking man wearing a small Stetson—Asia's version of the Marlboro Man. Moustached and smelling of wood and tobacco smoke, Dorje's eyes had a wild glint, and his movements spoke of someone far more comfortable out of doors than within the confines of walls. A smile playing at the corners of his mouth suggested that he found life amusing. Dakpa had earlier remarked, "You will love him; he is a very special person. He'll be with us for the segment to Lhasa. In the mountains, no one is better." Sitting down to join us, Dorje grinned and lit a cigarette. His scarred and callused hands seemed abnormally large, and strong. Dorje was, in the words of Dakpa, "part horse, part goat, and a tiny bit human." As I looked at him, I suspected that there was more than a hint of good-natured mischievousness in him as well.

Dakpa and I had spoken many times of the type of people we wanted with us on the journey. Physically able, yes, but of equal importance was that they understood that our intention was not to conquer a peak, race through an environment, or skim over the surface of a landscape in record time. One of the major components of the trip was the human element. Tucked away in valleys or perched on mountains were those few remaining men and women who had trav-elled along the routes, the last generation to have suffered the hard-ships of the incredible undertaking. The geography, stunning as it might be, was nothing without the journeyers who gave life—often theirs—to the Tea Horse Road. As well as the physical passage along what remained of the old trail, I wanted to visit these people, to record their words. I knew they had stories to tell and little time left in which to tell them.

Dakpa's ability to evaluate people was the reason he was in charge of choosing a team for our expedition. I could tell by the way Dorje looked at Dakpa that they shared a deep trust and respect. I was now anxious to meet up with the three other members of the team with whom I would be spending the upcoming months, living, sharing, and struggling.

Nomè, a relative of Dakpa's, I knew from previous journeys. In the three years I had known him, nothing about him had changed. Even his cheap runners looked the same. Steady and calm, with hazel eyes and a boyish grin, Nomè was an understated man and Dakpa's first choice for any major expedition. He would be joining us as do-it-all maintenance man and chef. His cooking abilities would be key in keeping our bodies, including our bowels and by extension our minds, in good working order. A cook who could after a day of misery raise the spirits without a word cannot be overrated. His moderation in all things—his speech, his gestures, his attire—would provide a centre point of balance. Long ago I had stayed with his family in a nearby town, and his entire clan had that same understated compe-tence. Nomè had once said to me that, in life, there were people who pondered and spoke, and there were people who acted. He was in every sense someone who acted.

Sonam, recently back from studying in India, was wiry, with cheek-bones that seemed to stretch his skin to the breaking point. He had an intense, respectful countenance that was at once schoolboy shy and sagelike. His English had taken on an accent from his years of public school in India. But Dakpa had told me not to underestimate him. "He is incredibly tough; he can go all day," Dakpa had said. Sonam's home-town, a day's drive north of Shangri-La, was a land of extremes, known for both its ruthless bandits and its ardent devotion to Buddhism.

The last to arrive at the restaurant was the team member I was the most curious to meet. With no real experience in the mountains or trekking, this young man had told a huge lie to his boss in order that he might come with us on the most difficult mountain segment of the journey. I was introduced to a short, thickset man with outrageously white teeth. This was Norbu, a local Tibetan news cameraman in his mid-twenties. He seemed mild mannered and exceedingly polite, but there was a determined set to his muscled shoulders, and to the look in his eyes. When Dakpa asked him how things were going with his boss, he shrugged and said, "There is no way that I am not going." With those words he cemented my confidence in him, and in his will. He would later tell me, "I need to see this part of my history. It is a part of our culture that is dying." Like Dakpa and me, he was passionate about getting to the elders and recording their memories and thoughts. He was exactly the kind of person we wanted to have with us on the journey. Will was an important characteristic that you couldn't fake and a quality essential for any trial in nature's mountain bastions. You either had it or you didn't, and Norbu seemed to be imbued with it.

In Asia, the notion of fate had long held sway over the decision making of the secular world, but for our journey we would need a balance of the two. Fate and will would prove far more important than any of us could have imagined. Vehicles, roads, electricity, and mobile phone shops may have pushed their way into the mountain abodes, but towering perilous mountains were never far away. Stone and snow still guarded the passes, harbouring unimaginable and unrivalled power.

THE NEXT FEW DAYS, our world consisted of maps, phones, papers, permits, and gear, with the required visits to Arro Khampa to eat. Bhaskar's curries and biryanis were consumed with abandon, with much of them ending up on maps and phones. It was during these meals that our team became just that.

Maps in Chinese, in English, and in Tibetan accompanied us wherever we went, poking out of pockets, folded into small squares to be opened and referred to time and time again. Maps can enthuse and feed the psyche far more than you might think. Dorje, in his increasingly frank way, voiced his rather cynical view of them. "For Tibetans, maps are but pieces of paper," he proudly told me. His statement was valid, for few show the extent to which paths, trails, and spurs access the towns, or the huge empty spaces in the Himalayan corridors. Waving his hand at a map's graphs and delineations in disgust, he told me that the tradition of the people of the mountains was to pass down knowledge and reference points to their children orally.

We planned to travel the two main strands of the Tea Horse Road, cutting each into segments. First we would follow the oldest and most vital of the two strands, the four-thousand-kilometre Yunnan–Tibet Tea Horse route, which wiggled and plunged its way from the south of Yunnan Province northwest into Tibet before heading west to Lhasa. From Lhasa we would head southwest along the arid highlands into northeastern India. The second route would be along the Sichuan–Tibet Tea Horse route, which originated in Ya'an, in western Sichuan Province, and eventually hooked up with the main Yunnan route. By rough calculations of to-ing and fro-ing, which included going off the trail to find the precious remaining elders, we figured that we would cover close to ten thousand kilometres in total. Breaking up the journey in this way was not an unusual way to travel the Tea Horse Road; seldom did a lado ferrying tea travel the entire route. Instead, the tea went through a number of handlers and was loaded and unloaded along the way. As the terrain changed, so, too, would the mules and muleteers, with subtropical jungle specialists making way for those experienced in the higher lands.

Shangri-La had been a transition zone, a place for those headed for Tibet to switch to heartier mules and the heartier-still muleteers capable of traversing the approaching high passes. It was here that the mighty Khampa (people of Kham) lados took over, if they weren't already a part of the caravan, and it was here that the six of us would begin our journey. We would start with the longest and most rugged section of the Tea Horse Road, knowing that if unforeseen delays due to nature, humans, or just fate were to occur, they would likely occur in these isolated passes of snow and rock. The spectre of injury, storms, and exposure hovered at the edges of all our minds; we knew that all our preparation and planning could easily come to naught in a blink of an eye. If we needed more time, it would surely be along what one old trader had called "the final test"—the segment from Shangri-La to Lhasa. A loose agreement existed among us that we would not "attack" this section but, rather, roll with the elements, our health, and the locations of the elders, taking it bit by bit. We had that one luxury of travel: a loose schedule.

One particular section of the first path we were to take, the sixteen-hundred-kilometre road from Shangri-La to Lhasa, held our interest: a virtually untravelled five-hundred-kilometre segment that made its way into the little-known Nyanqen Tanglha mountain range. One wrinkled trader had warned of the section, saying, "You are modern men and will wish you were at home in bed when you encounter the great snow passes." High snow passes, deadly blizzards, voracious rivers, flooded valleys, along with wind-shorn cliffs—these were obstacles we fully expected to meet. Distances were rough guesses and could significantly increase when circumventing landslides, washed-out bridges, or dead ends. The local mountain people refer to an often-repeated "Himalayan principle" when speaking of the area's geography: "There are no straight lines through the mountains." It was in this section that the lados of the past had made their names, or lost their lives. On this segment of the journey, we would be entirely on our own: it was one of the rare parts of the Tea Horse Road that was free of paved roads, traffic, and, that most stubborn of species, the tourist. Assuming the team arrived in Lhasa intact and of right mind, we would return by plane to Shangri-La, where I would begin preparations for the rest of the journey.

I am not one to use the word *if* often, but the ancient road was fraught with many ifs. Our team would be at the mercy of local guides and their availability, at the mercy of seasonal conditions, and at the mercy of a lot of unforeseen ifs. Organizing the journey was made more bearable with the help of charismatic Dakpa and two old hands, Tenzin and Yeshi, who knew not only portions of the route but, perhaps even more importantly, the exceptional people who had travelled it. Dakpa's local ties and knowledge of the route provided insight that no outsider could ever dig up on his or her own. All three men had some connection to the Tea Horse Road, whether they had travelled along it themselves, as Dakpa had, or had relatives who had journeyed along its formidable length. One of the three men would join me at a designated location for a portion of the journey, providing, of course, that I made it to each location.

Our base of operations was a corner office on the third floor of a building that sat between Shangri-La's old and new towns. Bodies were constantly coming and going, checking and rechecking and then triple checking the gear. Two days before our scheduled departure and five days after my arrival in Shangri-La, the team was to meet to review schedules, dates, and lists. Although Tibetans often wore watches, they rarely consulted them, and a person's acknowledgment of the time meant only that they had acknowledged it, not necessarily that they had processed it or planned to act upon it. And so I was surprised when everyone arrived for the meeting within a half-hour of each other—in Tibetan terms, on time.

Nomè was the first to arrive. Then Norbu and Sonam drifted in. Finally, Dorje arrived in a cloud of tobacco smoke with Dakpa. Nomè wasted no time in beginning our meeting, methodically going through the list of our supplies: *tsampa* (barley powder), butter, potatoes, oil, onions, garlic, ginger, turnip, pork fat, biscuits, quick-boil noodles, jam, chocolate, tea ... Dorje interrupted enthusiastically to insist that we take some *arra,* or barley whisky. A glance from Nomè instantly stifled Dorje's enthusiasm. Nomè continued running through his list—which fortunately did include *arra.* Good for digestion, *arra* was an old preventive remedy of the lados, to be taken before drinking water from a new source, though I suspected Dorje's desire ran beyond the drink's digestive properties. Sleeping bags, tents, bungee cords, nylon rope, medicines ... the list went on. To these items we would add our own gear.

With Tibetans, packing trek gear was simple. What wasn't essential wasn't taken. Their ensembles for the mountains were identical to their day-to-day clothes. Few changes of clothes, no high-tech gadgets, and no reasons to impress made packing a remarkably easy task. Most Tibetans of simple means didn't consider options but, rather, understood their limits—they know how far they can push themselves under physical duress in the environments. Their threshold for pain and appreciation for comfort was higher than most people's.

In his typical minimalist way, Dorje summed up the "excesses of people," telling me philosophically that the "more gear people acquired, the easier it was to hide their true nature, to hide themselves." Dorje always spoke in a simple and straightforward manner, and he seemed incapable of anything other than refreshingly honest directness.

Our spartan gear reflected our mission. Dakpa and I had agreed long ago to keep the gear and equipment to a minimum. We would rely on the generosity of local host families—*netsang*—for shelter and food, and when that was unavailable, we would camp, and make do with what the earth provided. We wouldn't use GPS or satellite phones. What we didn't need, we wouldn't take. To capture the essence of the old caravans, it was important to take in what they took in, and live the way they had lived, when we could. We were already too late for much of the caravan road: we would need to find a Jeep for those portions where a highway had simply been built overtop the ancient route.

Except for me, everyone on the journey was Khampa—eastern Tibetan—though from different regions. They all knew the importance of the trip. It would be in many respects a first and a last opportunity. It would be a journey into cultures, legends, and the realm of memories of old men and women.

We all spoke Mandarin, and the Tibetan members of the team spoke Khampa gè, the Khampa dialect, and quite different from Lhasa gè, Lhasa Tibetan. My abilities in Khampa gè were questionable at best, but I did have the requisite intonation for emphasis and frantic hand motions down. Dakpa, Sonam, and Norbu spoke English, while Dorje knew the word *fuck,* having learned it from an Australian climber who had used it liberally. Our language of choice was a mishmash of tongues, with the necessary hand motions, expressions, and intonations. The Khampa dialect was as expressive as any and, much like the people who spoke it, entirely direct. Tongues often waggle out of the mouth in wordless greeting to friends, no offence meant and none taken.

In the past, Lhasa highbrows saw Khampas and their informal speech as guttural and uncouth. The Khampa way was about wasting as little time on niceties as possible. Harsh landscapes and isolation were not conducive to time-wasting vanities. These "people of the east," as they were sometimes called, were by necessity tenacious and straightforward. These people alone could lead trade caravans over the top of the world.

In addition to undertaking our own expedition and meeting the lados, I was keen to peer into the mystical history and culture of tea, from its discovery in 2737 BC by the mythical Shen Nung (known in Chinese lore as the "Divine Farmer") to its undisputed status in Asian trade. The harvesting, packaging, transport, and, ultimately, consumption of tea had changed little over the centuries. Tea was at once exotic, accessible, nutritious, and utterly simple—hot water, tea leaves, and a thirst were all that were required. In the early days of the Tea Horse Road, tea passed from the hands of indigenous pickers to be steamed, formed into cakes, bricks, and balls for transport, and then hoisted onto the backs of mules for an exhausting trek that would cover thousands of kilometres and take up to six months.

Tea's importance in the history of the route cannot be overstated, nor can its importance to me. Tea in its myriad forms and colours, its culture and its lore, had charmed, stimulated, and addicted me ever since I had lived in Asia, almost a decade ago. Its regenerative abilities had been one of the few constants in my life, and it would join me on this journey along a thirteen-hundred-year-old trade route that carried its name. Of all the items that I might part with, the dried, unattractive lump of fermented Puer tea was the one I was least likely to give up. I had imbibed tea, studied it, written about it, and spent entire days marvelling at the high it gave me. From Taiwan's oolongs to India's Assam, I was a humble admirer of tea in all its forms. I was eager to visit the tea sanctuaries in the jungled south of Yunnan Province, where my green friend grew rampantly. But first the mountains awaited my attention.

DORJE WAS SLOWLY REVEALING why he was indispensable. Energy coursed through him, and there was no errand he wouldn't run, no task he wouldn't undertake, no embarrassment he wouldn't suffer. Not one day passed that a grin wasn't on his face.

The day before our departure, Dorje made a presentation. Awkwardly shuffling his powerful bulk, he placed a sand-coloured bracelet in each of our palms. He explained that it was made of *bagu,* a rare variety of small bamboo. "It is a tradition from where I am from to wear it," he said. "These will bond us together and keep our circulation in the mountains."

Bagu was cut at the knots and natural breaks along the stalk, then fire-heated and bent around the foot to form it into a bracelet. About one of every five attempts was wearable. The little band of bamboo rests upon my wrist still.

We were to depart from a valley known locally as Tapatang, just north of Shangri-La. An expanse of grassland, it was the traditional sending-off point for the ancient caravans. We were to spend our last night under the wooden beams and careful eye of the "Caravan Lady." All the local Tibetans knew her by this moniker. Her home in the tiny village of Ghonbi was just a few minutes' walk from Tapatang, and she knew well how to prepare those destined for journeys: her father had been a famous *tsompun,* or head muleteer, and her brother, a lado. Although her brother and father had travelled throughout the mountains on trading runs, her life had been, and continued to be, at home, making sure that travellers and traders had places to stay and that their bellies were full. Such *netsang* were to be found along the length of the trading route.

Our hostess knew well the potential plights of those who travelled the old routes. As owner of a caravan, with many muleteers and mules under him, her father travelled to and from Lhasa. Locals trusted him to both take and bring back items, paying him upfront. Tea, salt, sugar, noodles, pork, and copper were among the most prized items brought into Lhasa; incense, wools, textiles, and corals would make the return trip. Monks from the local Songzenling Monastery often travelled with him, and even entire families sometimes joined, believing in safety in numbers. Families that could afford to go would band into large caravans and travel the two months to Lhasa together, some members riding horses, while the lados walked alongside their *droo,* or cargo-laden mules.

Safe passage was never a given. The Caravan Lady's father, in order to dissuade his son from the perils of a life of as a muleteer, ordered one of his men to leave the son atop a mountain pass overnight in a raging blizzard. It was a cruel lesson learned early, and the teenager soon gave up his aspirations for a trading life.

Shingled and broad, as was the local style, the Caravan Lady's house reflected the wisdom of traditional house-building skills. Ground floors were used as livestock pens, while the living space was on the main floor above. In the past, two dogs would stand guard at every home in the area, one secured in the courtyard, the other outside the grounds, fiercely guarding the domain. But now dogs roamed freely, with the odd dreadlocked monster chained up.

Leading us up the stairs in the house, our tight-jawed hostess showed us to our sleeping quarters, which doubled as kitchen, social room, and, I was told, a dance hall. Whole tree trunks rose through the centre of the home, acting as anchors, and although little sunlight penetrated the low, square window, the home was one of warm hospitality. The Caravan Lady, in her sixties, was wrapped in an assortment of wool blankets and calfskins to ward off the chill. She served us freshly prepared *pu jia*, Tibetan butter tea, as her daughters, nieces, cousins, and grandchildren appeared about her and began preparations for dinner. In Tibetan towns and villages, families and neighbours play far greater roles in one another's lives than they do in the cities. When I asked how many people lived in the house, the response was a little shrug. "Everyone," our hostess smiled. Doors and homes were open and informal. People came in, assessed us, and departed, only to return again. Bodies blurred in the scant light, but I noticed Dorje's eyes lingering on one of the young women. His expression was easy to read, despite our cultural differences—already Dorje's playful spirit was revealing itself.

Every Tibetan town's tea was slightly different, accounted for by light differences in the tea leaves, the amount used, and the preparation of the butter, although each town, of course, claims its tea is the best. More and more, electric blenders were used to prepare the tea. But in Ghonbi, it was still prepared and mixed by hand, in the old manner. The object of Dorje's attention poured the frothy, lemon-coloured mixture from an old tin teapot, receiving a lengthy stream of *"karen, karen"*—"thank you, thank you"—from Dorje. Had she prepared a concoction of fatal herbs, I'm sure he would have swooned in joy, and probably lived.

An enormous black woodstove threw out waves of heat as we drank the tea and made the inevitable trips outside to relieve ourselves of the large amounts we were imbibing. Dinner was almost ready and still more people came into the room, including two elderly monks who lived nearby. The meal, or meals as it would turn out, consisted of *thukpa*, a thick meat and vegetable stew with freshly made noodles; endless trays of *momos*, or dumplings; a boiled mass of pork; and *palè*, slabs of homemade bread. After eating, I sat back, finally able to relax, only to stare in dismay as yet another stew was served. I was then christened by one of the monks, and given the name Norbu Medu, after a famed caravan leader, a successful trader, and a man known to be good to those under him. Norbu Medu came from the Tsarong area of southeastern Tibet and was successful not only because of his generosity to his muleteers but also because of his skill at conning others. Whether it was conning or convincing, the leader's effectiveness was key to a caravan's success. And although I had no intention of conning, I told the monk that I would do the name proud. With a wistful smile, he told me, "A little conning is sometimes necessary."

All of us were feeling the effects of the multiple dishes combined with the warmth of the fire. The local women were known for their incredibly high vocal tones, and song for many was a daily occurrence, whether in the fields or in ceremony. There were songs of welcome, songs of work, and songs of departure. On this night we were treated to songs and dances of joy, and of farewell. Dorje's interest was once again piqued as the young woman who had caught his eye took part, paying him absolutely no attention. Undeterred, he attempted to join the dance but was told in no uncertain terms to sit down. Smiling, he complied.

Hours later, we lay in our blankets on the wood floor, content with the world. Dorje hummed some odd little tune, his cigarette glowing orange. Drowsy from the food and the heat of the fire, I fell asleep amid the soft sounds of a dying day and the crackles of burning wood.

I woke to cold blue air, a hint of smoke from the fire. Fire was the great constant in Tibetan homes, the last one out and first one up. My watch told me it was a few minutes after six o'clock.

The morning of our departure started remarkably quietly. Dakpa and Norbu were attempting to ignore the fact that day had arrived.

Dorje had been up since five, and Sonam was murmuring his morning prayers. Our morning tea with *tsampa*—barley powder—was not just a drink but nourishing food, and its heaviness warmed us. The night chill hadn't yet given up its hold, and, outside, the village dogs were still lying in curled-up balls, waiting for the rays of sun to thaw them.

But the time had come to set it all in motion. Our departure was celebrated with a modest ceremony of prayers said by the two monks, a presentation of *katas*—white silk scarves slung around our necks— and the burning of juniper to cleanse the air and protect us on our journey. Both monks had done the route as young men and were giving counsel, warning us about Sho La, the first major pass along the Yunnan–Tibet route. "Be wary of the weather. It is still early in the season, and there will be snow. Sho La is often underestimated," one monk told us. The Caravan Lady stood, wrapped as before against the chill, smiling gently at us, while her five-year-old granddaughter, reddened by the sun, sang us a little song wishing us a safe journey. We were jumpy and eager, though our mules looked at us with some scorn, given the hour of the day.

The sky opened up, allowing us glimpses of a dense blue as our caravan made its way northwest. Behind us, the burgundy-robed monks' bare arms were raised, and we could hear bellows of *Kalèo*— farewell. After a long period without activity, the Tea Horse Road once again had travellers.

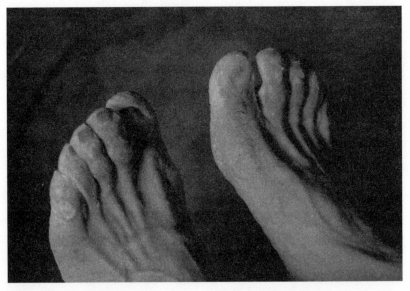

Dorje's feet, which caused us no end of grief, recover from frostbite after a warm soak.

2

Sho La Pass to Chamdo: The First White

Those who hesitate while crossing Sho La
in rough conditions will not make it.

—DAWA, KHAMPA LADO

GOUGED INTO THE MOUNTAIN, the narrow stone path in front of us
was more of a rock-domed passageway that plunged into a sheer drop
on our left-hand side. As we followed the contours of the mountains,
the trade route's genius was revealed to us. What from a distance
appeared impassable would, once we arrived, open to reveal further
strands—another narrow pass or a rut along the granite surface where
a faint track led still farther on. Some sections were more like a ledge
that had been cleared of debris—here we had to step daintily if we
wanted to continue. Trading families with much to gain, and lose,
often managed the trail maintenance for a given section, ensuring not
only safe passage for the caravans but also an active economy.
Landslides in the area were common, sometimes closing off important entries into the valleys and wiping out entire caravans. "It was the
mountain's thunder, and every lado's fear," one old muleteer recalled.
"Caravans would be completely engulfed, and bodies lay unfound for
months. Some still lie buried in the earth. There are valleys of bones
along the route." After a landslide struck, caravans simply salvaged
what they could of the cargo, if there was anything left to salvage, and
moved on. Grief in the mountains was by necessity brief.

Beauty, on the other hand, is raw and constant. Sand, blown by the winds up from the river valleys, had settled in ridges along the mountainsides. Slivers of barley fields tucked into rocky slopes shimmied in the winds. Dorje and Dakpa sang Tibetan songs of the trail. Notions of self-consciousness and false humility had never been popular among Khampa men, meaning the songs were belted out unapologetically. Dorje sang with the earnest effort of the tone-deaf, while Dakpa's vocal skills inspired and encouraged us.

Two days after leaving Shangri-La, Sonam and I broke away from the others near the artisan's town of Gonjo to trace a portion of the ancient tea trail that headed north. Silently treading along ledges had become a favourite pastime for the two of us and often provided a dramatic stage for Sonam's seemingly inhuman skills and his nonchalant daredevil approach to sheer drops and jags of stone. I was learning that the notion of risk was entirely relative. Upon rounding a bend in the path, Sonam muttered something about a shortcut. I saw only a ledge, a rock, and a drop. Without warning, Sonam's birdlike frame shot straight down a near-vertical incline, his lean, awkward legs striding in front of him, eating up metres in giant paces. Reaching what must have been a ledge some ten metres below, he simply held out his hand to me, not even having to catch his breath. Sonam was quickly christened "Spiderman."

One of Sonam's mantras was "Everything is in the mind." I chose not to comment that in *my* mind, gravity was a reality of the external world. Sonam's list of mantras was long, and shared in daily doses.

Where Sonam seemed to flit over space, Dorje stalked, and for each mantra Sonam repeated, Dorje lit up another cigarette. Dorje didn't walk upright but leaned slightly forward, his long arms dangling by his side. Whether in the steamy heat of day or the chill of night, he wore three layers of clothing, which included a pair of knitted maroon long johns, on permanent display thanks to the non-existent zipper on his pants. Dorje's only vanity was his daily moustache grooming, which he usually did as he smoked his first cigarette of the day. Using his forefinger and thumb, he delicately matted down the moustache, in an attempt to add a touch of domesticity to his untamed face.

When Sonam was not busy testing gravity's limits, he and Norbu spent hours arguing the finer points of Buddhism, and, judging by the amount of time spent on the discussion, there were many fine points. Norbu was seeing this land for the first time, and day by day was taking on the glow of understanding. Staring down at the steaming Yangtze River one afternoon, he whispered in a shaking voice, "These lados who travelled knew themselves, because they knew the land." This insight about his people and identification with his land was empowering to him. As one old woman of the mountains whom we encountered described it, the land was a "part of the soul of all people."

As we cut deeper northwest, we began to get a glimpse of snow-capped mountains. White-tipped peaks above us, sandy riverbanks in front of us, and racing winds that shot out of the Himalayas became our daily backdrop. Winds increasingly had that unmistakable waft of snow. Clean and cold, it was a distinctive scent that hinted at what lay ahead. Dust was whipped up in clouds, sending bits of debris into our mouths and eyes, adding to the gritty beauty of the ragged stone formations and impatient waterways. At each intersection of trails, my eyes traced the various paths as they wound up the cliffs and out of sight. Descending into a ravine along the Yangtze that was filled with cacti ("ghost's hands" in the Khampa language), I marvelled at the odd fertile patches irrigated by simple wooden troughs. Much in these valleys had remained contentedly unchanged over the centuries.

The night had a cool edge as we settled down to sleep. I thought back to Norbu's comment about the traders knowing the land and thereby knowing themselves. The traders' lives were lives of endurance, camaraderie, and compliance with the laws of the mountains. As I came to understand more of the Khampas and their nature, they seemed singularly able to live these lives.

Lados were aptly named. The word consists of two parts: *la* meaning hand, and *do* (rhymes with *low*) meaning stone or rock—no ambiguity there as to what was required of the men who chose to be muleteers. Hands of stone and no less were what a person must have to travel the route successfully. The life of a muleteer offered up hardship and freedom in a lethal blend and required simple principles of living and a rare tenacity. For the Khampas, this was a line of work custom-made for their character. Freezing nights, windstorms, *tsa du*—heat sickness—during the day, and being away from home for long periods of time required endurance and that most important of qualities that Dorje had in abundance: humour.

PONZERA, also known to Tibetans as Konzera, and to the Chinese as Benzilan, is both a town and a region in China, and once home to the most famous muleteers. We arrived in the town, nestled in a *rong,* or valley, two thousand metres above sea level along the rushing Yangtze, just four days after starting our journey. Here, eighty-five kilometres from Shangri-La, there was virtually no green life, only heat, winds, sand, and furrowed fields. Mountains soared in every direction, and pale dirt tracks feathered out along the mountainside to other towns enclosed in the valleys. From this arid land came the finest, most fearless muleteers. Their footprints along the Tea Horse Road traced as far west as Nepal and northern India. Ponzera lados had the twin gifts of casual charm and unerring horsemanship, making them the first choice of traders looking to recruit. Ponzerabas, as the people of Ponzera were known, were considered *rombas,* or people of the valley, and our own Dorje counted himself among these valley folk. They were lovers of the good life and could be counted on for light-hearted comic relief. They were also known for their fierce loyalties.

Ponzera had at one time been celebrated for its handcrafted tea bowls and embroidery, and no caravan passing through departed without a load of carved bowls, known locally as *porre,* and a stack of brilliantly decorated *chupas,* long wool jackets. In the noon heat, one local, a finely boned eighty-five-year-old tsompun called Neema, explained the prevalence of the barter system as recently as fifty years ago: "On our journeys, we would trade bowls or *cheril* [tea balls] for straw in areas where grazing was poor. What was money? Nothing." This ageless man had travelled first as a lado and then as a tsompun for twenty years. He summed up what was required to be successful along the trail in one word: "Discipline."

Wearing a hat similar to Dorje's, the old man's smooth skin, high cheekbones, and full lips prompted Norbu to whisper to me, "Lady-killer." Neema's wide travels had accustomed him to seeing foreigners, and the presence of an outsider in his hometown didn't faze him. "Where are you from?" he asked Dakpa. Upon hearing "Gyalthang" (Shangri-La), he let out a cackle. "We have a saying about that land: In Gyalthang, the water has no sound, the grass has no joints, and the people have no oaths." This is one of the treasures of the older generations—their memory of a time when towns and villages knew one another by reputation. Passed on orally, the legends always sounded poetic in a way that the written word could never quite duplicate, and yet the fact that they hadn't been written down and were oral histories only was contributing to their loss.

Ponzera had gained notoriety because of its inhabitants' practice of stealing brides. These were no brutal invasions by outsiders, no violent assaults, but, rather, carefully planned exercises by families who were often neighbours or friends of the targets. We had heard of young women in the past being taken along on lengthy journeys with their trading families, just so they could be watched over by their clan. Any young unwed woman from a good home was a potential target to be stolen away by a hopeful groom and his clan. Captured women were typically kept in a state of comfortable house arrest, and negotiations with her family would begin immediately, with basic ground rules—where and when to negotiate, and who would negotiate on behalf of each clan—established for the proceedings. However, if the woman had been abused or was suspected of being abused, a bloody battle was likely to ensue. Most often, though, negotiations ended happily for both parties—which translated into a more powerful union for the two families involved. Khampas, even the easygoing valley folk, carried vengeance in their hearts like few others, so peaceful solutions were preferred.

Norbu and Dorje had heard of the practice, though Dorje proudly exclaimed that only a coward would steal a bride. Sonam rolled his eyes, then quietly suggested that it was probably the only way some men could get a wife. As he spoke his eyes bore into Dorje, his insinuation clear. Dorje nonchalantly dismissed such a possibility with a flick of his cigarette. Norbu and I had come to welcome these wonderfully absurd exchanges. Sonam and Dorje had an uneasy but often humorous unspoken truce. Sonam was the embodiment of chaste discipline and formidable self-control, while Dorje, with his casual approach, was the more typical Khampa man. Their difference in character was encapsulated in their methods of addressing people: where Sonam used the ultra-polite and formal *la* after someone's name (thus, Dakpa was "Dakpa la"), Dorje would simple bellow out "O Dakpa," which was very informal and to many minds disrespectful.

Sonam was an ardent Buddhist. Like many of the devout, he believed that the blasé attitude toward religion that Dorje took was for cowards, those who couldn't adhere to anything. Dorje's view was, why devote yourself solely to one belief when you could devote yourself to many? When he said this, he winked and laughed his ragged, debauched laugh, leaving me little doubt as to what he was referring to. Yet, as with most things Khampa, there was unhesitating respect for one another's abilities. Both the pious, exacting saint and the charming ruffian were tough, and each one knew that the other was tough.

THE MORNING SUN rose slowly in the mountains, sending an ever-widening sheet of light into the valleys. Leaving Ponzera, we had crossed the Yangtze watershed and made our way one hundred kilometres northwest into the Mekong River's watershed and to the town of Deqin, or Jol, as it had been known in the days of caravan trade. We had been on the road now for just more than a week. Just ahead of us was the spectacle of Kawa Karpo—White Snow Mountain—one of the three most sacred mountains in Tibet.

A broad, 6740-metre monster, it remains unclimbed. For many Tibetans, it is the most holy of mountains. To the south sits "his wife," called Metzomo or Goddess of the Sea, an elegant mountain with fine, snow-covered ridges, and far more beautiful than the hulkish Kawa Karpo. For many Tibetans, a pilgrimage, often taking months, to the elevated white peaks is the spiritual highlight of their life. Sonam insisted that we give thanks to the mountains for allowing us good fortune so far. Kawa Karpo's spiritual and physical power is unquestioned by Tibetans. A doomed 1991 joint Sino-Japanese attempt to ascend the peak angered locals and seemingly angered the deities that dwelled within the mountains as well: all seventeen members perished in a storm at five thousand metres. In Tibet, mountains were viewed with reverence and were not the playthings of mortals. Our route would snake north to avoid incurring the deities' wrath, but first we planned to take a couple of days of rest, to learn from the locals the weather conditions ahead and also to give Dorje a little playtime.

The moment we arrived in Deqin, Dorje's eyes took on a mischievous glow. At around six every evening, while the rest of us tended to our clothes, inspected our toes for telltale signs of foot rot, engaged in debate about Buddhism, or explored the town, Dorje disappeared, returning quietly in the wee hours of the morning. He explained simply that he had gone out for a drink, but the look of satisfaction in his eyes spoke of more than just barley whisky. Even with only a couple of hours of sleep each night, he somehow was able to regenerate that limitless Dorje battery.

One evening as Dorje was leaving for his night out on the town, Sonam boldly asked him about his wife, clearly wanting to put him on the spot. Dorje just grinned. Sonam turned to us in puritanical indignation, snorting that if he ever started behaving in such a deplorable manner, we were to dump him off a cliff. Smiling, Norbu promised to oblige him. Whatever the nature of his nocturnal activities, Dorje would need his battery to be fully charged soon. Our time in Deqin was nearing its end: we had an appointment with an old man and a white pass.

Some places exist as entrances, as introductions to greater places; they are associated with something vast and formidable. This was the case with the town of Merishoo. Sitting on the west bank of the Mekong River, a half-day northwest of Deqin, it is divided by a dirt road that gives no hint of the town's former bustle. For centuries, Merishoo had been inextricably linked with the Tea Horse Road, serving as the base from which to begin the ascent of Sho La, the first major pass along the Yunnan–Tibet Tea Horse Road. In Merishoo, we were treated to the company of one of those rare men who carried the title of lado. In all my readings about and dealings with the people of the Himalayas, I had not once heard of anyone interviewing these living history tomes of quickly disappearing knowledge.

Sinuous and spry, Dawa had survived experiences few can imagine. More than fifty years ago, he had been one of the transporters on the Tea Horse Road. He had spent the last thirty years in India, recently returning "to die where I was born." From the look in his eyes, it was clear he had engaged in life and lived his eighty-one years to their fullest. He was one of those people who had a universal familiarity about them.

Dawa's home was humble and silent. The walls bore all manner of muleteer paraphernalia: saddles, girths, and plumes for the *shodrel,* or lead mules. They hung over his bed, as if in wait for their next journey. The sparseness of his belongings reflected a life of movement even now. We had woken Dawa from an afternoon nap, and he bid us to sit, disappearing and then reappearing minutes later, having donned a faded fedora and a stained shirt. When Dakpa told him he didn't need to get dressed up for us, he looked at Dakpa and said, "It's not for you, it's for me." Proud still, he looked us over as Dakpa explained our journey on the Drelam, or Mule Road. He listened quietly, then nodded his head. "Yes, it needs to be told," he said. "I cannot read, and I cannot write, so you must do this." Dawa soon warmed to the topic, his mighty hands gesturing constantly as he reminisced.

Dawa offered us butter tea, or *pu jia.* Its preparation, like everything that surrounded us, was unpretentious. Dawa's dark hands have done this for seven decades, and his actions were fluent. First he scooped a fist-sized chunk of yak butter into a wooden *don*—a long cylindrical wooden vessel—along with a generous helping of salt. Next he poured strong cooked tea made from the leaves and stems into this butter-and-salt mixture. (And *cooked* rather than *infused* is the right word to describe tea in Tibet: like a slow-cooked soup, the tea and boiling water meld into a hearty concoction.) The tea is then mixed with a *sula,* a plungerlike instrument. After a dozen powerful strokes to ensure that the ingredients were broken up and had released their flavours, Dawa poured the tea—a meal in itself—into a cheap tin kettle, then into small, tarnished bowls.

In these isolated regions of Tibet, little had changed in the preparation of *pu jia* over the centuries. It wasn't just the tea leaves that were valued but also the stems and stalks, because of their tannin and caffeine content. Tea was cooked several times daily to ensure that there was always some ready to drink. An old saying hinted at tea's importance in the lives of the mountain people: "Yak butter tea is a more lasting possession than a son." The sharing of tea was considered binding, cups of the thick liquid taking the place of signatures. When tea wasn't offered, it was a sure sign that there would be no relationship.

Tea in the mountain villages had never been taken for granted, partly because of the long journeys required to bring it there. Its preparation, so physical and time-consuming, served to remind one of its longevity. All of traditional Tibetan tea's ingredients were valued commodities, especially in the simple rural homes. Tea and salt came from miles away, and yak butter was a mainstay of Tibetan life. These treasured ingredients were offered without hesitation as a gesture to join and engage.

Merishoo was traditionally a resting and refuelling point, providing the last opportunity before Sho La to change horseshoes, assess animals, and, if necessary, upgrade to stronger mules. It was this exposure to a source of work that had led Dawa to join a caravan. With nothing to hold back his wanderlust, the teenaged Dawa had simply snagged a job with a passing caravan, spending years journeying thousands of kilometres to Lhasa and beyond into the north of India and Nepal, where he eventually settled. "The food, the weather, and life were better." His life mirrored many of the lados' lives. Limited employment possibilities at home and tough constitutions pushed many young men to adventure—anything was preferable to a life of toiling in the dirt.

Tibetans all dreamed of seeing Lhasa, the holy land, but few of limited means ever got the chance. Muleteering was low-paying and hard—at times life-threatening—but for the muleteers, any chance to get to Lhasa was worth the hardship. These men were both revered and envied as men who had not just dreamed but had done. When the muleteers arrived with their caravans in a town, they brought news of far-off riches, of wars and peoples, and of lands beyond the mountains.

Merishoo was the last trading town for a couple of weeks of travel; from there, the caravans crossed into dry valleys of heat. There was much hasty deal-making before the caravans headed out for the great Sho La Pass. Dawa recalled these times of his youth: "The town would flood with men and mules preparing for passage into the mountains. The grazing was good, and it was in the villagers' best interests to make sure that the lados and tsompuns were content. Many such towns lived and breathed thanks to the business the traders brought." Dawa's words highlighted the economic dependence many towns and villages had on the caravans. Beyond its geographic splendour, the Tea Horse Road was about trade.

Trade was an informal but serious affair, with all types of goods considered for exchange. Dawa recalled one villager long ago wanting to exchange a horse bridle for a hunk of the famed cured pork of Gyalthang a trader had. In both business and personal relationships, there was an emphasis on the future rather than on short-term gain. Cheating and corruption weren't tolerated, and many Tibetans have long and sharp memories. Agreements among the lados were often made with a handshake—and the sharing of a cup of tea—and kept. To renege on a deal brought dishonour to your family, home, and monastery. Over the course of our travels, we encountered many lados who lamented the loss of this honour system in the modern world.

Just as honour was cherished, nonsense and greed were met with typical Khampa efficiency. An old hulk of a man who had been a lado told us of a greedy chieftain who had been warned about his insistence that caravans pay him tithes in order to cross a certain mountain pass. The chieftain met his unfortunate fate when he was "carved up on the spot" by a Khampa lado. Although a few villages imposed duties on caravans for the use of grazing pastures, most dismissed this practice in the belief that it might undermine the trust that had been built up.

To me, Dawa had the character of the traditional lado. Calm, deliberate, and understated, he was gentle in a way that truly tough men were. All of this was brought into focus by a pair of sad eyes, eyes that had witnessed much. He spoke in a steady voice of himself, of the people, of the geography, and of the informal ways of the lados. At one point he stopped recounting to ask why a Tibetan wasn't writing the lados' story. Heads bowed. "It doesn't matter," he whispered, "just tell it." After all these years, his memories and knowledge had found listeners. "The young are not interested in any of this now," he said, looking off through a tiny window in his house.

Besides tea and horses, salt was one of the most sought-after items in the Himalayan corridors. Dawa called it "dirty white gold." Ancient brine wells in nearby Yenjing provided a valued commodity for the caravans heading west and for the ethnic minorities along the Mekong watershed. Naxi, Yi, and Lisu tribes and Tibetans all inhab- ited the area and benefited from its yields, cooperating and sharing harvesting duties.

The Tibetan saying "Wind is the origin of life" proved particularly appropriate here. For thousands of years, winds have whipped down the Mekong, which, along with long hours of sunshine, evaporate the water, leaving behind the salt in salt flats alongside the river. Mules carry the salt into otherwise inaccessible villages. Dawa told us, "I feel good to see that mules are still used. Nothing is more suited for moun- tain life, but no one took care of the mules like us. No mules were stronger or better looked after." His chest heaved in pride and, after a moment of thought, he pursed his lips and made a strange little sound, indicating that all this talk had made his mouth dry. He left us briefly, to return with a small glass of *arra*, or barley whisky, as if an honorary drink to the memory of mules was necessary. Taking a sip of the fiery liquid, he sheepishly confided that he wished he could stop but then insisted that it was his only vice. Looking at the eighty-one-year-old lion, I thought that it might not be such a bad vice to have.

When we asked Dawa which lados had been the best, he gave us the response we would get throughout our journey: "Ponzera—none were better." On the trail it was no secret where the best came from: "Mules from Minya [near Kangding in China's Sichuan Province], saddles from Wushe [near Lijiang in Yunnan Province], dogs from Deqin, lados from Ponzera, and tsompuns from Tsarong." Dawa allowed himself a little smile. "I wasn't bad either," he said.

Quietly acknowledging that he had outlived most of his generation, Dawa said softly, "The mind still wants to travel, but the limbs cannot.... I have my memories." He seemed to know the worth of his memories. When asked why he had survived when so many others had not, he suggested that perhaps it was to talk to us, as he was now. "My work kept me healthy, as I was always moving. People have changed now. TVs have become family members, and no one likes to talk any more." He took a long pull on his whisky. I had no doubt that, given new legs, this vigorous ancient would join us on the trail in an instant.

As we shared dinner with him, our talk turned to Sho La, the pass we would be heading to in the morning. Dawa's voice dropped and he looked at each of us in turn. He warned us that Sho La sometimes remained impassable for months during the winter. Its danger was "its ability to change instantly, becoming unrecognizable—even to those of us who knew it. Many have wandered off, getting lost in a storm, only to disappear for good." Both pilgrims and traders passed over it with trepidation; it was believed that ascending Sho La cleansed the mind and body of negative energy—that is, if it didn't demand the ultimate sacrifice of life.

IN MERISHOO, I was first to encounter two things destined to hamper my sleep on the trek ahead. The first had to do with an unwelcome odour that had been growing stronger since we had left Shangri-La, with no obvious cause. Soon enough, though, we discovered where it was coming from. Dorje's feet had started to rot, and their rank odour had crept into his boots, socks, sleeping bag, and, by unfortunate extension, our lives. We mentioned it once, then simply didn't have the heart to badger him, as he was helpless to do anything about it. But it became enough of an issue that Nomè, Norbu, Dakpa, Sonam, and I began a clandestine nightly lottery to determine who would have to sleep closest to him and his smelly feet. Discussions were had over the possibility of fumigation, and prayers uttered for divine intervention, but to no avail. While Dorje was happily ignorant of the attention that his feet were getting, Sonam joked that this "taint" might in fact be some protective deity.

The second disruption was Sonam's nighttime habit of grinding his teeth. The symphonic gnashing seemed preternaturally loud, and we often woke to the nerve-fraying sound of his clashing molars. If that wasn't enough, he often performed a duet of sorts: teeth gnashing accompanied by discombobulated talking and screaming in his sleep. Between the stench and the chorus, the nights were far from restful.

On being confronted with complaints about his noises one morning, Sonam countered that grinding teeth was yet another auspicious sign, and that our trip would be successful in part because of this and Dorje's smell. Leave it to our resident monk to find a benefit from two such unwelcome occurrences.

The next morning, we gathered in the town centre amid a throng of people. The entire village had shown up to see us off. For this segment of the journey we had enlisted new mules accustomed to steep ascents and two local muleteers who knew the passes. The six of us were politely shoved away while our bags were fastened to our mules by hands more adept than ours. A powerful woman quickly and competently secured a load, paying particular attention to balancing the cargo. Part of the trick with loading was keeping the girth tight enough but not so tight as to chafe the animal. This attention to detail was paramount in ensuring the animal's longevity in the trade: it was this consideration for the mules' well-being that allowed many of them to live healthfully for close to three decades, making dozens of voyages, and crossing tens of thousands of kilometres of terrain.

Not to be outdone by the locals, Dorje was attempting to help with the packing, despite being admonished for sloppiness by two elderly men. Nomè, on the other hand, had a natural ability with the mules. They seemed to sense his patience and allow him liberties, whereas they seemed equally aware of Dorje's slight lunacy and were not as accommodating. Our five mules looked like typical animals; nothing hinted at their cult status among people known for heroic strength.

In the past, lead mules were adorned with plumes and bells to signal their approach to villages and to oncoming traffic along the precarious cliffs. Ornaments dangled off them to ward off evils and ghosts, for the risks in travel were heavy enough without spirits to contend with. Walking ahead of the caravans, the *shodrel* were the eyes and brains of the operation, sensing conditions to such an extent that when one was injured or died along the route, the other mules often fell into temporary chaos, having lost their leader. Traders valued the lead mules above all other animals, and spoke about them with an affection that approached worship. Ancient caravans took their time: they knew that the success of the journey depended on the health of the mules.

As we continued to pack, one of the mules madly swivelled its hindquarters, intent on getting a few kicks in. Sonam narrowly avoided a punishing blow, then blamed some deity for the near disaster. The real instigators were more prosaic—locals knew the mule well and had been egging it on.

It was here at Merishoo that the remaining members of our team joined us for the crossing of Sho La. Our lead horseman, Tenzin—the first of many Tenzins I was to encounter—was a wide swath of a man with a massive chin. His understudy was an eager teenager of the Lisu tribe, who lived high up in the mountains. Dorje was carefully analyzing their skill sets, ensuring that they were competent, though I suspected he was just trying to cover his embarrassment at his poor performance loading the mules.

Wanting to see Dawa one last time, we headed to his home, but he wasn't there, and so we left town, veering into a deep valley that marked the trailhead to the Sho La Pass. An hour out of town, we saw a lone figure in the distance, loping down the path in long strides. As he approached, we could make out the tanned features of Dawa, dressed only in a pair of pants and a frayed shirt. He had risen before morning light to burn *duba*—juniper—for us in a small enclosed altar high up on the mountain we were about to ascend. Built specifically for morning prayers, which involved the burning of juniper, such altars were to be found throughout the Tibetan regions, the ancient ritual dating back twenty-five hundred years. Green juniper and its cleansing smoke were thought to not only eliminate negative past energy but welcome in a new day, a clean slate. It was a farewell that touched all of us, and even Dorje's perma-grin disappeared in a moment of genuine thanks.

Grasping each of us, Dawa wished us safety on our journey while emphasizing once again Sho La's volatility: "Those who hesitate while crossing Sho La in rough conditions will not make it—once committed, press onward." He knew the area well, and his words would prove prophetic. He stood there, seeing us off, until we were no longer in view. Dawa stayed in our thoughts throughout our travels, and he would come to represent a type of figurehead, a symbol, the face of the quintessential lado.

We made camp in the early afternoon as heavy rains pummelled down. We had ascended sixteen hundred metres of damp greenery. Mules were unloaded in minutes and freed to graze. Nomè effortlessly found kindling despite the onslaught of rain, and a fire was quickly built. Water could annihilate a person's will more completely than any of the other elements, and nothing was worse than soaked gear (although in the case of Dorje's footwear, we hoped it might offer us temporary respite). Rain's ability to permeate fabric and, with its constant droning, the mind, made it an unwelcome visitor. Tenzin said the rain was a bad sign: raindrops here meant snowflakes at the pass.

Setting up camp proved yet again Nomè's calm efficiency. In less than an hour he would unload his supplies, sniff out edible vegetation, and have warm food ready for us, usually including a traditional boiled concoction of sliced ginger and brown sugar, for energy. Caravans used a rotation system for the important task of cooking, each member taking on a specific role—water fetcher, fuel collector, fire starter, or mule caretaker; our group was only too happy to depend on master Nomè to do all this.

A nomad who had been looking for his two yaks for days drifted in from the dark dampness and joined us for our dinner of mushroom noodle stew. It was an unwritten law of the trails to share food with passersby without asking for payment. In the tradition of all mountain cultures, no one was turned away from food and warmth—only the wolves. The sum possessions of the nomad, now far from home, were a worn leather satchel containing a tin cup, *tsampa,* tea leaves, and a ball of butter. Bundled in layers of damp wool, reckless dreadlocks hanging about his collar, he was eager for a brief rest.

Dakpa often said, "For Tibetans, no life is left untouched by the mountains." Every aspect of life was honed down to the essentials, and if something wasn't needed, it wasn't kept. Our own caravan consisted only of requisites. In Dorje's case, his possessions fit into a tiny shoulder bag. I was to contribute one item to that meagre collection, a second pair of socks—an entirely selfish act on my part. Our first incident on the journey occurred when one of Sonam's socks, drying on a twig by the roaring fire, was engulfed in flames. The result was a toasted sock with a black-fringed gaping hole. That sock represented exactly one-quarter of Sonam's sock collection for the journey. Our group's sock supply had already dwindled to a critical level.

Night brought even more vicious rains, flooding one of the tents. With all of us piled into the other tent, we had little sleep. In the morning, Nomè's breakfast provided us fuel for the day, while my thick Puer tea revived everyone's spirits. Its scent alone brought me warmth. The black, earthy tea had come into my life like much of value—slowly. Years earlier, the fermented tea had been served to me by a teashop owner who was determined that I try it. Drinking it had gradually become a vital ritual in my life.

So fortified, we trudged ever closer to Sho La, as the air took on a freshness and the rains stopped. Mosses metres long hung like banners from the damp trees. Touched by the sombre, mist-enveloped beauty around us, we remained silent—all but Dorje, that is. He was burning off energy running up and down the caravan line, making sure everything was fastened and secure. Talking to mules, humans, and trees alike, he seemed a child of the mountains, secure in the knowledge that the gods favoured him.

Every so often a wet stone hinted at what had come before us. Grooves and welts like tiny pieces of sculpture worn and smoothed from long-ago traffic could be seen etched into the pathway. Ground down, they told of the passing of thousands of hooves.

Finally, the heavy forests cleared and we emerged into a grey, indistinct clearing, flakes of snow floating down from the sky. The snow cover was still light, but up ahead it lay in an ever-thickening coat. As we made our way toward the snow line, the light dipped as smouldering dark clouds obscured the sky. The wind had begun to hum. Tenzin said ominously that two bodies had recently been found frozen along the trail. The snow on the ground was deepening and we knew a different world was awaiting us. Hard pellets of snow and ice had begun to pelt down. The breath of the mountain was upon us.

Altitude only strengthened the elements, so despite the overcast skies, we all donned sunglasses. Dorje's pair had lost a lens and, without dropping the pace, he carved a replacement lens out of a green plastic Sprite bottle. This little feat of ingenuity took but minutes. Ever simple in his needs, Sonam refused offers of lip balm, saying, "If I get used to it, I will become addicted." He and his lips would come to regret that decision.

Our team strung out, making its way up a huge ridge that marked the way to the pass. Ascending in a zigzag pattern, we were only part of the way up when the wind was broken by a yell from Dakpa, behind me. One of the mules had plunged ten metres to land chest-deep in snow at the bottom of the ravine. Another mule was stuck in a deep trough of snow, unable to move. The snow was deep enough to buoy the loads atop the mule, making its exit doubly impossible. Dorje and Dakpa descended to join Tenzin in calming the animals and slowly digging them out.

One mule had a small gash on its haunch. Dorje promptly fiddled with his gaping fly, then urinated on the wound. This was a trick used by mountain men throughout the region to prevent infection: the urine acts as an antiseptic. Tenzin's expression had become hard. His fears were no different from those of his ancestors. A good animal was far too valuable to risk, and the Khampas of eastern Tibet, perhaps more than any others in Asia, knew the value of their four-legged companions.

The hazards to us two-legged creatures were not yet evident, but the deep snow concealed any number of rock traps that could easily snap the leg of a mule. The weather was intensifying by the minute, and the terrain had taken on a brooding beauty. The snow tried to deceive with its attractive blanket of uniformity, but we knew that the smooth, undulating curves were not to be trusted.

Tenzin moved ahead of our group and tentatively prodded the snow with his stick, gauging its depth and staring upward, grimacing at the risk involved. The mules could navigate the visible, but in the blizzard, many of the hazards remained unseen. Our second horseman, the young Lisu tribesman, put on his gloves and offered us a huge smile. Contained in his youthful smile was the pledge to follow us anywhere, and I sensed his innocent courage.

Dakpa's face creased as he studied the slopes. Reference points had all but disappeared as successive walls of snow coming down from the sky moved toward us. Dakpa had made the crossing in more temperate seasons only and now told us that "this is a different place from the summertime pass that I know. I have never seen it like this."

Dorje decided to do reconnaissance. After lighting a cigarette, he crawled on his knees and elbowed up a slope of white. He was the embodiment of mountain-bred men: unconventional, fearless, and strong. The rest of us gathered to discuss what we should do. We knew that later in the day a yak caravan was due to travel over the pass but, like much in the mountains, there was no guarantee of when, or even that it would show up at all.

Yaks had long been the choice of those requiring both plough and transporter. Slow and steady, they were stubborn behemoths, ideal for brutal conditions and high-altitude crossings, and our horseman had often followed in the wake of a yak team during the winter months. In the snow passes, all moving bodies were allies in the face of danger. This was one of the mountain's beautifully straightforward laws: cooperate or perish.

In the Tea Horse Road's peak years of trade and transport, the summer months were especially busy. While mules journeyed during the day, yak caravans would navigate the higher passes at night, avoiding the daytime rush hour. In my mind's eye, I could picture the patient animals plodding along with their huge cargoes, gently making their way along the precarious trails.

Then Tenzin spoke up, pointing out that if we were to try for the pass, we should leave immediately. Our window of opportunity was closing with each breath. Sonam and I were all for pushing onward, at least until we could better judge the conditions ahead. Sonam had enough knowledge of the mountains to know that the storm was only going to intensify. I recalled Dawa's words about the dangers of turning back. We were committed. No amount of research is as insightful as experience, and within the mountain regions, few could counsel like the old Tibetan mountain men and women.

Dorje returned from his scouting and informed us that conditions were worse up ahead, and that the snow was as "deep as a tree." Asking him how he knew would have been pointless; Dorje just knew. We quickly decided that Sonam, Dakpa, Norbu, and I would continue and make an attempt at the pass for as long as the elements—and our wills—allowed. Nomè, Dorje, the two horsemen, and the mules would wait for the yak caravan or for the weather to subside, whichever came first. Dorje's moustache bristled: he wasn't at all pleased at being told to wait, or with being away from the action. The mules would not be risked in attempting the treacherous pass with me and the other three, and Nomè and Dorje needed to stay behind in case the mules had to be led by hand across the pass, should the yak caravan arrive and plough the trail. Despite Dorje's wish to be everywhere at once, he would, for a time at least, be limited to one place. His untamed energy, crucial as it was to our team, was best used looking after the mules. Also, his infinite strength and keen sense of duty would ensure that nothing happened to our gear. Much like an honour guard, he viewed himself as a buffer between our team and anything unsavoury that might happen, and his desire to assist, protect, and clear away obstructions had to at times be funnelled into a specific purpose. Now for the first time since I had known him, Dorje wore a serious expression on his face. He clearly wasn't happy about being separated from his pack.

Carrying only the minimum of gear, we moved out. The speed that the light loads allowed should have worked to our advantage, but the wind was intent on bludgeoning us, and we walked straight into a vortex of shrieking air. For a few frenzied minutes, all our effort was spent trying to maintain our orientation and some sort of an upright position; the wind's whirling power abolished any notion of forward momentum. Without warning, our shuddering bodies emerged from the twisting vortex back into the only slightly less potent blizzard. As we trudged ever higher, Sonam's boots proved inadequate; snow had seeped in and soaked them. But since one of his mantras was "Complaining solves nothing," I didn't learn until later that his wet feet had slowly gone numb.

A call from Norbu above the howling wind alerted us that Dakpa was missing. Norbu motioned to us, his short, powerful frame chest-deep in snow. We waded back through the drifting snow, which erased our footsteps within seconds, then spotted Dakpa, or at least what was left of him to spot—he was nothing more than a smudge of colour in a froth of white. In taking a shortcut, he had sunk into a snowy vault. He looked bashful as Norbu berated him for taking a washroom break. Wind pulled air from our lungs as we heaved the snow from around him. After ten minutes of us digging, he was able to pull himself free, but his legs had gone numb. We gleefully pounded feeling back into them as the wind and snow closed in on us, aware that it could have been much worse had Dakpa been encased in the snow for any longer.

We continued through the grand abstraction of white and blue, stopping every few steps to regroup and reassess. Storms of this strength mock all those who try to get through them. Making ten metres of progress was exhausting, since each step measured mere centimetres. Simply plunging a leg hip deep into the snow and retracting it for the next step required huge exertion. Time ceased to exist, and it was impossible to know how long it was taking us to make even a few metres. Our focus was solely on the next step, and progress was incremental, foot by laborious foot, with all our limbs taking part in the effort. I fantasized about snowshoes magically appearing to transport us overtop the snow. Lados had told us that when the snow was too deep, they rode on the backs of the mules, but once the snow reached past the animals' knees, the potential for accidents increased greatly.

The mules would never make it in this, and I wondered if even a column of yaks could split the wall of white. Sonam and I continued on, with Norbu bringing up the rear, practically burrowing his way through the snow that was already filling in our path. Generally, tunnelling a passageway through the chest-deep snow allowed for the easier passage of whoever was behind, but the effort of leading was exhausting and often demoralizing.

We were making our way along a ridge that Dakpa thought led to the pass. If he was wrong, we would be at the mercy of luck and whichever mountain gods held sway. I hoped that the juniper Dawa had burned for us would have its intended effect. Dawa was in my thoughts as I climbed, his face and words vivid. I now fully understood his warning and imagined loaded caravans attempting the pass under similar conditions. Caravans had been buried alive in such raging storms.

Dawa had told us that in times of extreme snow, caravans endeavouring to cross the pass had two options. One was to simply wait. The other, which Dawa had taken in his journeys, was to unload the mules' cargo and lug each item by hand over the pass, then return to march the unburdened animals over in single file—but even then the mules' and lados' safety were not ensured. One lado might have between seven and twelve fully loaded mules in his charge, each potentially carrying two hundred kilograms or more of tea and other goods. Mules and men alike had been known to eat boiled leather in storms, if food supplies were low. The unflinching courage and strength of those men could not be overestimated, but as one lado remarked to us, "What choice did we have?" My appreciation for these men was increasing with each step; with only minimal baggage, we were using all our strength to simply maintain a forward momentum.

For me, part of the lure of mountains is their unpredictability: any venture into the mountains demands adaptability and will in equal measure. As we continued to ascend the ridge, our visibility dwindled to a couple of metres and nature's enforcer, the wind, had picked up from a howl to a roar. The four of us closed into a tighter unit, and I wondered at Dawa's words to us about pressing on without hesitating. Was it really too late to turn back? My mind began racing with thoughts of Norbu, Sonam, and Dakpa. These men had families, homes, and for the moment, functioning limbs, and I was in many ways responsible for making sure they returned home safely. As we huddled, I expressed my concerns, going hoarse as I tried to be heard above the wind. Dakpa, in a moment of humour, asked where we were on the map, and the ensuing laughs provided the answer as to whether or not to continue. Norbu's glowing eyes voiced his desire to press on, and Sonam simply nodded—his stoicism was his great strength, but I often worried that if he had a problem, I wouldn't know of it until it was too late. Turning around was no longer a choice for us; with Khampas, the idea of retreating was never an acceptable option. We all realized that our path was disappearing as we spoke, and tracking back would be just as dangerous at this point. It was the pass or nothing.

Snow and wind came at us in massive blasts; these ebbed, only to return in even greater strength, until finally there were no more ebbs and flows but just a white world of motion. I couldn't see past my arm held out in front of me. I began crawling on the surface of the snow, where there was less resistance from the wind, and Sonam and Norbu followed suit. We made slow progress.

One of the great dangers mule caravans faced in storms was disorientation, eventually leading to exhaustion as they tried to reorient themselves. This made the lead mule's ability to lead all the more critical. We, unfortunately, were tracing a ridge that was disappearing by the minute instead of following a mule with honed instincts. All our hope was pinned on an ambiguous white hump that marked the pass farther up the mountain. Should we stray even a few degrees off course, we would miss the pass entirely. Pawing our way, we half-crawled, half-staggered higher. Now and then we simply waited for the screaming winds to subside and let us push through again. As we climbed, the wind began hitting us from two sides at once, in an effort to crush us. I chose to take this as a sign that we were on the right path and that the wind was angered by our progress. Gathering together, silent and stooped, we made sure that everyone was able to continue.

So severe was the whiteout that we didn't realize we had reached the pass until Dakpa spotted the flags. Used frequently in Tibet to mark mountain passes, the *loong da*—wind-horse flags—were being savaged by the elements and rose barely a foot above the snow level. The three-and-a-half-metre-tall flags would be buried in snow within the hour. At more than forty-eight hundred metres, Sho La wasn't a giant, but it was the first of the high passes along the Tea Horse Road and it was not yet finished with us.

Numbers never properly explain the essence of a mountain, and asking a Tibetan a mountain's altitude simply brought a shrug. Instead, locals describe the mountain's *sheka,* or personality, in great sweeping gestures and stunning detail. They can describe the best route to take and how to interpret easterly winds and snow formations, but numbers and stats held no interest for them, and now I understood why.

Upon reaching the pass, we bellowed the traditional greeting of *Lha gyal lo*—"Victory to the gods"—to the ice-coated flags as thanks for our safe passage—thus far, at least. The words paid tribute to the mountain deities for allowing a being to journey unharmed to the summit. It was a shared victory, for the victory of the deity was the victory of humanity.

Sonam insisted on reciting the Tara prayer to Drolma, the bodhisattva of compassion and generosity. Hunched forward, hands together, he prayed for us amid the raging storm, reminding us all that whatever the senses might perceive, there were greater powers at work than lungs and quadriceps. The wind was pitching him about, and his words were lost to the air. I'm not sure Drolma could hear him, but she must surely have allocated some credit to his account.

Tracking over the pass, wind gusted in violent updrafts. Its pulverizing force had given way to cunning surges, which found their way into our bones. My face had long since stopped burning, and I started doing checks to make sure there was still sensation by thumping my gloved fists into my cheekbones and squeezing my nose. I wasn't entirely sure I could feel it.

For the first time in hours we were given glimpses of the terrain ahead of us. We could see blotches of grey and a vague sense of a trail. Huge snow drifts, an icy patchwork of snow and ice with the odd piece of granite poking through, gave some depth to the view. Just as the four of us stopped to adjust to this luxury of sight, the elements erased everything in an instant. The mountains had not yet finished their sermon.

We continued on. At some point in that first hour of descent, Sonam noticed that Norbu was limping far behind, struggling to keep pace. As he was the youngest member of the team and had a fiancée back home, we felt particularly protective of him. In the typical Khampa way, he said nothing, but it was apparent that he was in substantial pain. No one had seen the accident, as we were concentrating on our own struggles, but we learned later that a misstep had pitched him kneecap-first onto an exposed shard of rock, and that while trying to stand he had then twisted his knee and collapsed in pain. With each step he felt the knee tighten, until bending it became impossible. Any injury in the mountains could prove fatal. As the old traders said, the lucky ones die quickly; suffering would gradually deplete both energy and will. We let Norbu lead with Sonam so that we could keep an eye on him.

Descending at last into a temperate zone outside the storm, there came a strange moment where our ever-present nemesis the wind ceased and the air was still. It was as though we had stepped into a vacuum. And strangely, I missed the wind. The stillness and silence felt crushing and my understanding of an old trader's words became clear. He had spoken of the mountain's ability to "spoil the soul with its strength," of how once you had felt that strength, nothing felt the same afterward. The mountain drew you back again and again.

Lado Senge Karmo, the protective mountain deity, dwelt in a mountain far off to our left. It was Lado Senge Karmo that protected and warned lados and travellers traversing the mountain regions of conditions and risks. Locals held to the belief that if there was any snow on Lado Senge Karmo's banks, no attempts to cross the pass from that side should be made. Catching glimpses of Lado Senge Karmo in the distance, we could make out expanses of white.

Descending was hard on Norbu's knee, but he valiantly hobbled in silence. Dakpa, at the rear, was now also moving with difficulty. At a place called Mechod Pangang we plopped ourselves down for a brief rest, and to take stock of our condition. Breaks were always kept brief to prevent the body and mind from convincing themselves that they could fully relax. Many travellers in eastern Tibet frowned on long mountain travels without frequent breaks. This was considered macho and unnecessarily risky to the body. More practical was taking many brief breaks throughout the day to keep the limbs and senses fresh.

Mechod Pangang had once been a major camping spot for the tea caravans coming through Sho La Pass, and it served us well, just as it had the ancient mule trains. We sat in silence, humbled by the mountains that spread across the horizon, and wondered how Nomè and Dorje would ever make it over with the caravan—if indeed the caravan had arrived. Our destination was farther down still: we would take refuge in a *netsang*'s home in the aptly named village of Lado, once a stopover for caravans heading to Lhasa.

Lado was reachable via a series of steep switchbacks. Descending, we entered a hushed valley, a wedge of tranquility. It seemed unreal that this warm calm could exist so close to the reckless forces in the pass. All the requisites were in Lado in abundance: grazing for the mules and welcoming *netsang* to provide us with safe shelter for the night and respite from the wind, good food, and, most importantly, tea. Shuffling through a field, Dakpa began singing, to warn the residents of our arrival. It was with an eye to both safety and courtesy that he sang. Throughout the Tibetan regions, you announced your presence when arriving in a village or town if you wanted to be welcome. The massive Tibetan Do Khyi mastiffs still guarded their domains with brutal efficiency, though Dakpa let us know that the local canines were benign creatures and we had nothing to worry about.

With wind-burned skin, bloodshot eyes, and cracked lips we hobbled into the four-house village of Lado, population twenty-six, and into a rare vestige of traditional Himalayan family life: polyandry—the rare (and becoming rarer still) tradition of one wife having the joy and burden of multiple husbands. Our host family consisted of a woman, her three husbands, all of whom were brothers, and seven children, of which six were away picking mushrooms at a camp in the mountains.

The practice of polyandry had its roots firmly planted in practical, rather than paradisial, ground. The women usually married brothers; in this instance, two of the three brothers were handicapped. The youngest brother (junior husband) was deaf and the eldest (elder husband) had a deformed spine that viciously twisted his figure. Only the middle brother was "fit." It was he who had fathered the children—though the children referred to all three men as "father"—and it was he who was the home's decision maker. Married to the three brothers, the woman of the home essentially cared for two husbands, while being cared for by one. Without similar arrangements, many men deemed unmarriageable would simply live as hermits in isolation. As part of a united group they at least could contribute in some way to the benefit of the household. In the case of our hosts, the deaf brother was a respected master in the art of caterpillar-fungus finding and spent most of the season in the mountains—he was as strong as a bull. The crippled brother assisted his wife in light work around the house. Women held sway over much that went on in the households, which was only fair since they carried the vast burden of the day-to-day grunt work. Once again, these lands in the clouds issued their own law: adapt in unity or be vanquished.

In Lado, we quickly became acquainted with the notion of clan commune. The members of our *netsang*, who made up approximately half the village, were direct blood relations; the other half of the village was indirectly related. This held true for the animals too: canines and yaks, fowl and felines were all related to the other creatures of that species in Lado. But there were no obvious aberrations, and the relations among the humans were cohesive and tight, though Dakpa wryly suggested that an injection of new blood was necessary. Whether he was suggesting something or merely observing, I still don't know.

After hearing of our time up in the snow, the "main" father, the middle brother, sagely shook his head. "Sho La has claimed many in its time," he said. He told us of how novice lados, after experiencing the fury of Sho La, simply disappeared in the night, finding the lifestyle too harsh. He also reminded us that we had much distance yet to cross before reaching Lhasa. In his day he had travelled widely by caravan; now he shook his head and warned us not to be hopeful of our fellow team members arriving any time soon: "You are too early in the season, and for Sho La it is still winter."

The tireless woman of the house brought us jars of heated home-made *arra*, into which was stirred raw eggs and a little sugar. In times like these, it was the simplest of pleasures that gave the most satisfaction. We sat outside, soaking our raw feet in warm water and feeling the slow, soothing burn of the *arra* as it coursed through us. What luxury it was. But concern for the rest of the team, possibly stranded atop the wild pass, nagged at us.

Later in the evening we were told a group from another village had tried to cross the pass from this side, only to be forced back by the storm. It was clear that no caravans would be making it over. Would Dorje and the others try to cross? Nomè and the horsemen would know enough not to try, but Dorje was a different matter. With Norbu's knee swollen to a grotesque size, we decided to rest and rehydrate for a couple of days, and figure out what to do next. Sonam, his lips raw and scabbed from not using lip balm, reminded us in an earnest tone that in Buddhism, when faced with a problem or question, it was best to simply wait.

Our tiny room, with its simple wooden beds, faced the valley and provided a view of the staggering snow-covered peaks we were headed toward. The village was perfectly positioned: it had views of stunning power and beauty while remaining protected by the abrupt hills on either side. Upon discovering in a shadowy corner of the *netsang*'s home a stack of woven bamboo containers holding a huge supply of Ya'an tea from Sichuan, I knew that I could remain comfortably in Lado for days. My own stash of fermented leaves was (I hoped) still aboard a mule atop a snowy mountain. When I asked how the tea had made its way to Lado, my host's response was slightly incredulous: "By mule, of course. It is the only way to get any supplies in or out of the valleys." In all the centuries of transport along the trade routes, little had changed, and if modern technology and transportation were to suddenly disappear, one could still count on hoofed creatures to make the journeys. In the past, tsompuns often traded tea, sugar, or salt to *netsang* for the privilege of grazing mules and restocking yak-butter supplies. Items of trade often functioned as currency—tea being the currency of choice—as the inhabitants of these isolated areas had little use for money itself.

Caravans journeying to Lhasa stopped at the homes of *netsang* less frequently than they did on their return trips, often pausing only if desperately short of supplies or food for the mules. Returning later in the year, their job done, they would take full advantage of the hospitality, offering exotic items from India and Tibet to favoured households. Particularly spoilt were women who the muleteers fancied; *larang* (literally, "lados' gifts") were treasured as much for their exoticism as for their intention. A woman who was popular would receive all sorts of treats, including corals, teas, silks, and cottons. Romance had been alive and well along the trade routes.

The next afternoon we received a gift of our own in the ragged form of Dorje. Having made a solo journey over the pass, he was frost-bitten, sunburned, and shrivelled. His larger than life force now seemed vulnerable. Even his prized moustache looked limp and spent. But I knew he was still undeniably Dorje, for his easy smile remained intact. We crowded around him as he recounted how even the juggernaut of yaks had turned back, unable to breach the pass. Ultimately, Dorje had crawled over the pass alone through the still-raging blizzard to make sure we had made it. He had the same fears about our fate as we did about his and the others and he had argued against Nomè's common sense, saying that if he didn't attempt the pass, they would never know. He was to return the next day to carry the news back to Nomè.

As he gnawed on a bent cigarette, Dorje told us that Nomè had become snow-blind. After the four of us had departed for the pass, Dorje, Nomè, our two muleteers, and mules had waited, watching the howling storm gobble up the landscape, blanketing everything in bleakness. Hours later, a yak caravan had arrived, but even it balked at the force of the storm ahead. In the ensuing hours, the sun's seemingly diluted rays had damaged Nomè's eyes. He had started feeling the tell-tale needlelike pains in his eyes late in the day, then burning sensations and that sure sign, twitching, as his eyes struggled to lubricate the damaged surface. The waiting team retreated off the pass to set up camp and care for Nomè, whose eyes continued to worsen. Like many mountain men, Nomè scoffed at the idea of wearing sunglasses, at encasing his eyes in black plastic. I had been concerned, knowing that even when hidden behind furious snow and cloud, the sun loses none of its ultraviolet potency. The intensity of ultraviolet rays increases by five to seven percent every three hundred metres of ascent, reducing the time needed to fry the cornea.

Dorje told us of how he had urinated in the snow and used the resulting "yellow popsicle" to soothe Nomè's eyes. Nomè eyes began to mend quickly, thanks to Dr. D.'s quick-thinking home remedy, and I began to wonder how many other clever uses Dorje knew for urine. An image came to mind of Dorje running a mountain medicine clinic for travellers and doing promotional tours espousing the virtues of his celebrated healing methods.

Dorje's feet were themselves in need of some healing, as they had been frostbitten on his trek over Sho La. Peeling, misshapen, and swollen, they were not much more than lumps of rotting flesh. But Dorje took no notice as he quaffed a jar of warm *arra*. Dorje had one request: that we all sing and dance and be merry in an all-night party, so that on his return over the pass the next day he would at least be happy. Incredulous, Norbu asked him whether he could make the crossing again on his own. The response was vintage Dorje: "I made it once, didn't I?" His nonchalance belied his strength and resolve. His pack was well, and that was all he needed to know.

That evening, the children of the *netsang* came down from the mushroom camps, and the house shook with festivities. Each community, Lado included, had its own perennial mushroom-picking zone. But the exact location of the camps, where the mushrooms grew rampantly, was cloaked in mystery, and no one but the mushroom pickers' family was told. The mushrooms were sold and delivered to hungry markets often as far away as Japan through the inevitable chain of intermediaries. Mushrooms and other earth-bound delicacies (as we were to learn) were huge business. Now, with the entire clan happily squeezed into the home, the spirit of the evening embraced us and, for one night at least, the mountains were put on hold. Dorje was non-stop movement, playing the *piwang,* a violinlike instrument, whirling, dipping, drinking, and flirting. Norbu's eyes told of the pain he felt in his knee and he retired early. Slowly, dawn's hues ushered the rest of us, one by one, off to our beds in a contented haze.

With only two hours of sleep behind him, Dorje departed the next morning, stocked up with extra socks, dried meat, and a container of *arra.* We scheduled to meet up with him in the town of Beetoo, on the banks of the Tsa Yu Chu, one of the Salween River's tributaries, seven days later. He and the mule team would descend back to Merishoo without attempting Sho La Pass. As he was departing, Dorje eyed one of the *netsang's* elder sisters. He was visibly crestfallen when she said, "Have a safe return, *Aku.*" By addressing him with the title of *Aku,* or Uncle, she virtually ensured that any relationship between them would be forever platonic. Seeing that Dorje still had this incorrigible side of him, I worried less about the struggle he faced ahead.

We ourselves departed the next day. The only downside to our stay in Lado had been an infestation of fleas in the house. They had penetrated into our flesh despite our socks and thermal underwear. Our backsides and ankles were ringed with pink welts and scabs where the fleas had fed on us. Even though we were vigilant, tying up our sleeves and cuffs every night to keep the fleas off our skin, we still woke with new bites and welts. Our fresh blood and foreign flesh must have been scrumptious for the little brutes.

The fleas irritated us so much that Norbu said a daily prayer to the gods, asking them to rid the universe of the pests. Sonam joked that if the bites didn't heal, we could simply urinate all over one another in honour of Dorje. I tried smoking out the fleas buried in our clothes but to no avail: they were now a part of our unit.

Mules were frequently driven wild by hordes of hungry fleas. In keeping with the lados' respect for their animals, they did their best to minimize the mules' discomfort. Losing a mule to a landslide or snowstorm might be unavoidable, but neglect was unconscionable. The scabs from the flea bites would chafe, which could lead to sores and infection. To prevent the chafing, the lados ground a certain blue flower into a powdery paste and slathered it on to the mules' coats.

After a few nights of the fleas, I would have gladly painted myself blue, but sadly, the flowers were not yet in bloom.

Members of one of the families in town, relations of the *netsang*, had lined up on their roof to sing farewells to us. For Tibetans, farewell songs were often a way of covering up lament. But for Dakpa, it was yet one more excuse to sing his beloved Bollywood songs, and every song was accompanied by body gyrations to match. And so, with Sonam and Dakpa in full chorus, we left Lado to make our way to the Tsa Yu Chu. Songs about the river, with its notorious 108 twists and turns, have resonated through the valleys for centuries. Everyone who has travelled in the region knows of the Tsa Yu Chu. For days to come, we would follow its snaking course.

For the first time on our journey, we encountered unbearable heat as we entered the Tsarong district (its name composed of two Tibetan words, *tsa* meaning warm or hot, and *rong* meaning valley). Norbu was a silent but fierce presence as he limped along. His only request was for us to not speak to him. We had already learned that his impenetrable silences generally were not to be disturbed. Although his enthusiasm could be contagious, his darker moods were best kept to himself. Sonam referred to these states as "Norbu's angry meditations." The two men each had very different outlooks on life. Sonam in his soft monotone often spoke of how little in life is really needed for happiness and how returning to nature re-emphasized this. In response, Norbu growled that he would kill for a Coca-Cola, his girlfriend, and a bath.

Passing through the town of Gyalam—Wide Road—named after a common Tibetan name for the Tea Horse Road—we met two brothers in their eighties, the valley's remaining lados. One was tanned and squat, and looked as if he had been in every battle ever fought. He was clearly the dominant one of the two, and it was he who addressed us, welcoming us with a direct *"Chang tong"*—"Join us for barley beer."

We sipped homemade *chang* as we sat with them on the roof of their house. (A rooftop, one of the only sunlit places in a Tibetan home, often served as a patio of sorts. Traditionally, Tibetan dwellings had small windows to deter burglars; the windows allowed only a trickle of sunlight into the houses themselves.) The *chang* acted as an anesthetic on Norbu's knee, and he eagerly accepted the repeated offers of more. Sonam, on the other hand, tried refusing, but it was no use. The old hosts had not lost their sense of hospitality; after all, they were Khampas, imbued with Khampa forcefulness, and it didn't take long before Sonam capitulated, his hard, disciplined features relaxing and his eyes glassing over as he drank the thick liquid. Along with drinking the *chang*, the brothers were also snorting *nada*, or snuff, at regular intervals. Originally from India, *nada* was a major item of trade and, for many strict Buddhists, the only vice considered acceptable.

Many of the elders found our expedition noble, urging us to "remind the outside world" of what had passed, of the land and the peace amid the towering spires, and the brothers were no exception. The dominant brother waxed eloquent when we asked him about mules. His eyes softened as he described a particular mule that he favoured, and he shook his fist as he warned of the hazards of careless grazing—many of the mountain herbs had narcotic effects. Recalling a stoned mule plunging to a rocky death brought him close to tears. He made no mention of lost cargo; his passion was the animals. He attributed his own longevity to the same qualities that made a mule a good companion: hard work and not thinking too much.

The other elder, silent up to this point, tried to join the discussion but was promptly cut off by his brother, who broke into a long explanation of mules' diets, which was "most important." At least one month before a trip (in May or June in the Western calendar), the fattening period began. Allowed to roam freely in certain pastures, the mules would eat the weeks away, being fed treats of *tsampa* (barley powder), along with balls of butter for healthy coats. Beans, sugar, and even salt were added to the mules' diet to help them pack on calories, which would help prevent chafing from the cargo they'd be carrying.

Both brothers clearly felt joy at being able to recount and briefly relive their lives on the move. But the distant blush of the sun signalled that the day was on the verge of ending. Slightly buzzed from the *chang*, we departed for our *netsang*, a little wiser for the memories the brothers' had shared with us.

A ONCE GREAT MONASTERY now sitting in cheerless ruins welcomed us to Beetoo, a town of dust, one road, and numerous telephone shacks where you could buy rope, melted candies, and heaps of items years past their best-before dates. All the shacks had red telephones sitting on the counter. The phones were status symbols for the proprietor: whether they worked or not was unimportant. When someone made a telephone call, the townspeople gathered round, as though the call was something in which everyone could participate. The town was a place that had lost its soul. Chinese prostitutes, who serviced the local construction workers, wandered around nonchalantly with their hair in curlers, brushing shoulders with Tibetan elders doing their *koras,* or circumambulations, around a small temple.

Sonam drew the inevitable crowd when he tried to use one of the dusty red telephones. Workers, kids, and anyone who had nothing better to do pressed into the shack to listen, even more eagerly than usual since this caller was "exotic." Sonam became aggressive, shoving for space as he was jostled and prodded by listeners making way for more listeners. Before long, Sonam's lean frame was swallowed up by the mass of people. Minutes later, a yell rippled through the crowd and Sonam pushed and glared his way out of the shack. "It's pointless," he said. "I cannot hear and cannot be heard. How long do we have to wait in this empty town?" Our sage was fired up.

We had taken three days to reach Beetoo from Lado, slowed as we were by Norbu's injured leg. But in Beetoo we found a Tibetan doctor who, within twenty-five minutes, cut Norbu's knee with a knife and drained the blood and pus, applied a herbal compress, and sent him on his way. Two days later, Nomè and Dorje burst into town in a beat-up pickup truck. Men, bags, truck—all were covered in a thick coat of pale dust. But dust or not, it was a happy reunion and a night of celebrating ensued—well, not quite a night. All of us except Dorje were in bed by 9:30 P.M.; he was no doubt competing with the construction workers for the attentions of the prostitutes. With all of us reconnected, I rested easy.

MORNINGS ON THE ROAD usually began in the dark chill. My companions had two distinctive waking styles. Sonam's soft chants and murmurings rose from his bed as he performed forty minutes of solemn morning prostrations and prayer to the bodhisattva Tara, believed to protect and provide strength and fortune in any endeavour. This was Sonam's sacred time, a time of calm and a time of homage. Dorje, on the other hand, jerked awake in an explosion of motion and immediately lit his first cigarette of the day. He then peppered everyone with questions and comments, before breaking into song or even the odd dance, all still from his bed. Sonam meanwhile endeavoured to stay focused.

Travelling with my Tibetan companions day after day gave me an insight into their lives, their fears, and their quirks, and I know that they also were learning about mine. One of my joys was seeing their excitement as we took in more and more of the Tea Horse Road. It was a part of their cultural past and cultivated a sense of pride, yet it was easy to imagine a time when the mountains would reclaim the meagre paths. Travel through the valleys revealed massive swaths of mountainside that had been reconfigured by landslides kilometres wide. In many spots the paths were mere threads, crossed only by ambitious travellers and shepherds leading their flocks. And although the geography was, for the time being, still tangible, the lifeblood of the route was the lados, and there were fewer of these each year. The urgency of our endeavour became more obvious with each passing day.

Continuing our push northwest alongside the Tsa Yu Chu, we entered into the heart of Tsarong, a region of heat and poverty whose fittest native sons had become the most successful tsompuns. Although Tsarong had been an administrative seat, poverty had pushed the brightest and brashest to lives in the trade, and many of those with a quick-thinking and no-nonsense approach to life had attained fame as leaders of the caravans, never to return home. Even now there seemed an eerie inscrutability to the land and to the people. Desertion and silence reigned here, and an overwhelming sense of neglect. Dorje remarked that he felt ominous spirits at work.

Many of the minorities in Tsarong had at one time paid homage to the Tibetan trade families. Slaves had been common as recently as the past century, when Tibetans dominated the social sphere and, more crucially, the business trade. Before the 1930s, the region existed as a blank spot on Western maps. The eclectic British explorer and botanist Frank Kingdom-Ward was the first outsider to penetrate its shadowy lands. He had returned home speaking of dwarves and of a land of magic and secrets.

Up until now, Dakpa's charm had helped us be accepted by the locals, which in turn allowed us to participate in their lives, if only for a short time. Here, however, the locals ran and hid as we approached, re-enforcing the sense we had that we were treading where few had ventured. Shorter and darker than Khampas, the people of Tsarong more closely resembled the Burmese farther south. Eyes wide, they stared, and I realized that they were looking not just at me, the lone Westerner of the group, but at all of us. Our boots, clothes, and hair were inspected. Very little from the outside world had pried its way into this land and we must have offered up a feast for the eyes, if a somewhat ragtag one. Our group of swaggering, dirt-caked Khampas—one (Dorje) wielding a knife partly in jest and partly in warning—and an unkempt whitie was both curious and daunting, and Dorje's insistence on performing his versions of eastern Tibetan dances as we entered the towns did nothing to dispel their fear or interest.

Sitting just north of Burma, the Tsarong region held an important strategic position in the Tea Horse Road. It was through this corridor that the Tibetan armies of the Tubo Dynasty first accessed the Nanzhao Kingdom (the present-day Dali area in Yunnan Province) in the seventh century. In subsequent years, communication lines were set up along the corridor as relationships deepened. The route passed from Lhasa through Tsarong into the tea-growing regions of southern Yunnan and into Burma, and it was along this route that the Tea Horse Road was built. And so it is little wonder that the young men of this part of Tsarong were lured into a life of trade. History had been passing through for a thousand years. It would have been easy to join a passing caravan and make your way to far-off lands.

Withered by years of raging sun, ropes strung to act as railings along the perilous cliffs beside the Tea Horse Road hung ragged and frayed. Hunks of grey stone plunged off the path as we passed. Parts of the route were often nothing more than gashes in the stone. As we moved along the disintegrating paths, the smell of hot dust filling our nostrils, Norbu commented, "Once you live this way, once you see all of this and experience this way of life, you can never return to a life of habit." He was right. This life of travelling charmed in a way no stay-at-home life could. It was a charm that stayed with you for life and was seeping deeper into me each day.

Remnants of bridges littered the edges of the river, the bridges not having been rebuilt since trade had ceased in the 1960s. Fights between muleteers frequently erupted over who had priority on the bridges, since on many of them, the narrow passage allowed only a single-file crossing. One thickset lado still carried the battle marks— a broken nose and collection of scars—of such an altercation sixty years later. With a twinkle in his eye, he recounted the time at a bridge crossing when neither he nor his competitor would retreat and allow the other to pass. A fight ensued, and he received a thrashing. He was fifteen years old and leading his first "caravan" of two mules. With the Khampas' penchant for uncompromising directness, such confrontations were as much a part of life along the route as trade was for smaller caravans. Reputations were often made or lost based on these incidents. The route was not only geographically perilous but socially as well; lessons were learned quickly and often violently.

One incident in particular emphasized to me the isolation of the people in this part of Tsarong. As we bedded down one night in a farmer's home perched in an all but forgotten canyon, an aged grandfather gravely asked if we could answer a question for him. Staring into his callused hands, he asked if we had heard of "time differences"—he had heard decades ago from a fellow villager who had visited Nepal and India that the time there was different from that at home. Was it true that time was different, depending on where you were? It had been a question that had been on his mind for fifty of his seventy-six years. He had never left his tiny valley, nor encountered anyone who could answer it.

When Dakpa confirmed the "rumour," the old man was delighted. In a bleak and unexposed corner of the globe, an old man had finally found the answer. Although it may not make any difference to his life, he did say that now his grandson wouldn't be wondering about it into *his* old age.

Dakpa and I slept that night on a hay-covered roof, with flecks of rain tapping us. We preferred the open air and talked long into the night about our old host's joy with his new-found knowledge, and of how that confirmation had brought him a sense of enlightenment. He had reminded us of one of the great yet overlooked aspects to the Tea

Horse Road: its role as an information highway providing news and knowledge about the outside world.

MARKHAM HAD BEEN a major hub on the Yunnan and Sichuan Tea Horse Roads, but we headed west, bypassing it altogether. Our destination instead was the town of Dzogong, which would in turn take us to Chamdo, in eastern Tibet. Dzogong laid claim to being a vital link in both the Tea Horse Road and the postal routes of the Ming Dynasty (1368 to 1644). Resting between two of the great Asian waterways, the Salween and Mekong rivers, the town had certainly seen more traffic in the past than it did now.

Leaving Dzogong after two nights, after restocking our supplies, Norbu summed up my feelings when he said, "If I don't see mountains on the horizon, I feel trapped." Like me, he needed an unfettered view of the mountains, one not disturbed by buildings or signs. Apart from Dorje, who enjoyed the novelties and distractions, we were becoming almost anti-social. Each time we approached a town, we became antsy, and it wasn't long before we were overcome by the desire to head into the hills again. Now, the city of Chamdo awaited us, with distractions for Dorje and mountains for Norbu and me. Chamdo was considered mountainous even by Tibetan standards: more than ninety-five percent of its landmass was dominated by peaks and ridges that pierced the sky. We looked forward to the upcoming journey. After all, this was a land whose countless winding caravan routes gave it the name "the land of sheep intestines."

The ubiquitous and valuable caterpillar fungi as they appear when cleaned. Often added to bottles of local barley wine, they can withstand repeated infusions. Interestingly, few Tibetans actually consume the little creatures.

3

Chamdo to Lhasa:
Passes in the Sky

It is in changing that one finds purpose.

—HERACLITUS

FOR THE KHAMPAS, there are three kinds of men in the world: The *porap* is a strong man who crosses the mountain passes to make a name for himself, and who strives to improve his lot in life. The *poting* is an average man who makes himself a home, worries about the necessities of life, and "competes with wood"—an inanimate object—to ensure his own victory and so as not to be embarrassed by being outdone. The *pota* is a weak man who stays at home and sits by the fire arguing with his mother. This old maxim clearly encapsulates the Khampas' philosophy of living.

The Khampa lados seemed to flout the limits that govern most mortals. Restless, volatile, and quick thinking, these men were custom-made for a life of privation and punishing elements. A Tibetan friend from Qinghai Province, in northern China, once referred to the Khampas as the people who "prayed one moment and killed the next." Perhaps an unfair statement, but it did illustrate their reputations for piousness and ferocity in equal measure. It also partially explained why they were able to thrive as lados on the Tea Horse Road. With their own codes of conduct, these men were wary of what one old lado referred to as the "sweet tongues that resided in the big towns."

Many lados, having reached the big centres of Chamdo, Dege, Sadam (Lijiang), and Dali, were keen to do business, enjoy the novelties there, and leave. Their itch for movement and general distrust of city people made them long for the open roads and wind-blown spaces. And so it was with us: two days after arriving in Chamdo, we were anxious to be on the move once again, despite the rest our stopover afforded us. Our departure from Shangri-La almost a month ago had brought us more than eight hundred kilometres, but still we were jittery and uncomfortable when inactive. Even the always festive Dorje was edgy. Watching a television program showing trekkers clad in gleaming Gortex, carrying GPS receivers, and brimming with gear, Dorje went into an uncharacteristic rant, saying, "Those idiots wouldn't last a day in the mountains." His rant was indicative of the restlessness we were all feeling. Upon arriving in Chamdo, we had learned that an old lado we had come to see had just recently died, giving us even more reason not to linger. The legacy we had come to capture was disappearing fast.

Situated at the confluence of two rivers, the Za Chu and the Ngom Chu, and tucked into one of the most mountainous areas of Tibet, Chamdo marks an ancient Khampa stronghold. It was a major centre of commerce in eastern Tibet even before the late 1950s, when paved roads started being built. Postal, tribute, and trade routes all passed through the city, making it an important trade and communications hub for a millennium. Because it accessed the northern frontier lands, Chamdo was a stop on the Yunnan–Tibet route and on the northern Sichuan–Tibet route to Lhasa. It was also an important junction on any course into the desolate lands of the Tibetan nomads, Mongols, Kazaks, and Uygurs farther north. Encompassing ancient trade and migration routes that had been active for thousands of years, the northeastern region of Tibet had witnessed much, including Mongol rule in the seventeenth century.

Throughout Tibet, that invader the paved road had in many areas replaced the old routes. But the branch of the Tea Horse Road we were to travel remained unsullied by major roads, and it was these long-neglected branches that offered some of the most stunning landscapes of the journey. Many lados had spoken of the trail as being a punishing route of bandits, blizzards, and beauty. Entire caravans disappeared in raging storms along its length. On several topographical maps I had seen large tracts of the trail marked "relief data incomplete." This served only to beckon us to the long-forgotten routes, teasing us, stirring our minds, prompting visions of what might be there. Soon we would see for ourselves.

The ancient transit way bisected the titanic Nyanqen Tanglha mountain range from the northwest, then headed southeast toward the spiritual beacon of Lhasa, a route far more direct but also far more dangerous than the alternative routes. On its way it wound through the hidden lands of the Abohor nomads and the seldom-travelled areas of the great Salween Divide. Lados had spoken of the notorious Shar Gong La and Nup Gong La, two passes marking the divide that tested even the mighty Khampa traders. Thieves abounded on the passes, and if you were able to survive them, the cruel grey spires of Tro La, the last of the great passes before Lhasa, awaited to provide one last test of conviction. Lhasa welcomed those sturdy and fortunate enough to make the journey.

Every lado we spoke to had travelled the route at least once in their lifetime. Their insight confirmed to us that we had done the right thing using people, rather than maps, as primary sources of information on our journey. These men were never ambiguous about the route, and although none had seen maps of it, their ability to unhesitatingly recall distances and topography was remarkable. Their maps were their memories. As we talked to the old lados, this route of high passes became even more significant to us because it inspired that rarest of emotions among the lados: awe.

Norbu's leg had by now completely mended, and he exuded impatience. His injury early on in our journey would prove to be a crucial element in his introduction to expeditions: it had served to both caution and motivate him. It was not to be the last of young Norbu's trials.

Sonam used his time in Chamdo to meditate in peace, and shave the eight whiskers that had valiantly appeared on his upper lip. Dorje, in the meantime, had shocked us by shaving off his prized moustache. His naked face seemed foreign to me, but his Dorje logic was simple: "The local Tibetan women like a clean-shaven man." Unfortunately, Dorje's foot odour had lost none of its potency and had inundated the hotel room he shared with Nomè. The ever-diligent Nomè, meanwhile, disappeared for hours to purchase supplies for the upcoming segment of our journey. Dakpa and I pored over maps, peeled off sunburned skin, and drank gallons of Puer tea brewed from my stock.

As I entered Dakpa's room one morning, the sour odour of bile hit me, and at that moment I knew our undertaking had changed dramatically. A frowning Nomè sat on one of the beds beside Dakpa, who was curled up beneath a heap of covers. Frail and chilled, Dakpa smiled at me weakly. Nomè had taken him to the hospital after a bout of vomiting and feverous chills, and Dakpa had spent an agitated night there hooked up to an IV unit. Utterly spent, he was suffering from physical exhaustion. The successive days of trekking had taken a toll. "Sho La has done this," he said to me.

After making it over Sho La, he had never felt the same. He knew that he would be a potentially dangerous burden on us for the next segment and, to his credit, made the difficult decision not to join us. He knew what lay ahead: a long grind through areas that hadn't been accessed for decades, locales with little or nothing in the way of supplies, and an area lados referred to as "the most physical part on the Tea Horse Road."

In the years I had known Dakpa, it was his ability to accept and move on that I most admired; it was his consideration of others that made him one of the few truly noble people I know.

Dorje, ever loyal and eager, decided to accompany Dakpa back to Shangri-La. Two men down, we would be four to Lhasa—Sonam, Norbu, Nomè, and I would continue on, plunging into the next section. Dakpa's compassion and his unparalleled ability with regional dialects would be missed. As for Dorje, we had lost a source of entertainment, and a power force in the mountains. The emotional turmoil caused by his desire to stay on the trek and his undying loyalty to Dakpa was clear, but in the end it was loyalty to his friend that won out. I felt privileged to have had such men as travelling companions.

THE NEXT DAY WAS SPENT packing and repacking, again minimizing our gear to the essentials while still making sure we would be ready for the great expanse of rock and snow that awaited us. The vast and deserted stretch of Tsa Gochentang would be short on both fuel and water. Making our way south from Chamdo by Jeep on Highway 214, we turned west onto a dirt track on our way to Da Noo Tang—Horse Weeping Grasslands. The plain was the starting point of Tsa Gochentang, one of the most physically exacting portions of the Tea Horse Road. The horses, mules, and men all suffered here under winds that one ancient said were able to wipe out footprints in the snow and loose earth in mere minutes. Stray mules were usually given up on quickly. The area seemed to gobble up life. Men who went searching for lost mules often disappeared themselves. It was fascinating, and intimidating that such a massive space could simply swallow up men and mules. As I watched the mists choking the horizon, I felt adrift in its vastness.

The ancient lados faced unforgiving winds, impetuous weather, and ingenious bandits. Now, although the climactic conditions remained the same, the bandits at least had retired for the most part. In the past, as the mountains and valleys approached increased in height and width, so, too, had the bandits' creativity—it was no small feat stealing from the notoriously tough Khampas. Small caravans were, of course, most at risk. The thieves generally took one of three strategies. The most straightforward attack involved brute force. If the lados had weapons, this strategy was risky, especially since many of the lados were Khampas, ferocious fighters who rarely steered away from confrontation. Never without their heavy knives, they were murderously proficient and enjoyed a little "physical activity" now and again, as one lado put it. One old Khampa had said to us, "What did we have to fear? We are Khampas." Whether accidental or intentional, violence was part of the life, and rarely in our travels did we meet a former lado who didn't have a scar, a gash, or some appendage missing.

A second bandit strategy also involved some degree of brute force. Approaching the caravan as fellow travellers, the villains would share tea or discuss the weather while assessing the value of goods and the risk involved in grabbing them and making a run for it.

The third strategy was the nocturnal switch. An audacious plan, fraught with risk, it involved replacing the desired items, usually tea or salt, with bricks of earth or cords of wood of about the same weight and resealing the containers. Tea was transported in brick or cake form, wrapped in tight bamboo sheaths, and wrapped again in yak skin to protect it from moisture. Salt was simply bagged and plunked into bamboo carriages. After unpacking the mules for the night, the lados kept their cargo nearby them, sleeping on top of the most valued goods, such as silver or cash. The mules were free to roam and graze. Bold thieves were surprisingly successful unless caravan dogs forced them to rethink their strategy. Then, with less time to switch items, not only was the cargo targeted but also the mules. Many a mule was miles away by the time the lados realized it was gone.

Penalties for being caught were harsh. It was in the lados' interests to make examples of those bandits unfortunate enough to be captured. Their livelihoods at risk, the Khampas were unforgiving, often hunting down bandits to exact justice on the spot. Bandit life became even riskier when lados started carrying guns.

On our first night of camp, we made an unpleasant discovery as we unpacked our gear. It seemed we, too, had been victims of a switch. Somehow Dorje's fetid sleeping bag had been packed onto Norbu's bag. Our sleeping bags looked identical, and we had no way of knowing whether Dorje had made the switch deliberately. Either way, Dorje's unwanted contribution would join us for the trip. I wasn't the only one whose sympathy for Norbu was quickly replaced by relief that my sleeping bag hadn't been the one switched. Sonam, Nomè, and I shared a moment of silent celebration, while Norbu looked like a beaten man.

Ahead of us, the trail looked forlorn and forgotten. In the distance we would see lone motorcycles buzzing their way toward us. Nomadic riders covered in ankle-length wools, black balaclavas, and oversized sunglasses raced past us, their arms raised in salutation. Fat vultures marked our passing with the patient interest of master survivors, as snow squalls in the distance teased us, temporarily obliterating the landscape. Villages were nearly devoid of people, and finding hosts, mules, and supplies was, as we had suspected, proving difficult. Norbu joked that the "prized worm" had emptied the valleys.

In fact, the worm Norbu was referring to wasn't a worm at all but a fungus. Known locally as *yartsa gunbu* or simply *bu* (summer grass-winter worm), the ten-centimetre-long (and sometimes as much as ten centimetres in diameter) *Cordyceps sinensis* fungi have long been instrumental in providing nomads and isolated settlements with much-needed profits. During the spring and summer months, there is an exodus of men, women, and children from villages throughout the Himalayas to the high mountains, where they set up camp, living there while they harvest the precious fungi. The little treasures are worth gold, and, much like the mushroom camps, the location of the camps are shrouded in secrecy.

The tiny fungi start life on caterpillars that have burrowed into the earth to hibernate for the winter. Eventually the caterpillars that have been infected by the fungus spores die, leaving their bodies as a host for the fungi. The purported health benefits of *Cordyceps* are countless, but its primary claim to fame is its ability to increase nutritional circulation to all parts of the body, with one particular organ benefiting greatly. The fungus has reached cult status in Asia as a natural sexual stimulant, and it commands exorbitant prices. Nomadic families of four or five could, in two months of diligent gathering, harvest two or more pounds. A local "fungus man" told me that a pound could fetch up to $1400—an amount that could easily keep that nomadic family, with their very basic lifestyle, fed and warm for two years. Local middlemen made fortunes selling the fungi in turn to Chinese dealers. We were to become well acquainted with them before long.

Late one night, days into our trek, a trio of mountain girls had barged into the ramshackle hut in which we were staying to try to sell us the fungus. Still covered in damp earth, the musty-smelling little creatures were freshly harvested. They were cleaned off with small brushes to reveal their tawny bodies and then gently laid out for us to inspect. In China's bigger cities, one might sell for a hundred yuan—between $10 and $15; the girls were asking ten yuan. We inspected the slightly soft bodies that sported the tiny black heads of their once-living hosts. Some were plump, others anaemic-looking, and I had to wonder about the properties they were said to have.

Once we had decided to buy a few, bargaining began in earnest. Not knowing how to judge, we prodded the fungi, smelled them, squeezed and weighed them, frowning in pretense that we knew anything about them. Sonam went so far as to test one with his teeth, prompting a warning sound from the girls. He told them that this was the way it was done in his hometown—a lie, of course. "Very well then," they indicated, clearly under the impression that we easterners were not only odd but barbaric.

When bargaining with Tibetans, it was not clever tactics that won out but blunt words and forces of will. We had long ago agreed that a team approach would be used in all our dealings, as each of us had certain strengths. Now, Sonam tried to drive the price down as Norbu feigned disinterest and Nomè operated as moderator. In this case, my role was simply to look and act ignorant, which was rather convenient considering I was neither accustomed to the style of bargaining nor familiar with the valuable product. The bargaining was a game, not so much about money but about having fun. By this time, the townsfolk had shown up, crowding into our room to witness the proceedings. The lead girl refused to budge on the price, and despite all of Sonam's rakish charm, the price remained fixed at ten yuan.

We bought twenty of the fungi. Delighted with themselves and perhaps with us, the girls assured us that our performance would benefit. Norbu smiled, while Sonam shuddered. We immediately added a few of the fungi to our wine supply, to ensure that the benefits would be shared by all.

LHATSE WAS A TOWN that appeared to be in constant gloom, a village of damp, dark fogs that had narrowed in on itself and retreated. Sitting in a valley, it wasn't a place where the sun often ventured. Lonely curls of wood smoke rose through the roof slats of a few of the houses. We were there in search of a trader who was said to have made dozens of journeys along the various arteries of the Tea Horse Road. Learning that his wife had died four days earlier and that he himself was coughing up blood, we were prepared to forgo meeting him and leave him in peace. But upon hearing of visitors, he insisted on speaking with us. A powerfully built grandson quietly led us into a stone hut of three rooms and served us tea. The grandson's eyes took us in carefully, then flitted to his grandfather. The young man in an instant would cut us off and possibly do worse, should his weakening grandfather become upset by our questions.

It was at first hard to make out the bald old man, propped up in the bed and deep beneath wool blankets, his long, lean hands resting in front of him. The muted room had two windows that let in only dim light, which, combined with the sense of his recent loss, gave the room a sombreness. Every corner of the room seemed infused with his sorrow.

At eighty-nine, Dandee Pinchu's skin was the colour of burned butter, creases like black welts lining his face. This face had led caravans into screaming winds and snow and had borne the brunt of many seasons in nature's great stone garden, the Himalayas.

We settled ourselves around him and waited for him to speak as our eyes slowly adjusted to the dim light. He was aged, yes, but still commanding. Speaking in the Lhasa dialect, which was more common than the Khampa dialect, Sonam explained to Dandee our interest in the fabled tea horse route. Sonam's soothing and respectful voice always put these rare personalities at ease. Dandee nodded his head slightly as he gently massaged his temple with his hand. We waited patiently. He exuded a lonely strength that so many of the lados seemed to have, and we had learned not to rush them.

"We had to urinate while walking, so that the mules didn't get mixed up, or worse." His rumbling voice was as startling as his words cutting through the dimness. "It was the most difficult of lives, but we didn't know it at the time. The mules had more difficult lives than us. Horses were too finicky, yaks too unwieldy; mules alone were the perfect partners for the journeys by the men with the hands of stone." Our host shut his eyes, and I suspected he was remembering the days of old.

"I was a lado for a Lama from Xiangcheng [in Sichuan], and the bandits didn't dare bother a Lama's caravan for fear of their afterlives." Monasteries often had their own caravan teams to transport tea, incense, salt, wool, and religious relics, and for much of his fifteen years of roving, Dandee had been a handpicked member of a high Lama's entourage. Thanks to their business acumen, monasteries made fortunes trading goods in the city centres, able to profit because of their power within Tibetan society. The caravans also provided safe passage for monks and Lamas. Other caravans often linked up with the holy convoys, so that their own shipments would be secure under the auspices of both secular and spiritual forces.

Tea was often presented as gifts to Lamas, and most caravans made donations of tea to the big monasteries when passing by, in return for blessings and merit points in the next life. The monasteries often hoarded tea in dark chambers, storing it until the prices rose and then selling it for huge profits.

When I asked about the discipline of the caravan teams, Dandee's voice rose and his hands coiled, somewhat rejuvenated. "The tsompun's attitude affected the quality of lados. The leaders had to be shrewd, compassionate, and, most importantly, respected. Relationships were built on trust and smarts. A tsompun not only had to make sure his cargo and men were secure, he also had to nurture relationships with host families and maintain the confidence of his employers, the powerful trading families."

Dandee was riveting and forthcoming, and showed no trace of vanity. But he began to wheeze after long exchanges; speaking clearly exhausted him, and at times his words tapered to a moan, or he was racked by a phlegmy cough. There were long pauses while we waited until he was ready to speak again.

"What direction have you come from?" Dandee startled us by speaking.

When Norbu told him that we had come from the east, Dandee murmured something about the "two faces of Sho La." Our interest peaked with the mention of our old nemesis, the Sho La pass. We told him of our ordeal on its slopes, and he nodded slowly in understanding. Any remaining barriers had come down: the Sho La we knew was the Sho La he knew, and we were bonded in the knowledge that we had all struggled and succeeded.

"The cold ate at me, and it would freeze the tea in minutes," he said, then passionately recalled how ice would form between the horseshoes and the mules' hooves, causing the animals incredible pain. In extreme cases the horseshoes had to be removed, the ice shaved off the hooves, and the shoes replaced, all while still on the pass. The lifestyle of the lado would "kill the youth of today" he said with a long sigh as he cast his eyes downward and shook his head.

Did he miss those days? we asked.

"No, no ...," he faltered, "but in the valleys we would have tea and we would talk too much, but they're gone ... yes, I miss the *tsapo*," referring to the tea and food breaks.

I wanted to stay longer with this man, to absorb even more of his spirit, but it was time for us to go. One by one, we rested our hands on his gnarled, callused ones in a respectful gesture as we quietly departed.

For all the romanticism I have attributed to the lados' adventures, theirs were lives of simple truths, struggles, and mountains. There was nothing vague in the mountains, and one of the great appeals of the men was that there was nothing vague about them: they were fully engaged in life.

SHAR GONG LA, the Shar Gong mountain pass, was one that had been at the back of our minds for weeks—it had reached a special status among the four of us. It and its big brother, the perpetually snow-covered Nup Gong La, had become synonymous with the Tea Horse Road's physical dimension. An unofficial gateway into the greater Nyanqen Tanglha range, Shar Gong La would lead us out of the Khampa stronghold of eastern Tibet into the realm where caravans encountered their greatest trials, and where we would encounter those of our own.

Our first priority upon arriving in Pemba, the final town of any size before Shar Gong La, was to find mules and a horseman who knew the mountains, but two days of searching yielded nothing: the caterpillar fungus had once again foiled us. Most of the mules, along with their proprietors, were already high in the hills on their annual pilgrimages to the "land of the worm." We were also hearing rumours of avalanches. One local told us, "You cannot cross over Shar Gong La." We had two choices: wait indefinitely until we had secured the mules and horseman and the danger of avalanche had passed or head out on our own. Perhaps it because of our successful experiences with pushing forward and knowing our limits that the option of waiting held no appeal to any of us. But it would be our resident "Mr. Steady," Nomè, who in the end decided. In his typically straightforward way, he said simply, "We can do this." Moderate and practical in all things, he was the voice of reason, and his was the voice we listened to.

We found a driver and Jeep, packed up our gear, and made our way toward Shar Gong La, intending to get as close as possible before going by foot the rest of the way. As we drove, we spotted figures hunched over the earth—fungus pickers. After about forty kilometres, we stopped. Ahead of us, a metre-thick wall of white blocked the road: an avalanche had obliterated the dirt track ahead of us, and this was as far as wheels could go.

We unpacked to re-edit our gear, repacking only the *absolute* absolute essentials. As I deliberated over the equipment, I wondered what exactly "essentials" were. For a lado, his life belongings could be wrapped in a single leather satchel. After shaving down our belongings, we were left with about thirty kilograms of gear per person. I recalled old Dandee, his voice rattling, gifting us with an old maxim of the caravan trails: "Mountains are nature's editors." How often had we in the course of our travels eliminated items because of the mountains' demands? Our driver was dubious about our plan and recommended we return to Pemba with him to wait it out; we were too early in the year, he said, and there might not be any transport at all beyond the five-thousand-metre pass. But Norbu, dwarfed by his load, was already walking toward the white horizon. Turning, he said, "We are Tibetans" and continued on.

ISLANDS OF CLOUD slipped through the sky and the sun burrowed into us. On the horizon we could see the massive peaks marking the divide of the Tsangpo and Salween rivers. The Nyanqen Tanglha range ran east-west, a magnificent barrier accessed by tight gorges and glacial rivers. Locals believed that a sea once occupied the great valleys between the Shar Gong and Nup Gong passes.

Ascending the pass on the single footpath path, where the snow had been beaten down by previous travellers, we encountered four nomads casually carrying a motorcycle across the avalanche and a young man whose eyes twitched horribly with the beginnings of snow blindness. It was just another day in their lives in the mountains. We had a bag of cheap sunglasses we had bought in case our own broke, and which came in handy as small offerings to fellow travellers, and so we handed him a pair. The nomads told us that all the mountain passes were snowed in and only the valleys were clear.

But winter still had its hold on the access roads leading into the valleys. Nature dictated the speed and the route of our travel—and whether we could travel at all. After about two hours, we finally reached the pass. The landscape opened up into a vast expanse of beauty that numbed our senses with range after range of white-sheeted mountains. The snow's insulating silence muted everything but the wind. If Sho La had been furious nature, Shar Gong La was a grand breadth of it. Below us, valleys wound in every direction, and all was glittering ice, snow, and the dark ridges of stone.

Sonam's nickname of "Spiderman" had not been given in vain. His wiry frame seemed to flit about unaffected by gravity. I had long since stopped worrying about his exploits in the mountains, since Norbu constantly reminded me, only half-jokingly, that if Sonam did fall, his light weight would hover for a second or two before gravity kicked in, giving us time to rescue him. Gesturing to us that he had found a shortcut along a narrow ridge, Sonam did a little dance that was his way of testing the path. Not believing in walking sticks, he used his feet and hands like multipurpose tools. Winds had shorn the undulating snow from the path, and his shortcut proved easier going than the main route, which lay deep under a white blanket.

Careful to secure each foothold before taking the next step, I soon became aware that on Sonam's shortcut, a misstep to the left would launch me onto a fifty-degree slope, shooting me into a canyon. Sonam's shortcuts often called for an acrobat's nerves and just a touch of insanity. We joked that there was a very real possibility that Sonam intended every one of us to perish.

Sonam and Norbu walked ahead, Sonam in the lead, their bulky shapes dominated by their packs. Nomè and I followed some metres back. At one point, Norbu stopped and pivoted slightly toward me; in that instant his feet shot out from under him and the weight of his pack sent him rocketing down the snow-packed slope. Sonam's shriek as he watched Norbu was almost inhuman. In an explosion of strength, Norbu managed to flip himself onto his front. Even as I heard

Sonam's terrified screams, Norbu was digging in his hands and feet to slow himself in a spray of white. I knew that in that one movement he had saved himself—and the rest of us a lifetime of grief. Incredibly, a few hundred metres down, he ground to a halt. Carefully scuttling down the slope, we found him sitting quietly, smiling slightly, with only a small tear in his pants. Sonam's face was strained as he looked beyond Norbu to where our friend might have ended up. Another twenty metres or so and he would have been pitched into a rocky gorge, to become a modern-day casualty of the Tea Horse Road. So often, it seemed, the distance between a tragedy and a miracle was minute.

Only slightly ruffled, Norbu told us that he knew he would be all right even as he was shooting down the slope. "Sho La was a good instructor," he said softly. We came to refer to the incident as "Norbu's number two," number one having been his Sho La experience. Sonam sarcastically asked what Norbu had in mind for number three, his stern expression masking his protective feelings for our youngest team member. After a tea break to bring our pulse rates down, we continued down Sonam's shortcut without further incident.

My thoughts were never far from the lados, their stories and experiences, and cargo, and so, as we walked, I found myself thinking of those delicate green leaves—the tea, packed tightly and bound to mules—making their way over snowy passes to distant markets. Journeys from *jaiyul*—tea areas—in southern Yunnan Province to Lhasa could take six months, and just as the character of the terrain changed, so did the tea.

The tea Tibetans craved was not the tea of the West. The most consumed beverage on the globe still struggles for an identity beyond the cultures that grow, harvest, and live with it. The West, long duped into believing that the tea they were imbibing was a quality product, would scarcely recognize the black brick of tea carried by a mule. A plump bag of Lipton's best would taste like nothing more than dusty hot water to a drinker of the powerful black teas so loved by Tibetans.

Grown in more than thirty nations, tea or *Camellia sinensis,* as it is known to botanists, is categorized into three main varieties: *sinensis, assamica,* and Indonesia. Despite the many names, most tea comes from either *Camellia sinensis sinensis* (a small-leaf shrub grown mainly in China) or *Camellia sinensis assamica* (a big-leaf shrub grown in southwest China and India). Tea's essence and character, and its colour designation, are established only after the leaves are picked. Greens, yellows, and whites are lightly fermented if at all; oolong—known as *ching* or blue in China—is partially fermented; and red and black teas are fully fermented and often aged. All these teas may originate from the same tea plant. The vast majority of teas grown in Asia have been cultivated as an economic commodity, then spread through trade and often hybridized. From the birthplace of tea, in China's deep southwest, the first varieties of tea made their way into the remote mountain areas of Tibet. Parts of India's tropical Assam region, in northern India, have also been home to indigenous or wild tea for thousands of years. Tea from these areas has been nurtured, talked to, and fawned over, then sent off into the very peaks we were now ascending.

Under the scorching eye of a high-altitude sun, tea leaves start to ferment. What began the journey as freshly plucked green would emerge from its hold dark and pungent. This tea was not only stronger and earthier in taste, but it had also developed medicinal properties. It was the arduous journey, rather than any deliberate manipulating, that led to the drink Tibetans have preferred for a thousand years and more.

TRYING TO FIND SHELTER with caterpillar fungus pickers along the route inevitably led to suspicions that we might be rival pickers. When asked directly if we were, Norbu would point at me and casually ask why a foreigner would travel all of this way to pick fungus, joking that foreigners had aphrodisiacs of their own. This evidently satisfied the pickers, and the hospitality they then extended would almost always embarrass us. Still, many tried to sell us some of their harvest, and if we replied that we had already bought some, the pickers would insist on inspecting them. Some, much like antiquarians, would nod in approval of the size, the shape, and the striations on the bodies, while others would roll their eyes, shaking their head at what they perceived as an inferior or prematurely picked crop. All our interactions with the pickers we met seemed to revolve around the creature. I came to refer to stories of our encounters as "the chronicles of the worm."

We were making our way into the lands of the semi-nomadic Abohors, people who lived in the remote valleys between Chamdo and Lhasa. And, as Nomè reminded us, we were also entering a world effectively still cut off from the outside—we would have to deal with any emergencies that arose on our own.

The reputation of the Abohors preceded them. One lado, with typical Khampa directness, warned us of the "despicable character of those people," while Dawa of Merishoo had suggested that the Abohors had been "spoiled by the profits of caterpillar fungus." I asked a Khampa trader how Abohors differed from Khampas. "A Khampa will steal if he can but be the first to help, whereas an Abohor will hesitate to steal and hesitate to help," he replied, pursing his lips in disapproval. Isolated and not having travelled as traders, the Abohors kept to their hills and their fungus, whereas the Khampas had been fearlessly wandering, pillaging, and trading in the Himalayan corridors for centuries. Where the Khampas confronted, the Abohors held back.

We finally tracked down a horseman outside a town called Chini Bela. Finding a mule or pack horse to help with our gear was not easy even here, and the old volunteer had to be convinced that we would make it worth his while. The negotiations perfectly exemplified the significant differences in character and manner between the Khampas and the Abohors. Negotiating for the horseman's services and that of his horse was complicated, lasting more than an hour, and I was glad to sit back and watch this cultural exchange of sorts. For the Khampas' services, we paid a lot but had all the details settled in twenty minutes. With the Abohors, negotiations were almost a performance. Surrounded by a good portion of the townsfolk, Sonam tried in vain to quickly conclude the deal, but the horseman kept asking the townspeople for their opinion on the matter. But this was new ground for them: offers for a pack horse's service didn't happen here often. Arguments ensued, with some urging him to accept and others ridiculing the offer. All the while, Sonam's face grew more sinister. Semantics were not kindly tolerated by the fierce tribes of Kham, and Sonam's quivering jaw muscles warned of a pending blow-up.

Children stood silently watching the debate as the crowd grew ever larger. When at last it seemed a price had been agreed upon, we heard a voice raised in protest that we were being cheap. And so it continued this way until Sonam halted the proceedings with a burst of impatience and a growl of indignation. Looking straight at our horseman, he said, "If you are a man, you will decide now, or we will leave." Sonam's hands were tense, his body bent in resolve, and his gentle eyes had become dark with that Khampa menace I had learned to appreciate. Sonam's approach was both provocative and effective: the horseman quickly agreed to the terms.

I loved Sonam's boldness of spirit, his unpretentiousness, and Norbu actually applauded the display. We paid more than we had initially offered, but we had an old tea kettle thrown into the deal. Nevertheless, the incident made me realize that Sonam was not an effective enough negotiator for us to get a bargain. Now, as with the fungus the girls had sold us, we ended up paying too much. So I suggested Norbu begin acting as our bargainer, which pleased him to no end.

We were to have a 6 A.M. departure the next day. Our food pack contained biscuits, noodles, radishes, a chunk of yak meat, garlic, chocolate, and a bottle of *arra*. From a local woman we bought *palè*, homemade barley bread, and a five-kilogram hunk of pork fat, as well as a bunch of green onions. But the next morning, our horseman, Lobsang, didn't show. This sent Sonam off into a diatribe about humanity. Although himself ethical and moral to a fault, he remained sceptical about humanity in general. With all his cynicism about people, he still expected the best from them and went into tirades when he felt let down. He went so far as to say that the Khampa lados' appraisals of Abohors people were right, and that they were undependable ditherers with no honour.

Sonam disappeared, intent on finding our horseman, to return an hour later, having woken the still-inebriated man. As they approached us, Sonam looked grim and the swaying horseman slightly dazed, but the crucial horse was in tow.

We travelled under sheets of blue for days, meeting many people who as children had witnessed the caravans pass through their towns. "We could hear the tinkling of bells of the *shodrel* [head mules] coming down the valleys long before we could see them. The lados would walk beside their mule teams, which formed long columns," one man whom we encountered told us.

Order among the caravan teams was generally strict, and it was a credit to the lados' sense of duty that we never once heard of them behaving poorly in the towns. One lado recalled an informal and eccentric rule of the road particular to his caravan team. If, during the course of the journey, a tsompun was discovered to have been intimate with a woman without allowing his lados the same freedom, he was bound and then had stones tied to his genitals until he agreed to some form of compensation for the muleteers. Compensation could take the form of better food, a day of rest, extra pay, or a gift of tea. Luckily, Dorje wasn't around to hear about the perils of pursuing women on the trail.

Tragedy along the route was not limited to caravans, as we were to learn during a lunch break. Chewing our dried yak meat and onions, our recently acquired horseman, Lobsang, gestured at our green surroundings and explained how the town of Alando once sat in this valley, and how as a child he had roamed the area and dreamt of having a home here one day. Looking around, there was nothing to suggest that life or structures had ever existed in the little nook. Sitting at the confluence of two rivers, it had been a tranquil paradise until one fateful night when flood waters ripped through the canyons, wiping out eight families along with their livestock and homes. All that remained were flapping prayer flags in honour of the lost town and the lost lives. Tibetans viewed such tragedies as retribution or karma for some misdeed or a warning to leave a particular locale. No community would ever settle here again.

Joining us for a spell was a young rider who had come to pick the caterpillar fungus. His long frame, large hands, and reckless good looks marked him clearly as a Khampa. Though only eighteen years old, he looked thirty, and, typically for a Khampa, his abilities with horses were enviable. Riding into our camp, he wanted to share food and company with us. After tethering his two horses, he opened his bag of food for us and we did the same for him. I had long seen the value of the informal way in which things happened in these parts. The overly polite manners of those in big cities struck me as superficial, whereas here the unpretentious way in which strangers addressed one another appeared genuine. A camaraderie existed in the mountains, one based on a shared geography and a shared struggle. Whatever other differences might exist, with this commonality and understanding communication could be brief yet meaningful. It was good for our group, too, to have the company of another Khampa; the body language and complaints struck similar chords.

And so our tiny caravan grew by one man and two horses. Our newest addition conversed with Lobsang about horses, and they studied each other's with curiosity. As we continued our journey, our young Khampa selflessly shared his mounts with us when there were flooded ravines to cross. All of us were far from home, and this bonded us.

We met another rider along the route who told us that our plan of reaching the town of Ala Jagung before dark was unrealistic. It was just past noon, and Ala Jagung, at 4390 metres, was still more than thirty kilometres away. He hadn't taken into account that for Khampas, limits were something to flout.

We did reach the outskirts of Ala Jagung just as dark began to dominate the light. We had covered more than forty-five kilometres that day. Our priority now was tea, followed directly by bed. Approaching the town in the dusk, we came upon three drunken Chinese men who were finishing up work on a building site. It was strange to see them in the middle of nowhere in their heavy overcoats—even by Tibetan standards this was a remote area. They seemed bored and belligerent.

Norbu muttered something about "trouble coming" just as one of the men drunkenly grabbed at the reins of one of the young Khampa's horses. The horse rose on its hind legs in protest. Not to be dissuaded, the man then tried mounting it, inadvertently kicking the horse in the ribs. His two comrades roared in laughter. The young Khampa, his handsome features tight with fury, let out a blood-curdling roar. He had brought his own mount up alongside the one the drunk was on, raising a horse strap high to deliver a mighty blow to the man. Only Lobsang's quick intervention prevented a potentially lethal beating. He positioned himself between the young man's strap and his target, while Nomè grabbed the horse's reins. The young Khampa wailed in anguish at not being able to deliver his blow. His wail cut into my being, stirring something deep in me; it was like a call to arms. The young Khampa's fury was the fury of the just, and it was a terrible and beautiful thing to behold.

It finally dawned on the drunk what was happening. Fear sobered him in an instant. His two mates, meanwhile, were stunned into inaction. We crowded around the young Khampa, trying to soothe him and head off a second attempt, lest blood be spilled. Again I was struck by the thought that it was this ferocity, this driving force, that had made the Khampas of eastern Tibet so dominant in battle and business.

Throughout the incident, Norbu and Sonam had remained calm; being Khampa, they understood our young friend's reaction. Now they eased the horses and the man away from the Chinese trio as Nomè and Lobsang warned the three of the perils of messing with a Khampa's horses. Trigger points for Khampas can easily be summed up: honour, land, and horses. Anyone who encountered a Khampa quickly learned that he had to be firm, honest, and careful if he was to remain breathing. The horses and his scant belongings were likely all the young Khampa had, and he would protect them and his honour with a rare kind of spirit, a spirit that had been passed down from a generation of people who travelled with not much more than will, pack animals, and a devil-may-care attitude.

We all felt drawn to the young man and urged him to join us as our horseman for the upcoming section, and even Lobsang, who would then return home, encouraged him. The young man thanked us, but said he wanted to get to another fungus camp before the season ended. We parted ways the next morning. Bloody interfering fungus ...

ALA JAGUNG had been a favoured resting place of caravans. Whether preparing for Nup Gong La or exhausted by its crossing, the town provided a haven where caravans could rejuvenate. The four of us were in desperate need of rest: our throbbing heads and limbs were threatening to stop functioning. We had trekked thirteen hours that day above four thousand metres and our mouths—and brains—felt dried up. Some locals offered us a nourishing stew, which we accepted graciously, eating noisily until our shrunken stomachs became bloated and hard. They then showed us to a bare-bones wooden hut where we could spend the night. Little did I know that the next morning I was to receive my first offering from the gods, a gift from above.

I was walking along a path to a small stream for my morning ablutions when I was struck by a sharp, silent force from above that dropped me to my knees. Searing pain ripped into me. Stunned, I reached up to my left shoulder and felt the dampness of blood. There was a gash along my collarbone where my skin had been sliced open. Clutching the wound, I looked up at the mountain to see what had caused the blow. In the distance, I saw nimble goats leaping from ledge to ledge, dislodging stones that then plummeted down the mountainside—offerings from above. Even though the offending stone was only the size of a small walnut, it felt as though my left shoulder had been hit with an axe. Later Nomè would tell me that it was a good omen, that it could have been a larger stone.

Meanwhile, Sonam had found a man, about fifty years old, keen to serve as our horseman—but he first had to ask his wife's permission. He returned to us, permission secured, only to have to excuse himself again to ask her what the price should be. Norbu giggled that no Khampa would ever ask his wife's permission, no matter what the reason—"at least not publicly."

Our horseman arrived at our hut the next morning with two horses. One well-muscled animal he would ride, and the other, an old grey, would carry our equipment. The grey was an antique whose best days had been years ago. Nomè, who knew horses well, blanched at the sight of the poor thing. The horse's hind legs quivered and quaked just standing still, and it looked bashful, as if in apology. With Khampas, horses' health and well-being were paramount, and they would have long ago sent the poor animal into retirement. Uncomfortable with the state of the horse, we begged the horseman to reconsider his choice, but to no avail. The two horses were all he had, and he wasn't about to consider riding the aged, slope-backed mare himself.

Not wanting the creature to expire on us, our humane solution was to load the horse with only a bare minimum of gear. Surprisingly, the old grey held up well for the entire first day, though it did have a troubling case of gas. On every incline, however mild, we were treated to a session of loud detonations issuing in perfect rhythm from the horse's rear. Every effort was made to stay well ahead of the horse, its alarming reports marking our progress along the trail and echoing into the rocky canyons. At only a foot wide, the path required full concentration at all times, and the horse wasn't helping.

Approaching the formidable Nup Gong La, the old muleteer pointed us to a lone nomadic community consisting of two yak-wool tents. A small naked child with dreadlocks played in a stream, barely taking notice of us. It turned out that three generations of women ran the little encampment. Sitting around the fire, they welcomed us, then sprang into action to prepare tea, bread, and *tè*—sour yak cheese— and also to put together a care package for us. It was here that we were reintroduced, all too briefly, to earthly delights.

A young woman who had been working outdoors came into the tent and everything seemed to stop. Tall, lean, and stunning, she smiled at us and sat down. Picking up a sleeping child from beneath a blanket, she showed us her *pomo*—girl. I'm not sure any of us even looked at the child, so transfixed were we by the mother's robust beauty, with her black hair pulled back over gold-specked eyes and full lips. Unlike many of the Abohor women, she was unadorned with jewels or stones. We were hopelessly unsuccessful in our attempts not to gape, and Sonam's monotone had become an unintelligible rasp, while the usually stoic Nomè was locked in a shameless trance. Norbu wore a blissful grin on his face as he stared idiotically at the woman. As for me, I had ceased to feel my legs the moment she walked into the tent. Urging us to eat and drink more, she pushed the food and tea at us, unaware that she was on the verge of creating a mutiny. We accepted bowl after bowl of tea so as to prolong our visit.

It was not uncommon for lados to fall for such women while travelling. After spending long months on the road, it was only natural that some would be attracted to a life of relative comfort and warmth over a lonely life on the trail. Many, having fallen in love, abandoned the trail and stayed where they were. Quitting a caravan was an informal affair, unless you worked as an employee of one the big trading companies, and even then, staying behind for a woman was considered acceptable grounds for leaving. The caravan would simply continue on, looking for a new recruit with horses.

Eventually, we left the nomad's tent, a silent, introspective bunch, secretly glad to be clear of our wandering thoughts. Had the incorrigible Dorje been with us I could only imagine what might have happened.

DOTOK, literally translated as "stone roof," is a nomadic settlement made up of one large extended clan. At 4630 metres, it was also our last stop before crossing the 5468-metre Nup Gong La. Flat dwellings of broad stone stood low to the ground. It was easy to imagine them becoming undetectable mounds under a white shroud of snow during the winter months. As we arrived, our old grey horse let out a final wail of gas, as if to point out to us all that it had successfully made the journey, despite its appearance. Having delivered us to Dotok, the horseman took his leave immediately, which surprised us. We joked that his wife kept him on a short leash.

Dotok was once a stop along one of the ancient postal routes. Mail up until the 1950s was transported through a series of runners or horsemen, and postal stations often consisted of nothing more than fresh horses and a warm fire.

The Dotok men wore their hair in braids. Our host, whose ancestors had been postmen, was the clan head, and he prepared a yak stew that we ate with an abandon that would have pleased even my Hungarian grandmother.

Just before turning in for the night, the village matriarch brought us bowls of thick, sweet *omah*—yak milk—and like kids we slurped our way into what I figured would be a deep sleep. Safe from the winds, our stomachs full and the fire crackling, we bedded down in a corner of our hosts' dwelling, ridiculously content even though the space was no more than two metres wide and forced the four of us to be tucked tightly into one another. But it would turn out to be a night to remember—for all of the wrong reasons.

That night, Sonam's teeth came into full chorus earlier than usual. Once that finally died down, the hyperactive highland rodents, the *avra,* began to run riot. Throughout the Himalayas, vast networks of tunnels teemed with the voracious little monsters, some the size of a small marmot—or so it seemed to me. Evidently, they also inhabited the stone dwellings of Dotok. The sounds of scurrying and scratching increased in frequency and volume, reaching a crescendo before dissipating, only to surge again. To make matters worse, Nomè, Norbu, and Sonam were all in the depths of an exhausted sleep, so while they slumbered, I alone struggled to remain sane.

I turned on my headlamp, which I always wore around my neck when I slept, and one of our hosts gasped in shock as the blue light cut into the darkness. Quickly extinguishing my light with mumbled apologies, I felt the night come alive as miniature bodies shuffled madly about. The odd skirmish broke out here and there between rival rodents as they battled it out over a crumb of food or, perhaps, a prospective mate. It was clear that they were lords of the domain at night. Before long, they were bumping into my sleeping bag. Jolting upright as one bold rodent streaked across my feet, I cracked my forehead on a low-hung shelf with enough force to snap my head back, and I was tempted then to grab my gear up and sleep under the stars. Instead, I buried my head deep into my wool hat and tried to retreat farther into my sleeping bag. This tactic worked until, just as my pain from the bang on my head was slipping away and sleep was mercifully arriving, Norbu turned over in his sleep, thumping me on the nose with his elbow hard enough to bring tears to my eyes. For moments that night I had murder in my heart; daylight could not come fast enough for me.

When I woke up, I saw that the wound in my shoulder from the rock had seeped red deep into my clothes and sleeping bag. Sleepless, bloodied, swollen, and stiff, I was a silent mass of wrath and ugliness and couldn't help but glare at everyone as we prepared for another day of trekking.

Our *netsang* offered us as much food as they could, and we gratefully stuffed dried *palè*—homemade barley bread—and wads of yak meat into our packs. In need of an extra therapeutic stimulant, I used two tea balls, rather than the usual one, to make tea for my Thermos.

Our ascent of Nup Gong La was slow. We were carrying all our belongings—the locals had refused to risk venturing up with mules, telling us that, even though it was June, the snow was too deep and dangerous—and our packs were heavy. But I didn't care about anything other than tea and movement: every time we paused for a rest, my swollen nose, scabbed head, or bloodied, aching shoulder made themselves known. In more than a month of travels, I had never felt so on edge. Nevertheless, I still had that feeling of autonomy that releases the soul. Should everything collapse around us, we had what we needed. Nup Gong La awaited, and I knew that I couldn't waste my energy on hating rats or obsessing about a lumpy nose, though, in a way, my misery motivated me. Sightlines stretched for miles ahead into the blue sky. The thick snow reflected not only the warmth of the sun but also a vicious glare. At first, the sun was pleasantly soothing; all too soon it started to pound into us, and before long we were covered in sweat.

We then became aware of a strange sensation. The wind had died down and silence descended in pure heat. The wind had given the sun the opportunity to show its power. We continued to climb in gentle steps through the waist-deep packed snow, and every once in a while a foot would plunge into a deep cavern—these air pockets under the snow were what put mules at significant risk. Using bungee cords, Nomè strapped both his packs onto his back. Usually we carried one in front, but Nomè's packs were unwieldy, despite our packing only the barest of essentials, and he was always tinkering to find the most efficient way to carry them. And although it helped with balance, carrying a pack in the front hampered your ability to see where you planted a step, and each blind step was potentially dangerous. Nomè cut a strange, misshapen figure, hunched as he was with the massive bulb hanging off him, but he had the balance to carry it off.

Picking out chunks of exposed stone or sculpted snow forms as landmarks, we mentally cut the ascent into smaller segments, resting as we reached each landmark to sip tea. We avoided eating the snow, which, if it had sat for months, could bring on bouts of cramps and diarrhea—as tempting as it was to soothe my tongue, pulpy from the heat.

Rather than calling for bursts of strength, the grinding ascents required carefully measured steps. Nomè warned us that we would dehydrate if we ascended any faster, and that heroics under a high-altitude sun inevitably backfired. Heat became a major factor three hours into our climb, when our mouths began to feel as though they had been sponged dry of every drop of moisture. My thermometer read thirty-two degrees Celsius, and my skin and lips were starting to fry. Several times I simply planted my face into the snow and let it cool my skin. Even down to our shirtsleeves, we felt the debilitating lethargy that only intense heat can bring on.

We had crossed from the east side, leaving the heart of the main Nyanqen Tanglha range. Heaving through the deep snow, we finally reached the summit, where we treated ourselves to a spoonful of jam each, one of our favourite pick-me-ups. A jar of very average marmalade had turned into a highlight of the week, and we rationed it like it was the last jar of jam on Earth.

It was time now to begin our descent. Nomè and Sonam tobogganed down the slopes on their behinds—until Sonam narrowly missed being cleaved in two by a black slab of stone. Tso Dungwu Ngi, the mystical ice-covered twin lakes, sat off to our left, groaning with the spring thaw. Having crossed Nup Gong La, we had officially left Arig district and entered Lharigo. But in the mountains, where maps were alien, there were no formal borders, no fences, nothing other than tree lines, snow peaks, and rivers to mark which land belonged to whom. Continuing our descent, we were confronted by two young men who were acting as watchers of the pass. Once again, the caterpillar fungus demonstrated its incredible sphere of influence. We had crossed from one unofficial zone of fungus picking to another. Norbu and I weren't pleased about having to explain ourselves to the young men, and I was tempted to say something belligerent. As the two pickers sized us up, I wondered aloud what they would do if we simply moved past them without their permission. It was probably fortunate that the men didn't understand English. But Sonam reminded me of where we were and what was at stake for these people. The fungus was one of the only commodities that the mountain peoples could trade for profit. Fortunately, the two decided that we were not there to take their fungus, and we were allowed to move on.

Oddly unfriendly, the nomadic encampment of Tsachuka reminded us once again that we were far from the unquestioned hospitality and directness of Kham and the Khampas. Villagers walked by us barely acknowledging our presence. In any number of cities in the world, this would be normal, but in a nomadic encampment of about seventy people in a desolated area, it was more than peculiar: it was downright bizarre. We were, however, learning that where caterpillar fungus was concerned, all bets were off in predicting the behaviour of locals.

Sonam approached some young men with questions, but they simply walked away from him. After fifteen minutes of this, Sonam lost his temper, screaming at a man, "This isn't my Tibet ... what's happened to Tibet? We give tea to travellers, we give warmth ... you don't even talk. Why don't you speak ... *why?*" Sonam's sinewy features were strained. Principled and not prone to explosions based on mood alone, Sonam was disgusted. Norbu looked tense and aggressive, and my own thin temper was ready to snap (though partly, I had to admit, in anticipation of having to exorcise my rodent demons again that night). Nomè whispered to Sonam to relax.

The four of us huddled together. The incident was a reminder of how isolated we were, of how very much we needed the good graces of locals. By now twenty or so villagers had gathered, staring at us and our gear. Norbu cursed and made as if to move toward them. But then I realized as I looked at the faces around us that we were surrounded by fear, not malice—not what I would have expected from a hardened mountain community.

Addressing Nomè—strangers often picked up on Nomè's role of mediator and his approachability, just as our mules had picked up on it so long ago—a man explained that the community's headmen had warned the people not to talk to outsiders, in case they tried to get information on the location and quality of the caterpillar fungus, or even try to rob them. Sonam muttered something, obviously finding the explanation distasteful.

The villager observed that our group was made up mostly of Khampas, his voice hinting at the respect, and a touch of fear, that our team often inspired. Nomè nodded. Even in this isolated community, the Khampa legend was alive and well.

The tiny village had been on the frontline of fungus intrigue, and the villagers' paranoia was extreme. It was a sad little place with a sad bit of history. The Khampas in their time had travelled and traded far, learning the worth of other goods, learning the invaluable skills of negotiating. Here, there was only a worm.

OUTSIDE TSACHUKA, we found an empty nomadic dwelling to use as a foundation for our tents that night, and Nomè put his talents to work. Rearranging slabs of stone and turf, with a bit of direction to us, he built a windproof, rainproof nook in ten minutes.

Throughout our time in the mountains, we made these temporary shelters and actually began preferring them to a hut or *netsang*—not because we didn't like the *netsang* hosts, or the treats they provided, but because the shelters were clean, flealess, and totally of our own devising, which added to our feeling of independence. The system was simple: we lined up our sleeping bags side by side, positioning our heads on the high ground, and jammed our boots into a corner, to keep their odour as far away from us as possible. We put stones in our socks and placed them next to the fire, to warm. (Norbu, still with Dorje's unwanted sleeping bag, had tried smoking out the odour, but the stench was entrenched.)

Nighttime brought a new world as the blue-black blanket of mountain air erased in just moments the grand geographies of the daylight hours. The cold night air would hurtle into our little abodes, relentlessly searching us out. Evenings consisted of eating, piling more layers of clothing on, and then unceremoniously stuffing ourselves into our sleeping bags. This night, we heard approaching footsteps. A gang of Tsachuka men appeared and proceeded to check out our shelter, admiring the bungee cords and sleeping bags. We all tensed, unsure if they had come to confront or simply look. But they wandered around the tent silently and respectfully, even though Sonam glared at them, almost daring them to say something. His anger hadn't abated yet, and he didn't care who knew it.

Then an unexpected thing happened: a man asked Nomè if we needed hot water. It was an offer we couldn't refuse, and I certainty was not about to. Nomè and I prepared some of my heady black Puer. It was at times like these that tea provided not only respite but also an offering of something beyond histories, beyond needs and economies, and even beyond the worm; it was an invitation to share that was understood throughout the lands. Tea was integral to community life and no decisions were made, no treaty signed, no celebration marked that didn't include tea. And so, for fifteen minutes, a silent bonding took place. By offering the tea, we expressed to the locals that we understood why they behaved the way they had. I wondered how many confrontations could be thus avoided.

SONAM WAS CONSTANTLY on the lookout for opportunities to prove himself—and perhaps to make amends for his temper having got the best of him. One day, not long after departing from Tsachuka, through the *whoosh* of the pelting water in an ice-cold driving rainstorm, we heard eerie bleats. We decided they needed investigating. We made our way in the direction of the noises, eventually coming upon a goat destined for a slow death. The weak animal was neck-deep in a muddy swamp. Sonam's eyes lit up and he skilfully made his way toward the goat, grabbing it without any hesitation by the horns and eventually releasing the muddied and skittish creature on dry land to enjoy another day. Norbu sensibly suggested we consider having a meal of goat to mark the good deed.

Bogs and gloomy skies gave way to open plains, with tiny communities sprinkled here and there. We could see isolated showers off in the distance, reaching for the earth. Greenery gave way to a geography of brown. As we rested next to the path, sharing a Thermos of tea, a nomadic herder greeted us in passing, then led his yaks to an open grazing area about fifty metres beyond us. Not five minutes later, I noticed him shaking oddly. There is nothing ambiguous about an epileptic seizure, and I began hurtling instructions to the team as I raced toward the man. Three of us reached him to find bile gurgling out of his mouth and his pupils dilated into huge discs. We rolled him onto his side and cleared his airway, then waited with him while Norbu somehow tracked down his family, who fortunately lived nearby.

When his son showed up, we moved the father to his simple dwelling. It was touching to see the huge son embrace his father, nuzzling him and cooing, *"Aba, Aba"*—Father, Father—undeterred by our presence. His big eyes thanked us in a way words could not. The father, having recovered, silently touched our hands. I was reminded how quickly death and suffering can occur. We would, however, be constantly reminded that here, joy was equally swift. Our encounter that day made an impression on each of us, and we continued on in silence.

Atsa Tso the town and Atsa Tso the lake, although adjacent to each other, seemed to be in different worlds. The town was going through a boom of modernization, with nothing quite finished, while the sacred lake outside town was a multihued calm of shimmering green. For us, it was time to rest and have a rare treat: a hair wash. Sonam, ethical as always, decided to announce our arrival at the local police office in town. (In Tibet, you are required by law to register when arriving in a city or major town.) So Sonam and I, passports and travel permit in hand, walked into the office—and straight into the troubling figure of the officer on duty. Dressed in a lumpy suit, his eyelids swollen, he looked like a lazy brute, and I felt in my bones we were in for some kind of incident. For all of Sonam's genuine outrage in the hills, he was a gentle creature when confronted with authority, folding his hands and dropping his head in a show of inadequacy. His reaction inevitably started my blood boiling in a blend of protectiveness and a desire for him to show some spirit. We knew that our documents, which were wordlessly ripped from Sonam's hands, were in perfect order. This must have peeved the officer, for he seemed intent on finding error. Sonam continued to gaze at the floor.

Heat was coursing into my neck and shoulders, and I felt my eyes go dry in a surge of loathing. Tugging at his suit in what I assumed was meant to be a gesture of superiority and almost screaming at Sonam, the official demanded to know exactly what we are doing, where we are going, and for how long. In a little voice that made me shudder, and through the numerous interruptions from our inquisitor, Sonam gave a precise rendering of the whats, wheres, hows, and also the whos and whys. But the official had made up his mind about us long before, driven by that deadly condition known as boredom. I felt a choking desire for Sonam to assert himself and our documents' legitimacy, and to cut the boor's performance short. I kept humming to keep my anger in check.

If anything was missing from our permits, the officer could easily call the issuing office to confirm. But instead, he wanted to throw his weight around, and Sonam's meekness was only protracting the situation. Being held up by a storm was something we couldn't control, as were both altitude sickness and shattered bones—but this situation was different. I wondered whether the counter that separated us from the man was a blessing or curse. In rough Mandarin, I suggested the officer call and clear up any issues with an "authority," hoping that by my use of the word *authority*, he would understand that I didn't regard him as such. I could feel Sonam's frame go slack beside me, and for an all too brief moment I had the pleasure of watching the officer's conceited eyes go blank. He moistened his thin, cruel lips by his tongue as he composed himself and considered his options, not sure how to take the waiflike Sonam and the agitated foreigner. He must have decided that there might be trouble from higher powers, for he shoved our papers back at us and waved his hand in dismissal. Leaving the police office, I ranted about how assertion was sometimes necessary. Sonam peered at me, saying simply, "Our ways are different, but we balance each other, yes?" I suppose we did. Sonam had more than a bit of clever politician in him after all.

ONE MORE MAJOR PASS awaited us before we reached Lhasa. Tro La— or Crying Pillar Pass, as the muleteers called it—inspired another deep emotion in people: fear. The pass wasn't on any map I'd ever seen; at times we even doubted its existence, but as we approached, we all felt its presence. This legendary pass was the last bit of physical anguish to be inflicted on travellers before they reached civilization. It would take us south, out of the great ranges, out of that great belly of mountains, to where our journey turned west and headed on to one of the bastions of faith.

A collection of yak dung piles and stones marked the long-forgotten path to the pass, and it was from here that we departed one pale dawn. In preparation for Tro La, muleteers would sometimes grind together ginger and dried mushrooms, add boiling water to the stimulating mix, and slurp it back—and only then attempt the pass. Our own inspired diet that morning consisted of an added shaving of chocolate. I ripped off some dry tea leaves to keep in my mouth, the bitter tonic waking my body and stirring my mind.

Traders and horsemen alike had stressed to us the secular nature of business: gods and nature's grand forces had little place in the world of economics. And Tro La, or Crying Pillar Pass, was not given its name for any otherworldly spiritual qualities it might possess but for the suffering and misery it dished out.

Covered in shale that sat on a layer of rubble that in turn sat on a base of permafrost, Tro La was a lethal combination—it was landslide heaven. Shale gave way in great tracts that started slowly, then slid down in great ugly clumps to echo through the canyons. At one snow-covered part, I was forced to do a variation of a crab crawl as I tried to keep my weight as widely distributed as possible. Sonam was inadvertently skiing down sections, only to nimbly skip back up, while the indefatigable Nomè was moving impossibly slowly, calculating every stride.

During our dozens of crossings of mountains, peaks, and passes, crossing Tro La was the only time we kept our heads down not to see our next step but in concentration, summoning up our energy. It would take us almost half the day to ascend the five kilometres to the summit. We might have uttered a total of eight sentences the whole way up. Finally, we reached the top. Winds whipped over us in reminder of what had passed, and the four of us silently embraced. It had been a time of peace for us, blissfully ignorant of dates and times as we were. For nearly two months, ever since leaving Shangri-La, we had been up with the first light, down with the dark. Days were just days and had no names, and while numbers—of temperatures, altitudes, distances—do not reflect life, they do hint at the rigours involved in travel along the ancient Tea Horse Road. As troubling and daunting as the segment had been, the equally grand pleasures and rewards were well worth the effort.

We had covered almost sixteen hundred kilometres, not even half of the route. No clouds parted, no snow fell; nothing marked our arrival at the summit other than our laboured breath and the wind. It felt lonely here, as though the mountains missed all the ancient traffic. The jagged blades of grey stone were handing us over to the next phase of the journey: we were entering the Himalayas' holy land.

A rare moment of unity—both emotional and physical—in front of the holiest of holy locations for Tibetan Buddhists, the Jokhang Temple in Lhasa. From left to right: Yeshi, Jeff, Dakpa, Tenzin, and Sonam.

4
Lhasa to Litang:
Holy Lands

As long as there is a sky, as long as the earth is not emptied,
there will be no discord.

—TIBETAN NOMADIC PLEDGE OF FRIENDSHIP

LHASA THE DREAM, the centre, the holy.

For the many lados, Lhasa was one of the main reasons to become
a muleteer. It was a centre point of faith, a place that called spiritually
to every corner of this nation of isolated valleys and windblown mountains. A simple lado returning from Lhasa to his village was greeted
as a hero, a man of stature, a man who had *seen*.

Lhasa was a place where all things led. Trade routes, postal routes,
pilgrimage routes, and tribute roads; beggars, traders, and warriors all
converged in Lhasa, a valley on a plateau of stone, before leaving
again. It was here, too, that the various paths of the Tea Horse Road
came together, only to splinter off the main route again. From this significant juncture, the main route continued into northern India, while
smaller subsidiaries continued west and north along the Himalayas.

Having arrived safely with their cargo, many lados would stay the
winter, though some remained for the rest of their lives. One thing
both lados and tsompun did without exception while in Lhasa was
visit that most sacred of places to Tibetans, Jokhang Temple. The
temple's construction began under Songtsen Gambo, the Tibetan
king who married the Chinese princess Wencheng, and it is the most

precious building in all of Tibet. Songtsen Gambo's other bride, the equally stunning and clever Princess Chizun, was from Nepal and it was toward her homeland to the southwest that he faced the temple, in tribute. Since the middle of the seventh century, the most sacred Buddha image in Tibet, Jowo Shakyamuni, has rested within Jokhang's walls. This sacred statue, it is said, was brought to Tibet as part of that celebrated dowry of Princess Wencheng. The princess's high status in Tibetan history is because of two items in her dowry, one belonging to the secular world—tea—and the other belonging to the spiritual world—Jowo Shakyamuni.

Our own arrival in Lhasa was one of sensory overload. We slowly took in the throng of humanity and the endless motion. Norbu was delirious with joy and expectation; this was his first time in Lhasa. Arriving in Lhasa also meant that, at long last, he could escape the suffocating stench of Dorje's sleeping bag, which, incredibly, had not lost any of its potency over the course of the trek. I began to wonder if it was Dorje's way of reaching Lhasa. Sonam was in one of his semiconscious trances, and ever-steady Nomè seemed nonplussed. As for me, I felt delirious joy from having arrived at this fabled destination of prayer and sanctuary. Yet, I also felt a peculiar sense of loss at having abandoned the jagged peaks that had shepherded us intact for so long.

Our first two hours in the city were spent in a kind of urban rehabilitation, as bodies, dust, and sounds competed for our attention. None of us was quite sure how to deal with the wall of movement and the fact that we had actually arrived in this metropolis. The mass of people thrilled and terrified us. Having become accustomed to being alone with the sky, mountains, and stars, it was all rather unnerving. But our days along the trails and our talks with the many who had made this journey, and the many who hadn't, had given us a sense of reverence for the city, and particularly Jokhang Temple. In travel, you adapt or perish. Part of my adaptation had been to develop a fresh perspective on Lhasa based on my experience and time spent with lados, as I heard of the physical struggles they went through to travel the road and ultimately visit this sacred place. We, too, had battled to get here, negotiating rivers and mountains that two months ago had been but names. Exposure to the hardships and personalities associated with the route inspired an intense appreciation of our destination's significance.

But soon, my preoccupation became more self-centred, for I realized that the mysterious odour that had been with us for some time was emanating from me. In the open expanses, or even in our windswept shelters where we often passed the nights, the elements had dispersed the odour, so we hadn't been able to detect the source. Now, in the confined spaces of a city, truly enclosed interiors, I realized that it was me who had taken on a raw edge. Weeks of consuming tea, pork fat, butter, and cheese, along with gruelling exercise, had altered my metabolism, resulting in this interesting odour emanating from my pores.

All of us were filthy. The condition of our feet had long since gone beyond acceptable, and we were covered in dust, dirt, and dung. Glacier streams had provided bathing waters, but the temperatures didn't encourage long soaks, so while we had washed, we weren't squeaky clean by any measure. So we headed to the Flora Hotel, a short walk from Jokhang. Shown to my room, I stared at the door, not quite sure what I was looking at. In just two days, we had moved from stone encampments bristling with wind to neat little rooms with numbers on the doors. The room was quiet and totally foreign to me. Emotionally, I was still out in the mountains. I had to control an urge to bolt.

After shaves and drip showers, thanks to the low water pressure, we rushed to Jokhang to join the swelling mass moving around the temple. Our clockwise *kora*—circumambulation—was part of something ageless and understood, something soothing, something safe. It was thanks.

Powerfully built Khampas, wool-covered nomads, the new and the ancient all joined in the rotation. The Tibetans here ran the gamut: enormous monks from Kham; shaggy-haired men of Amdo, in the northeast of Tibet; young mothers from Tingri, on the Nepali-Tibetan border—all had come to demonstrate their faith, a faith evidenced by bruises, callouses, and perspiration. I felt moved being able to participate in this incredible ritual in an age where sceptism ruled.

On our journey to Lhasa, a rheumatic muleteer we had met summed up the business element in the city when he said, "Business is not within the realm of gods; it is the mess of earthly men. We never prayed for success. That was up to the mountains and men." He added, "It was after the business was done that we could pray for our souls, and those of our loved ones." Lhasa offered both a wealth of material things and a wealth for the soul. It was the centre point of both.

Caught up in the movement, we continued the *kora* for hours, well into the night, none of us wanting to let up or leave the crowd that had become comforting. Sonam, with his prayer beads, joined in the chorus, reciting prayers in his soft monotone voice. Excited and wide-eyed, Norbu let us in on a little secret: he had lost eight kilograms since leaving Shangri-La. Sonam promptly berated him for having such vain thoughts within earshot of the sacred Jokhang. Norbu quietly accepted this judgment with a tiny smile, then sputtered how his wife-to-be would be delighted with his new-found form. Sonam's "*kaakaa,*" a Khampa term signifying displeasure, demonstrated his outrage. Nomè and I howled at the exchange. Nomè himself seemed most interested in the hundreds of stalls lined up on the *kora* route, tempting him with gifts he could bring back for his wife and children.

For some, like Sonam, the arrival in Lhasa marked a spiritual high point. For Norbu, it was a dream turned reality, and for practical Nomè, it represented an abundance of trinkets to bring back for his kids from a place they might never see. But we all also felt a sense of humble accomplishment. Finally, we halted the *kora,* stopping at the entrance to the Jokhang, where Sonam, Norbu, and Nomè prostrated in devotion. They were not alone: the rich, the impoverished, the pious, and the corrupt all bowed on knee and belly to the centre point for Buddhists throughout the Himalayas.

LHASA HELD LITTLE in the way of reminders of what had transpired there so long ago. Certainly, not much of that essence remained in the central markets of Barkhor, one of the city's older neighbourhoods. Products that were once valued by and vital for the caravans were now considered novelties. The horse markets were gone, replaced by stalls selling gold tooth caps, something of a local trend. Elders had believed that a gold tooth protected against poisoning, but the reason most

Tibetans now sought one had more to do with the look. I contemplated buying a gold cap myself, before succumbing to tea-stall gazing. There were still tea stalls selling tea bricks from Ya'an in Sichuan, and it didn't take me long to find them. Prices were four times what they had been in smaller towns. This tea would have arrived by truck via a paved road.

Barkhor had a bedlam charm, and I could only imagine the sights and sounds the lados would have been a part of. Many had described it as a manic, exotic wonderland. Banaksho, the main market area in Barkhor, had in the past been a one-stop "shop." Jade, musk, copper, horses, salt, silk, corals, and tea would have sat on display, beckoning travellers. These goods from India, Nepal, and even the Middle East made it to this holy city by caravan, and it was these exotic imports that were prized and taken back into the hinterlands of Kham by caravans and lados alike. Another commodity was available too: sex.

Not only were goods, worship, and flesh all available to the new arrivals, they were within easy access of one another. Some lados upon arriving in Lhasa would visit Jokhang in much the same way pilgrims would, lighting a butter candle and circumambulating the temple. Dots of golden light danced about as the butter lamps burned with their offerings of energetic fire, illuminating light, and valued butter—the very same pale-yellow yak butter used to make Tibetan tea. After the *kora,* many pilgrims would visit another local establishment, a place concerned with the pleasures of the flesh rather than the purity of the soul: a brothel.

"If a lado went missing in Lhasa, his companions would search the local brothels. Lhasa was a health risk," an aged monk had told us in a horrified tone. Arriving on the south shore of the Kyi Chu, the Lhasa River, the caravans would camp there until the tsompuns had secured buyers for their goods. Only then was the cargo brought into the city. Once a tsompun had sold and delivered his merchandise, he paid the lados—with tea, with the currency often used within Tibet before the loss of independence, or with silver ingots. The lados were then free to leave the caravan—and to visit the brothels, if they so chose.

One distinguished ninety-year-old tsompun with whom we had sipped *chang* told us that his operation didn't pay wages per se. Upon arrival in Lhasa, he provided lados with clothes, horse gear, knives, and, if a lado had been skilful and efficient, a load of tea of between twenty and eighty kilograms. This tea was something a muleteer could trade or sell. In market towns throughout the Himalayas, tea was more valued than gold, and as early as the fifteen century, it was used as a currency of sorts. One good horse was worth up to 120 kilograms of tea, 70 kilograms got a decent animal, and 50 kilograms would get you an animal that at least had four legs.

One veteran who worked for the same trading family for years happily told us of how he and many other veteran lados were permitted to bring their pack animals laden with tea along on the caravan. Reaching Lhasa, they could then trade their items, or sell them and retain the profits. "Tea and trade items were the currency of India, Nepal, China, and Tibet. We didn't need money if we had something to trade," one old Khampa told us.

When Tibet's currency was officially replaced with that of China's sometime in the mid-1950s, many traders lost a great deal of money. But those who had traded for or bought up tea, wool, silks, and other tradable items had what the old Khampa called "a fortune—items like tea and wool rarely lost value."

Lhasa's three major monasteries, Drepung, Sera, and Ganden, received visits from the tsompuns and lados entrusted with donations from villagers, businessmen, monks, and other monasteries. Upon presenting these donations, the tsompun or lado was given a *jolen,* or receipt, by the monasteries' *nyeba,* the treasurer, to be passed on to the donors.

In all our talks with lados, tsompun, and merchants, not once did we hear stories of dishonour among the tsompuns or lados in their handling of the donations. But several men, including Dandee, told us that such a system today would never work. When Norbu had mentioned paper contracts, one astute old merchant muttered, "If someone needs a piece of paper to seal a promise, that person must be a liar."

OUR ENTRY INTO LHASA had been by foot, but our exit was to be by a winged metal beast, which would fly us back to Shangri-La in less than two hours—a far cry from the two months our trek had taken. A day's drive north of Shangri-La, in the daunting landscape of western Sichuan, a nomad named Tenzin, one of Dakpa's business partners and yet another Tenzin in a long list that I was to encounter, impatiently awaited my return. He would be my guide for the next segment of the journey. And so, it would be back to the ancient Tibetan province of Kham and the indomitable Khampas for me.

I was once again somewhat at the whim of guide availability and the elements, and I was eager to get back to Shangri-La given the small window of time in which the conditions were right. Tenzin had secured the services of two horsemen of nomadic blood, which made them ideal. My venture ahead traced a leg of the Tea Horse Road that the nomadic caravans had taken but that, as far as I knew, no Westerner or Chinese had travelled. Notorious among the muleteers, this desolate route would offer a peek into the Litang nomads, the fierce Litangpa *drokpas,* and their connection to the caravan trails. From Lhasa, a place of the spirit, I was headed into as pragmatic and harsh a land as any in the Himalayas.

The half-empty airplane allowed us extra room, but as I sat in my assigned seat, I felt disconnected from the land that had held us safe for so long. The mountains had tested us, had threatened and taken from us, but ultimately, they had ushered and protected us as well. Now we had stepped into a machine that took us far from those mountains, a machine that rose above them. The giant blue blade of sky cutting across the mountain ranges provided a backdrop to this flight that we would later refer to as the "Nomè Show."

Nomè had never flown before and his anxiety was clear from the moment he boarded the plane. His eyes flickered about while his fingers explored the various controls on the seat arm and played with the fold-down tray. He knocked on the small window next to his seat to make sure it was sturdy, and he kicked at the floor to make sure no gaping holes were waiting for him beneath the carpeting. The Chinese flight attendants tried to reassure him, all the while keeping their distance, perhaps viewing him as a touch wild.

Takeoff wasn't a problem for Nomè—most Tibetans I know are speed enthusiasts—but when the choice of two meals was offered in Chinese, he sat perplexed for a moment before answering in

Mandarin that he couldn't eat two meals and that one would suffice. On being presented with his one meal, he looked at the bemused Sonam and asked loudly where the kitchen was. As we passed over an icy lake, he insisted that we had crossed nearby just days ago, his finger banging on the window in glee. Peaking down on a spot of blue, I would have gladly glided down to once again be in all that space. The "civilized" world we had come back to had not yet impressed me.

Our ninety-minute flight covered more than 1100 kilometres, and the concept that it was taking us back to Shangri-La seemed unreal to Nomè. After landing and disembarking, I realized that Nomè in his innocence had summed up this unreality for all of us. Looking around the two-room airport, he said that the transition had been like pushing a button, meaning it was that quick, that possible, in our modern times to go from one world to another.

Dakpa was waiting for us in the airport, and his welcoming smile helped eased the transition. Still thin and drawn from his Sho La adventure, Dakpa studied us carefully, taking in our changed appearance. With a sad smile he told us how, upon returning to Shangri-La, he had been taken up with "administrative life" and "trying to gain some weight back." Dakpa informed us that "mighty Dorje" had forlornly returned to his small town, a half-day's drive north of Shangri-La, and like an overly worried mother, was calling Dakpa hourly, day and night, for updates on our condition, location, and return dates. After a while, Dakpa no longer answered Dorje's calls. Dorje's wife later told me that, upon returning home, Dorje had sat chain-smoking and staring out the window, nervously stroking his moustache, cursing us for not calling him and letting him know our status. Sleepless, bored, and irritable, he was a man whose mind was very much elsewhere. I was to see Dorje again very soon, though I did not it know at the time.

Geographically, Shangri-La was a central base for the various chords of my journeys along the Tea Horse Road; logistically, it was a supply base for reconvening, repacking, and recovering. Now, my companions of the last two months and I would separate, as I was scheduled to meet up with Tenzin farther north, in Litang. Norbu would return to his work and an impatient boss, Nomè had a family to return to and a home to finish building, and Sonam would race to his remote town to visit his ailing father. My own brief time in Shangri-La would be spent procuring clean underwear, enjoying a meal or two of Bhaskar's wicked culinary treats, and re-editing my equipment.

The trip from Shangri-La north to Litang could take as little as thirteen hours of hard driving, depending on the weather and road conditions. The four-by-four I had hired took twelve and a half. The drive was fast and competent—to a point. After a food break, progress was punctuated by tea breaks and pep-up talks to the driver, who had the terrifying habit of increasing speed while nodding off—the weight of his drooping chin seemed to apply even more pressure on the gas pedal.

The destination was an old haunt of mine. Over the years, my path had repeatedly led to Litang, and I had spent time studying and living with the nomads. So, in a way, arriving in Litang would be a minor homecoming for me. The place held an allure not only for me but for all Tibetans. Litang's rough charm has much to do with its nonchalance toward tourism. Its setting wasn't kind to everyone. Many Chinese who passed through called it "nosebleed central" because of its four-thousand-metre altitude. It wasn't only the altitude that had made the Litang region dangerous to outsiders: it was also the traditional homeland to the most feared Tibetan warrior tribes, tribes that had fought everyone, from the central Tibetans to the Chinese, from the Mongols to the southern kingdoms, and they had no hesitation in fighting among themselves. They and their abilities in the "blood arts" were well known.

I don't know if there is anyone more dangerously competent with a 150cc motorcycle than a Litang teenager, peeling down the road with photographs of Lamas taped to the gas tanks. Little had changed since my last visit. The outrageous panache of the young men was marvellously intact, continuing a tradition of reckless masculinity that was a vital part of their character. It was this adherence to their character, this ambivalence toward modernity, that I cherished. A local had once told me that cell phones, while convenient, were useless in a town where someone wanting to talk to a friend simply walked over to see him or her.

During the Chinese invasion of the greater Litang region in the 1950s, it was the Litangpas, with their unequalled horsemanship, who gained renown for their fearlessness and daring raids. Thanks to their wanderlust spirit, they had settled as far west as northern Pakistan and Ladakh in northern India. Sword-wielding Litangpas on horseback inspired fear as warriors who were just as happy hacking through bodies with a dripping blade as they were firing a rifle from afar. Even today, they carry knives strung from their belts while atop their mounts—though this, too, is gradually becoming a tradition of the past.

Living and thriving in the highest, most extreme conditions on Earth, it is their unity in the struggle with the elements that has made the Litangpa *drokpas* so daunting. Rather than weakening them, their geographic isolation strengthened them. Anyone choosing to venture into their lands had to grasp this truth quickly. Their forcefulness of character had served the Litangpa *drokpas* well but had also kept them socially and physically distanced.

Sitting on the eastern extension of the Himalayan Plateau, 145 kilometres east of the Yangtze River, Litang was known for its mazes of mountains. In the past, rival tribes had been separated by the mighty Yangtze River, but now the river serves to mark off the Tibetan Autonomous Region (TAR) from the rest of China. The region is historically important as the birthplace of Tibet's seventh Dalai Lama and as an eastern hub of Tibet, although uncompromising nomads and bandit clans made travel through it a frightening task, even for hardened lados.

An old trader from Ponzera had laughed when I asked him what he feared most on the route, proudly stating, "What did we have to fear? We were Khampas." But upon reflection, he had added sombrely, "The Litang nomads could be frightening, if one didn't respect their lands and traditions."

Tenzin had once told me that "the *drokpas* fear nothing except themselves." Then he changed his mind, saying, "No, not themselves either."

One of the refreshing aspects of the Balitangpas, the people of Batang and Litang, was their straightforward informality. Words were not wasted, nor were expressions. Theirs was the language of essentials, honed by life in the mountains, living on the edge of nature's wrath. Nuances and gracious eloquence had long ago been edited out of their dialect as unnecessary. One well-placed look from a local was enough to end a discussion. It was perhaps with an eye to these talents that the famed warriors of the north, the Mongols, during their various invasions, recruited heavily and even copulated with the robust eastern nomads, astutely deciding in many cases that any people with such fighting skills were worth more as allies and partners than as adversaries.

But for all their fearsome martial talents, it was the Litangpas' shrewdness in business along the tea road for which they were best known. The nomadic tribes had their own paths to access the market towns along the Tea Horse Road. Apart from the caterpillar fungus, which I had come to accept as omnipresent in the mountains, the region was known for its rare mushrooms, many of which sold for immense sums, and for its famed *da,* or horses. The annual Litang horse festival, which began long ago as a ragtag affair for the nomadic tribes to trade and buy horses, had become a huge tourist draw in recent years. Once, horses from across the region were brought to the *tang*—the plains—of Litang to be sold, traded, or just admired. This scene played out in isolated towns all along the Tea Horse Road. Again, isolation had preserved this traditional venue of trade: the old ways were still alive and well.

TENZIN'S DEEP VOICE welcomed me "home." His dark features reflected the elements, and nothing of his intensity had diminished. Within minutes of my arrival he got down to details, updating me about the team for the next segment and the conditions we were likely to encounter. We would be four people in total (that number would later increase to five). His younger brother, Onshu, and his cousin Tenzin (a name as ubiquitous in Tibet as the fungus) I knew from past expeditions in the mountains. Both were rugged outdoorsmen who had intimate knowledge of the terrain and the people; they also happened to be two of the finest horsemen I had ever met. Onshu and cousin Tenzin were waiting for us just outside Dranla, a day's drive southwest of Litang.

Midju, a friend of ours in Litang, had heard about the upcoming journey. In her thirty-one years, she had rarely left Litang and was so obviously interested in our trek that we invited her to join us. The smile she gave us was magnificent. Powerful and patient, she was the essence of a Litang woman and would be a steadying female force. She would also prove to be indispensable thanks to her culinary talents. We had no worries about her capacity for endurance, for, as she often reminded us, she was a Khampa.

As for the weather conditions, the elements "know why we are coming, and will be good to us—*Jo rombo* [I swear]," Tenzin said. He had been born in the very mountains we would be travelling through on the Kangnan Plateau and had what seemed like an innate knowledge of them. Our route was "between 140 and 170 kilometres," Tenzin estimated, *"Jo rombo,"* and would take about two weeks. (Although I had learned to not take the statements Tenzin's *"Jo rombo"* accompanied too seriously.) Rather than travelling on the highway that linked Litang to Batang, we would shoot south and come around by foot in a grand sweep over the grassy highlands until we arrived in Batang, farther west. Although it wasn't the most direct route through these lands, for the nomadic caravans, it had been the most important.

Our alternative route to Batang had remained exactly as it had been for hundreds of years, unspoiled by roadways. It had been an essential access point not only for the caravans but also for the nomadic peoples bringing goods to Batang's markets to trade. I wanted to touch these nomadic links whose history had been largely overlooked and unchronicled. One of the unique aspects of the Tea Horse Road was its association with nomads and the most isolated of communities on its way to the main centres of commerce and trade. The people of these remote areas were purveyors of precious rare high-mountain medicines, which included our constant friend the caterpillar fungus, as well as various mushrooms and tubers. Yet their contributions were rarely acknowledged by many Tibetans.

The village of Dranla, where we were to meet up with Onshu and cousin Tenzin, had been a stop for caravans travelling west from the tea regions and markets of Ya'an and Dartsendo (also known as Kangding) in Sichuan on into Lhasa and even farther south into Nepal and India. This caravan route, part of what many called the Sichuan–Tibet Tea Horse Road, extended from the tea regions of Sichuan to eventually hook up with the Yunnan–Tibet Tea Horse Road, which brought tea from farther south. Nowadays, the Sichuan–Tibet highway covers what was once an artery along the Tea Horse Road, taming the terrain and erasing the vestiges of a thousand years.

After buying supplies and gifts for Tenzin's relatives, we set off along a road that year after year challenged the buttocks of any human who travelled it. Tenzin was in some way related to everyone in this nomadic corridor, and the driver of our Jeep was yet another cousin, whose name, not surprisingly, was Tenzin. We arrived at our destination to find camp already set up and warm soup waiting. Onshu and cousin Tenzin's understated greeting made it feel as though we had seen them just yesterday, even though it had been a year. Onshu, handsome as ever, continued quietly collecting fuel for the fire as cousin Tenzin nodded his head in welcome. Long limbed and muscular, Tenzin embodied the classic Litang male. His strength visible in his comfortable movements, he had that enviable mix of easy power and complete confidence that had been honed by years of outdoor life. He had already suffered the harshness of his environs: although not yet thirty years old, he was already a widower, his nomadic wife having died suddenly not long before. I noted a bashfulness about him when he was in Midju's presence, his hard features softening ever so slightly. A year earlier, he and I had almost come to blows over a misunderstanding that involved language, exhaustion, and a Jeep, but now we simply nodded at each other, smiling at the memory.

Midju immediately went to work unpacking and setting up for the meal. Used to work, she rarely sat still, and she clearly derived joy from providing for others. Magnificent cheekbones and waist-length hair set off her long traditional dress. Invariably, she wore a smile, and although her nomadic mother was from a nearby village, she had never been to this region. Indeed, this was her first outing in years, and we felt privileged to have her with us, and perhaps a little spoiled.

TENZIN'S MORNINGS, no matter where he was, invariably began with Nescafé. It made a strange sight, this man of the mountains, his mass of hair tumbling around his shoulders, gently nursing a small cup of instant coffee, which he made hideously sweet. He was not himself until he had a minimum of one cup. Talking to him before that was pointless, and physical activity of any kind was out of the question for him until he had drunk the muddied water. We had different dependencies, he and I.

My pouch of tea was along with me as usual—I knew I would need the odd break from the rich butter tea the nomads drink. After Tenzin had his cup and I had mine, we packed up, the five of us with our six horses, and headed into Dranla to meet with a villager who remembered the days of caravans, before being on our way. In the courtyard of a huge house, this relic of a man told us the legendary tale of the wicked people of Wondo. "Wondo's citizens had preyed on the tea caravans for years," he said, "stealing tea and worse. Some traders were killed. We needed those caravans, for it was they who brought tea and news from the outside to our little village."

The people of Dranla issued a warning to the Wondoans to stop the banditry, but to no avail. Finally, a local Lama prayed for the demise of the village of Wondo. Over the next year, misfortune fell upon the citizens and their crops. The crops were destroyed, a rumour has it by guerrillas, and eventually, the last of the eighty families was murdered one night. Whether it was the work of guerrillas, nomadic warriors, or the heavens, Wondo was no more. The moral of the tale was irrefutable: Do not disturb the caravans.

As we left Dranla to begin our journey, Tenzin thought of his boyhood. "Five-day journeys were nothing for us children," he said. "We travelled to eat, to herd, to move, to survive; it is why we are restless."

Not all children, though, could make it in the harsh climes. Coming to the confluence of two streams, Tenzin briefly bowed his head. It was here that children who had perished before their seventh year were buried. One bit of green looked as though it had been upturned recently. Midju looked from the graves to the water and then back again.

The graves were somewhat unusual, since Tibetan nomadic burials normally took the form of either a sky burial, whereby the body is cut into pieces and placed on a stone platform in the mountains for eagles to feed on, or a water burial in a river, where the body is weighted down with stones and simply allowed to settle at the bottom. Children of the hills, however, were buried in earth near a stream, together in one spot. Only children could be buried like this. It had been that way for as long as Tenzin and his family could remember. It was thought that by giving children an earth burial at the confluence of two rivers, their ills and misfortune would be taken away by the flow of the water and encourage a healthier next generation of children. In the nomads' world, those not vigorous enough simply perished. As Tenzin briefly summed it up, "Nomads cannot afford sickness. The weak die and the strong live and that is all." This also explains why the nomads have remained relatively untainted by the outside world: strong nomads, needing few modern amenities, were able to stay isolated. If the sick lived in a weakened state, help from the outside would likely be sought. Each successive generation carried the survival of the last in its blood, validating themselves by surviving childhood. There were no half-functioning members of the communities because there simply couldn't be in these extremes. It wouldn't work for the household, the family, or the community.

I had spent a good chunk of my life in these places in the sky among these people with their simmering violence and huge hearts. From them I had learned to listen differently from how I was used to, as a Westerner, and to ponder less. An uncle of Tenzin's had once told me, "Here there is that which matters and that which doesn't and nothing in between." Their decisiveness was dictated by their day-to-day lives rather than by ignorance or simplicity. It was this quality that allowed them to settle and resettle, to travel and adapt where others withered. It was also what made the men gifted horsemen and feared lados.

A lado we met had spoken to this. "The Litang nomads were slower to prepare the mules," he said. "Their loads often totally disorganized, but if foul weather or bandits arrived, there was no one better to have along. They had no fears, and thieves wouldn't go near the drokpas."

As we turned away from the graves, the sky turned black. Onshu and cousin Tenzin left with the horses for the little town of Laykundo on a route that would allow their mounts to run full out, while the rest of us continued to follow the trampled pathway heading southwest that still carried local four-legged traffic through the mountains.

Arriving in Laykundo, we made our way to a wide stone house, where tea was waiting for us—and about a dozen men. They were waiting for Tenzin, who brought medicines when he journeyed to these areas. Aspirin, creams for joint pain, and headache medications were favourites. Greeted by a chorus of yips and huge smiles, he carefully distributed the medicines into their waiting hands.

And so, things have changed even here. Traditionally, ritual prayers and herbal compresses were the nomads' medicines; medicines from the outside have only recently become preferred. Medicines now rank as one of the top imports for anyone coming into the mountains. Yet the process is similar to that of a century ago, when a caravan brought hard-to-acquire items to trade with the locals, and had the horses fed and their *tsampa* bags replenished for the continuing journey.

As we continued on our way, rain fell in clean, cold waves. Our horsemen Onshu and cousin Tenzin tucked themselves into multiple layers of wool blankets and moved on up ahead with the horses. Unleashed in the mountains, Midju happily strode ahead. Her long dress billowed in the wind and the rain jetted off her rimmed hat.

Twelve years ago, when she was nineteen, Midju and four other pilgrims set out on a journey, prostrating on hands and knees from Litang to Lhasa, taking a route that was more than twelve hundred kilometres. Distances and days were measured by the number of prostrations performed. Five hundred prostrations marked one kilometre; roughly five kilometres were covered each day. That made for about twenty-five hundred prostrations a day, through hail, snow, and ailments. Their seven-month journey, literally on their knees and the palms of their hands, was another grand epic of Himalayan travel. We were not worried about Midju's abilities to endure in this enormous landscape.

Onshu and cousin Tenzin had moved on ahead, leading the horses, while Tenzin and I trailed in the downpour of grey. Midju now and then wandered fearlessly into the forests, curious of the land that she had heard so much about. We were travelling along one of a series of strands of the Tea Horse Road that wound their way along the valley floor. Massive *goliaka*—eagles—flew overhead.

We set up camp on a little peninsula jutting into a stream, the rain adding to the swell. In the wall of wet, Onshu effortlessly managed a fire while cousin Tenzin acted as the unofficial head horseman. No horse whispering here, but rather grunts, clicks, screams, and yells. I had assumed the duties of the tea man, and Midju had taken over cooking duties from cousin Tenzin, which pleased us enormously. High mountain streams provided us with an unending source of water. Much of the Tea Horse Road ran beside waterways, whether gentle rivulets or gushing rivers, as these watercourses offered nourishment and were easy landmarks to follow.

Just before darkness raced in, the torrents of rain abruptly stopped and the wind dropped off. As the clouds parted, we were given a glimpse of snow-clad Mount Genyen above us, and we experienced a moment of veneration before this sacred mountain worshipped by the nomads. It bode well for us.

Sleep arrived under a million winking stars.

TENZIN'S MOAN OF CONTENTMENT sounded as we entered a valley just south of Mount Genyen. Lengu, also known as the Naygo monastery, sat before us in a desolate, silent valley. It had been home to Tenzin in his earlier years as a novice monk (sporting considerably less hair then), and seeing it stirred him still. Our path led into a narrow gorge of glorious green, fitted dramatically between the vertical grey. Lush valleys populated by enormous boulders, as if cast down by giant warriors, went on into the distance. Off to our left was Mount Genyen—or the "Pursuer and Seeker of Virtue," so named for the legions of monks and pilgrims who came for the magnificent spaces and murky caves in which to meditate. A home like no other, the monastery, with its tiny stone huts surrounding the main structure, looked to have been born of rock. It was remote and powerful, a place of patience.

Upon reaching the monastery, Onshu and cousin Tenzin unloaded the gear in its tiny courtyard. A distinguished, delicately built man stood off to one side, gracefully wrapped in the burgundy robes of a monk. His calm eyes welcomed us. Tenzin's uncle, a man in his eighties, had spent much of his life here, had seen caravans, had been a part of them, and had travelled widely, though always returning home. "Why would I ever leave here?" he said, gesturing to the mountains.

Evening found us curled into the corners of a small room lit with butter candles, a stove in the centre glowing with heat. Midju had stationed herself by the stove, coaxing yet more heat from it and watching over the gurgling kettle. Our octogenarian host sat with his robes tucked elegantly around him.

Although formal titles aren't generally important to the Khampas, I was to learn that this wasn't always the case. When I unwittingly addressed Tenzin's uncle as *aniè,* a term of respect for an elder male, Midju firmly admonished me, telling me in no uncertain terms that he was a *rinpoche.* The title *Rinpoche* was given to those who are divined to be the reincarnation of a bodhisattva or an enlightened being. Tibetans hold these reincarnates in particular esteem, for it is these beings who remain in human form on Earth to assist others humans in their earthly struggles. Midju's intensity when she corrected me was moving. The ageless *rinpoche* laughed as his eyes shone with forgiveness.

As a thunderstorm bounced through the valley, Rinpoche told us of the luxuries the caravans had brought. Nomads would travel from every valley, from every rocky dwelling place, to welcome the traders on their passing. Caravans returning from Lhasa and India often stopped at the monastery to present gifts of incense, snuff, and silks. From the east, that absolute necessity, tea, was transported on its way west to Batang, Markham, and beyond into Tibet. These travelling markets gave the isolated communities a chance to access rare and exotic goods. For these, they traded their own valuable herbs and mushrooms. It was in this way that many *drokpas* did their "shopping" or trading, without ever having to leave their remote homelands. This is what made variant routes like the one we were on so special.

Along with grain, which the nomads didn't grow, two other items of trade were particularly prized: gems and aprons. Any trader of these two items knew they had guaranteed sales. The first, gems, found its way from distant Calcutta, sitting at the mouth of the Ganges, where the mighty river meets the Bay of Bengal. Brightly coloured stones and corals from the depths of the Bay of Bengal were transported by caravans heading north to the highest plains on Earth. From Calcutta to Kalimpong in west Bengal or Gangtok in Sikkim, the mule caravans travelled along extensions of the Tea Horse Road into

Tibet bringing jewels to adorn the nomads. Much of the brilliant turquoise loved by the nomads had made its way east from as far away as the Middle East via other ancient corridors.

The markets of Lhasa, similar in style to those of the Middle East and India, swelled with sparkling gems and ornaments. Caravans bound for the nomadic regions would hoard what they could to bring into the hinterlands, eager to please their nomadic hosts. Like much of value to the Tibetans, these ornaments had travelled great distances, evoking a sense of exoticism. Harsh and vigorous lives spent in isolation were brightened by these brash blue and orange stones. They were one of the rare extravagances of people who lived in full view of nature's brutal splendour, and the fickleness they exhibited with the ornaments and trinkets that they wore made an interesting juxtaposition to their otherwise simple, uncluttered ways.

The other item of trade treasured by the nomads was more practical. Aprons from central Tibet, called *pomden,* were worn by most Tibetan women yet were hard to find except in the big market towns. They flew off the mules' backs when they arrived in the nomadic districts. The more colourful the patterns, the better.

Many hours later, in the dead of night, Rinpoche bid us goodnight with an observation of the nomads' lives and of our own: "You must always remember to remain simple in life. The nomads stay simple because they must to survive. So many complicate their lives, only to come back to simplicity. Don't waste your days." With that, he shuffled off to his simple wooden bed that lay beyond a curtain. A little cough and all was silent.

TENZIN'S ANCESTRAL HOME, Dziwa, waited for us in the distance. The caravan routes were claw marks in the high mountain greenery as smaller trails broke off to rejoin the main path at a later point. Trees had waned, they, too, finding the altitude too great. Maps did not even hint of what lay here.

Suddenly, a high yelp cut the air. Onshu and cousin Tenzin had urged their mounts on, and now they streaked across the plain. The three packhorses under their loads did their own little jig to follow.

"They need it," said Tenzin as Onshu and cousin Tenzin disappeared into a valley.

Mount Genyen, at 6360 metres, was pivotal for the nomadic tribes of western Sichuan, who believed that many mountain deities resided within it. Now, it appeared once again off to our right, whispering to me, as it had done in the past, for reasons that I have never understood. Its fierce peak and shields of snow drew me closer. With its sombre peace coupled by its brutal strength, it seemed not only to define the nomadic lands and people perfectly but also to strike a chord in the individual, championing the spirit of independence. Some mountains are spectacles, stunning natural creations that force the eyes wide with their power, while others attract with a mysterious and dangerous allure. To me, Genyen had always felt to be a mountain that was very much alive, harbouring unseen forces. Many mountains have beckoned me, but few held sway over my mind like Genyen did. Through the swirling clouds and masses of ice, this mountain seemed to pulsate and radiate life.

Looking to Midju and Tenzin, I told them I felt a need to be closer to Mount Genyen. Tenzin simply said, "You must go then." But Midju frowned; the locals saw mountains as dwelling places of gods. They were not humps of rock for travellers to scale—to do so would invoke the fury of the deities and, perhaps worse, the fury of the locals. Although local tribes were Buddhist, they fervently worshipped the gods they believed dwelt deep within the mountains. These gods alone could settle the disputes of the mountain people. Indeed, only Brongri—the wild yak mountain god—was thought capable of unifying tribes in times of conflict.

For the next hour I criss-crossed up past the undulations of snow, then wandered along a ridge where patches of snow gave way to a higher zone of perma-ice. The mountain seemed to go up forever. It had drawn me to be with it and reminded me that its people hadn't forgotten it, and I couldn't help but admire their wisdom. They hadn't abandoned their gods of the mountains; their faith had remained vital and intact. Their devotion, like most else, was tested by time and now simply accepted by the locals. Such is faith.

My spirits invigorated, I descended toward the two black specks of Midju and Tenzin, my thoughts wandering to tea. How nice it would be to plop down with a bowl of pungent tea right here surrounded by this white grandeur. It seemed only fitting to drink the sacred within the realm of the sacred. Hailstones interrupted my thoughts. Suddenly pounding down, they sent me racing along the mountainside, my head tucked into my jacket. Tea would have to wait. In my mind, I could hear Sonam chastising me for even thinking of tea while engaging with the divine.

Onshu and cousin Tenzin had waited for Midju, Tenzin, and me to catch up to them, and together we continued on to Dziwa. Huge black yak-wool tents separated by large parcels of land sat facing south. The yak wool rippled in the wind. Used to make the nomads' tents waterproof, sunproof, and rugged, this fabric of the mountains had been marking the landscape for a hundred generations. I spotted yak herds higher up on the hills. Shepherds raced toward us over the turf, laughing.

As we approached, Tenzin's sister, Lashi, came running toward us, alerted by the children's yells. Weeping, she fell to the ground, grabbing at Tenzin's legs. Their mother had passed away only a few months earlier, and this was the first meeting of the siblings since. On her knees, she tore at Tenzin in happiness, in sadness, and in mourning. Rising, she put her arms around him, and for a few moments the two stood in an embrace. Then Lashi looked around at us and smiled. Sorrow was short-lived here. Time and the wasting of it were both luxuries.

I hugged the children whom, a year earlier, I had lived with for a month. Their short pronouncements of my name—"Jepoo"—filled the air, sending me into laughs of joy. Familiarity in this most beautiful and bleak of places was a gift to me.

Midju introduced herself to Lashi and off they went to Lashi's tent to prepare tea. A friend had once observed, "[Tibetan] women run the households, and men run everything else." The women's power could not be overestimated in these communities, and it was often the woman of the house whom people addressed first.

Lashi's tent was a home with none of the physical or psychological divides walls bring. Everything was shared: combating the elements, suffering, and celebrating were all communal activities. Cousins, uncles, nieces, more uncles, and still more men named Tenzin descended on the tent, where we had joined Midju and Lashi, to bombard us with gossip, complaints, and their list of needs, and to lavish upon us food and, thankfully, tea. In the middle of the tent was a stone fireplace. Above it, a flap in the tent allowed the smoke to escape. Beds, or rather, blankets, had been pushed back to the edges of the tent, along with clothing. The cooking area consisted of some knives and a couple of large chunks of wood, used as cutting boards.

Lashi ripped a hunk of dried tea off the brick. For centuries, these people had been repeating this simple procedure up to six times a day. The nomads intuitively knew that tea would provide them with the nutrients they lacked in their high-fat diets. Yogurt, butter, and meat were broken down in the body by the tea's amino acids, tannins, and minerals. Tea also provided many vitamins found in those fruits and vegetables that would never find their way to this distant land.

Lashi's daughter, Ajie, motioned to me that both my hair and hers had grown. She was clearly pleased with this development. Sitting watching the faces around me, I admired how their features had not lost character, had not been covered with the blandness that so often comes with complacency. Their voices were raw with a lifetime of wind and smoke, their wizened features borne of effort, their faces perceptibly marked by life's trials. Nomads' expressions were frighteningly direct, reflecting an uncompromising self-sufficiency. There was an efficient economy to their movements, a physical prowess that stemmed from the understanding of the land and the limits imposed by their surroundings.

Outside, more men and boys gathered around the horses, studying haunches, hooves, and head shapes. The odd hand would lift the tail of the animal so the mob could stare at the uncovered rear. Nothing had changed. This is the welcome ancient caravans had received. News of the outside world, supplies, items for trade, and seeing old friends all called for a celebration. Horses and everything horse-related attracted interest. Bridles, girths, saddles, and animals' genitalia were studied and commented on in great detail.

On a previous journey to a nomadic settlement, I had been fortunate to witness an ancient ritual that deepened my appreciation for just how much horses meant to the people. Nomadic horsemen done up in their best garb, their animals groomed and gleaming, had gathered for a ceremony. But first, there was a ritual to cleanse both the ceremony and the participants—including the horses. It was a cleansing much like those morning fires of juniper we had encountered on our trek; the difference was in the scale.

Piles of juniper were lit and once the dense smoke had blotted out the sky, dozens of dismounted horsemen silently circled the smoking juniper with their horses, letting the smoke roll over themselves and the animals, muting their dazzling garments. I was mesmerized by the silent procession as it moved clockwise, figures disappearing in wafts of smoke, only to reappear a moment later. More men joined in, their animals walking behind them, sweat mixing with the scent of the burning juniper, mixing with the hypnotic motion. My senses were engaged as I, looking on with the women and children from the sidelines, was drawn in spirit into the churning movement.

This cleansing ritual, called *sondon,* had traditionally been performed before battle or ceremonies involving competitions in an effort to rid the men (and horses) of negative energies, previous defeats, and bad memories—the smoke doing its part to remove this residue—so that all was new and fresh. Once the cleansing was complete, the brave horsemen would depart fearless and secure. But there was a certain humility in the ritual, a sense that there was something greater than those present. Smoke was considered special by Tibetans for its effortless ability to ascend into the heavens, and at these altitudes, that journey was brief.

In Dziwa, though, everything was brief. Such communities shift, as they have for centuries, six or seven times a year, doing a circuit of sorts throughout the year until they return to Dziwa, their summer home. All they did and all they possessed were geared to these seasonal movements. Seasons above four thousand metres were not the seasons the lowland world knows. Rather, with even a subtle change in weather, the merest hint of pending change in temperature set off a migration. Late September saw communities move into more temperate valleys to avoid not just winter snows but bludgeoning wind; early spring saw communities move higher into the mountains in search of grazing lands for their precious herds of yak—availability of food for the yak took priority over the nomads' own comfort. The nomads had nothing that couldn't be packed up in fifteen minutes and heaped onto the backs of yaks and horses, mules, and sometimes even sheep. Within hours, an entire population of people, tents, and animals could be on the move. Of all the peoples in Tibet, it is perhaps the nomads who can most empathize with the lados and their continuous journeys.

Our own brief time in Dziwa would be spent doing as the locals did—waking, eating, collecting fuel, taking rest breaks to drink tea. But first, a young, sun-stained cousin of Tenzin made us *sohie,* a traditional nomadic treat, one made for caravaners in the past. "Aged milk that had formed around a wooden plate," was the quick explanation. The plate consisted of a wooden rim encompassing a net of dried yak entrails; it was left to soak and ferment in the milk for twenty days, the milk gradually stiffening in the container.

The resulting skin, minus the yak goodies, was then mixed into a dish of yak cheese and butter. Rich and filling, it could sustain hunger for hours. In my case, though, the buttery richness of the cheese and fermented milk proved lethal. Within half an hour, my bowels had conspired to send me white-knuckled out of the tent to a nearby "zone of tranquility," where I could relieve myself in the most glorious of expanses.

I returned to the tent, feeling considerably better, and was promptly presented with a bowl of barley powder to "firm up the insides." There is a hard and fast rule when eating anything powdered, and that is to avoid talking and, more crucially, inhaling. But when Tenzin asked me something, I forgot that rule and started to answer. Inhaling a mass of ground barley flakes into my lungs, I exploded into a series of powdery barks that sent the laughing villagers running for cover.

At just below five thousand metres, the oxygen available for inhaling is about forty-five percent of what it is at sea level, so the recovery time for lungs heaving out chunks of barley purée is about the same as it would be for a quick sprint up a mountain. There was only one cure, one simple and soothing solution: a bowl of tea.

Although almost all tea in the area has traditionally come from the region of Ya'an, in western Sichuan, the tea most coveted has always been the *jia kabow*—bitter tea—of southern Yunnan. Older Tibetans usually drink strong teas, and although more expensive than others, the Yunnan teas can produce many successive bowls from the same tea leaves. But, in the remote areas, access to Yunnan tea was very limited. A bowl of lukewarm Ya'an tea was shoved into my hands, and I gratefully gulped down the welcome fluid, which helped ease my heaving stomach.

THE MORNING FOR US TO MOVE ON arrived. Lashi was again in tears. Living in these inaccessible lands where few venture, with little knowledge of the outside world, you got used to departures, she explained, but still, you never knew when you were seeing a person for the last time. Her husband prepared our horses, insisting that he himself load. It was in this way that he could contribute to our safe passage. *Gyapkè*—loading a mule's cargo—and *gyap po*—unloading a mule's load—was a tradition with hosts: whatever plights might befall their guests, they knew the loads would at least be secure. There was an added bonus for us in the form of Lashi's young son, Gelanab. He had begged to accompany us part of the way, and his parents had given him permission to join us. He took the reins of the first pack-horse and started off steadily, already showing the skills and strut of a muleteer—a lado in the making at only twelve years of age.

Departure was a simple affair: numerous checks of our horses and cargo, some nods of the head, a few words. As we were leaving, I gave some of my *cheril*, or tea balls, to Lashi's daughter, Ajie. She knew immediately that it was a token of thanks, something for the entire family, and she pocketed the little bundles. "Words are for fools," a Khampa had once told me.

Gelanab stayed with us until we hit a rare high-altitude forest, his signal to turn back. Without ceremony he flashed us his wild smile and, bidding us well, headed back to his village on foot, turning once to wave. He and his ever-present slingshot would be a match for any living threat he might encounter.

As we made our way into a valley that stretched kilometres in every direction, Tenzin stopped and studied some tall blades of green grass. They looked identical to me. Then he traced one down to its base and, digging carefully, extracted from the soil a small onionlike bulb, which he put in my palm. Midju's nod confirmed that she, too, knew of this local specialty. "We call this herb *do*," Tenzin said, "and we have picked it for generations. The Chinese call it *bee moo* and have long treasured it for its abilities to cool the body and aid in respiratory ailments."

Besides caterpillar fungus, this was one of the most important local commodities. Many people from the cities had tried to find the various valued herbs, mushrooms, and fungus to pick, but only the nomads knew where they were and when to find them, and they weren't about to share their secrets. That mountain people used these products helped give them a special appeal. Many pharmacies in China's main cities emphasized the altitude and remoteness from where they came—"high mountain, Himalayan, picked by Tibetans"—in promoting them. This at least has benefited the local peoples.

Just as with the fungus and mushrooms, the bulb Tenzin now put in my hand had been a flash point of violence and treachery: clans double-crossed each other just to lay claim to the prized mountain products, and all hell broke loose, with no rules, once the killing started. Tenzin told me of a dispute he was called in to settle just the previous year. Two rival clans (both sides relatives of Tenzin) were "at war" over the picking rights in the nearby mountains. Not surprisingly, there had been deaths, as these commodities were one of their only sources of revenue. Knives, screwdrivers, and rifles had been used in attacks, and once the violence began, nomadic blood oaths were made to avenge previous killings. The spiral would continue until everyone died or someone mediated.

After my own recent experiences travelling through the Abohor lands near Nup Gong La, I understood these picking rights. Given the choice, I would rather have a dispute with the Abohor than with a Khampa nomad. With the nomads, dialogue would be brief and action guaranteed.

A few days after Tenzin had shown me the bulb, an incident involving Onshu and his horse reminded me of the dangers of clashing with a Khampa nomad. We had just finished lunching on dried yak meat and curd. Onshu was sorting out gear to load on to one of the packhorses just feet away from us. No one saw what happened, but we felt a dull thump resonate through the earth. We turned to find Onshu bent over, holding his thigh above the knee, his face hidden by his mane of hair. His mount had carefully lined him up and deliberately cracked him with a rear hoof. It must have been a murderous kick—perhaps it was an old vendetta that the horse had decided it was time to repay. Onshu was silent in his pain, but as he lifted his head, I saw a nomad's cold fury. He had become a vengeful demon. Eyes gaping and teeth bared, he quickly mounted the horse and tore off across the plain, shrieking.

We were not to see Onshu and the horse for close to an hour, and when they did return, it was a different horse and a different Onshu. Atop his horse, his wild hair flung back, Onshu glittered with triumph: his vengeance had been satisfied. His mount was a slavering wreck of perspiration, despondent strides, and glazed eyes. Onshu had ridden the proud animal into submission. Beating did not play a role in their relationship. It was a simple battle of wills between two powerful creatures and, for the time being at least, it seemed to have been settled.

Man and beast alike earned their loyalty, and nothing was taken for granted. Like the people, the horses were wild, defiant, and strong. Tibetan nomads took a special approach in corralling the horses. They didn't use ropes or incentives. Instead, a nomad carefully crawled up to the horse, grabbed a foreleg just above the hoof, and, with his hands, slowly worked his way up the leg toward the neck, to clutch the horse's mane. If this was successful, the horse was claimed as his. Such sessions often took hours or even days, the nomad attempting to tame a particular horse dozens of times if he was convinced of the horse's pedigree, with no guarantee of success.

The undersized horses from the nomadic areas of Tibet, only slightly larger boned and taller than ponies, became the prize of the Chinese cavalry during the wars with the Mongols and also of the invading northern nomadic Jin and Liao tribes during the Song Dynasty (960 to 1279). The horses, like so much in the nomads' world, came with the caveat that durable and fast wasn't always controllable.

WE HAD MADE IT OVER yet another pass, into yet another valley, a valley of hot, still air. I felt like I was suffocating. Even the impenetrable

Onshu looked distraught under the unusual shroud of heat. Midju, who had been an absolute titan in the mountains, walking all the way and wearing her long skirts day after day even through passes and gorges, finally looked pained. Her face had turned an unnatural red. Tenzin remained mounted on one of the horses for most of time, and I was starting to feel an intense loathing for the sun. The sweltering heat brought a sense of monotony, an awareness of each step, each bend of the knee, each crease of wet skin. I felt close to delirium as we continued to weave around the mountains, over clear, gushing glacier steams, and up passes.

Heat was not our only challenge once we encountered the *djonbu*, the huge honey flies, as the Litang nomads referred to them. The droning, black-winged insects didn't waste any time in assessing the quality of their targeted meal. They drove straight into our faces, intent on taking chunks out of us. They were piranhas in flight. The horses were also suffering from the repeated attacks. Onshu's mount looked skittish, as though longing to be let free to run. Well aware that that old battle of wills could rage anew at any moment, Onshu held the reins tight. We kept moving, covering up as best we could against the attacking insects, until they gradually dissipated. We had made it through with only the odd bit of flesh being taken from us.

No towns dotted the route, no pastures for the mules, no yak herds, no passing caravans, and I felt the remoteness, the separation, and the vastness of the land even more than elsewhere, if that was possible. Unlike the Great Himalayan Range, which flows east-west, the mountains on the eastern cusp of the Great Himalayan Range ran north-south, as though mirroring the people of the east, who did so much so differently from other Tibetans. Open plains where each of us could choose our own path gave way to one tight trail ascending in a series of switchbacks. As the mules made their way up, one of the animal's front hooves slid on a rock, sending the mule into a frenzied dance in an effort to get traction. All of us stopped, willing the mule to find firm footing, which it finally did.

For the most part, this region of Kham lulled one with its gently rolling grasslands and immeasurable vistas. But the vastness hid danger. Coming upon a turquoise lake, Tenzin sensed my desire to dive into it and said firmly, "Don't, Jeff." My inevitable "Why not?" was

Our caravan makes its way up to Sho La Pass.

Young Khampas still display the horsemanship and fearlessness that made them so famous in the past centuries as warriors. One piece of advice offered to people new to the land of the Khampas is not to touch their horses without permission.

Eastern Tibetan Khampas continue an ancient tradition of passing through the smoke of burning juniper. Believing the smoke purifies bodies and cleanses spirits, the young men lead their horses through it in preparation for a horse festival near Niarong, in western Sichuan.

Salt flats, such as these in Yenjing, eastern Tibet, have existed unchanged for centuries.

A Tibetan woman works on the salt flats near Yenjing in eastern Tibet. The salt wells, like the one pictured top right, have been active for centuries, and there has been little change in the harvesting methods.

Our caravan slowly ascends to Sho La Pass. Down below, one of the mules has exhausted itself trying to free its legs from chest-deep snow. An hour after this photograph was taken, we decided that the mules would not make the final push to cross the pass, as the dangers of broken limbs and deep snow proved too much of a risk.

Wind-horse flags mark spots to give thanks to the mountain gods for letting one pass unharmed.

Dawa in Merishoo told us about his life as a muleteer. A gracious and welcoming host, he was happy to know that the story of the route would be told.

An "ancient" of the Lisu tribe, which populates southern Yunnan, northern Thailand, and Laos, sits alone outside her home. Tea for many of the minority tribes has been a staple in their diets for as long as tea has grown.

Nomadic women dressed up for a festival. Many of the women have kilograms of ornaments hanging from their hair and often end up bleeding from the scalp.

Sonam, Nomé, and Norbu walk along a section of the Tea Horse Road marking the great Salween Divide near Pemba.

The Tea Horse Road angles in from the left through the old abandoned town of Tenda in central Tibet. The valley in the past provided grazing and supplies for the caravans. In the background lie the Nyanqen Tanglha mountains.

Within a nomadic dwelling, *palè* (barley bread) is prepared over a fire as dawn arrives. Using scarce fuel, cooking is often done on flat stones that conduct heat, and everything is reused season after season. Little has changed in centuries for many of the nomadic tribes.

Early morning charm: one of our horses gets grumpy.

The "First bend in the Yangtze," known as Shigu, in Yunnan, was a traditional divide along the Yunnan–Tibet Tea Horse Road, as well as the first significant bend in the eastward-flowing Yangtze.

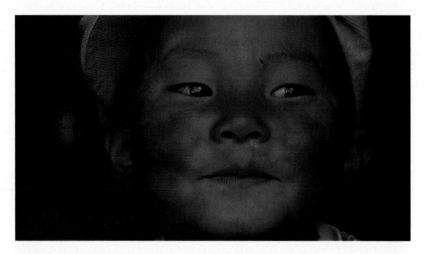

The sunburned cheeks and mischievous eyes of a young boy near Litang delights not only us but also his mates, who encouraged him to pose for a photograph.

An elder prepares the candles in a monastery by cleaning and replacing the cotton wicks. Many volunteers contribute to the daily chores performed in and around monasteries throughout Tibet.

A path hanging along a cliff leads to a monastery tucked into the mountains near Lharigong in central Tibet, the ever-present snowcaps providing a frame.

Countless bridges were crossed like this one near Ala Jagung in Tibet, along the Tea Horse Road, as the route meandered along rivers and through valleys. The simple but proven engineering has stood the test of time and floods.

A crucial step in advance of serving tea is to prepare the pot. Hot water is poured over the outside of the pot to preheat and prepare the clay before water is poured inside. The delicate clay pot is then resistant to cracking.

A lonely, wet portion of the original Yunnan–Tibet Tea Horse Road in Yiwu town has remained virtually unchanged for centuries; many of the original flagstones are still intact.

Tea gardens, which are more accurately tea landscapes, go on for as far as the eye can see in many parts of southern Yunnan, such as here near Simao, unofficially known as the "home of tea."

Tea leaves being "cooked" by hand in Yiwu town in southern Yunnan. This cooking must be done immediately after picking the tea leaves to eliminate moisture from the leaves. One of the most essential steps in tea production, the cooking is often done right in the tea fields.

Our guide to all things tea, Napu of the Lahu tribe, near Menghai, delicately searches for tea buds on an ancient tea tree near Nano Mountain.

The sun goes down near the Tibetan–Nepali border, just kilometres from Mount Everest.

One of the few surviving yak-skin boats gets loaded up for a daily passage—increasingly rare in Tibet—near the village of Saga, west of Lhasa. In many areas, such boats were once the only way to cross rivers.

In Kalimpong, India, Ashi Penzon prepares one of her formidable meals as pork dries in the window.

met with a shake of his head. "Very bad for our trip and for you." This tiny body of water, like the grand peak of snow-capped Genyen, was a sacred resting place and home of divine beings: a site not to be disturbed. Onshu's grave expression signalled his seriousness. I had long ago learned to heed locals' advice. My action would have put a jinx, at least in their minds, on our journey. The primeval forces at play here far outweighed my desire for a quick swim. Mountains, trees, and lakes were often sacred in the Tibetan regions, and to defile them by climbing them, cutting them, or, in this case, swimming in them was to tempt fate.

"Here," said Tenzin suddenly, gesturing to an ugly peak of black stone. "Many died there. *Jo rombo.*" Tenzin had a story to tell. He dismounted his horse, and as I poured tea from my Thermos into cups, Tenzin told me of one tsompun's tests of toughness.

Alo, a famous nomadic tsompun, had built up a reputation as a local hero. Through his familial ties in the valleys around Dziwa, he became one of the sole providers of goods to the nomads. He was known to be fair and sympathetic to those in the remote communities, but he was also known as a shrewd businessman, able to buy cheap and sell cheap. His caravan consisted of ninety-nine horses, and he would consider only nomads to work as his lados, with one proviso: before working for Alo as a muleteer, the prospective lado had to pass a feat of endurance and strength.

The black-stoned peak now before us provided the test. Anyone wishing to join his teams had to scale the summit of the peak within a certain time. Often, the candidates were required to carry a load on their backs. Failure often resulted in death, as many expired on the way up or fell into crags and were never found. "I think there might be many, many bones up there," Tenzin whispered as we looked up to the uneven crags and crumbly passes.

In a nomad's mule team, all-important loading skills were still secondary to the lados' strength, which was why nomad caravans might take a little longer to reach markets, hampered as they were by their awkwardly-bound loads, but were seldom targeted by bandits. I could picture bandits up in the folds of grey stone, waiting for their quarry, and watching as the nomads arrived, their hair braided, wool *chupas* (long jackets) tied at the waist, prayer beads hanging from around their necks, and huge knives hanging from their belts. Few bandits, unless desperate or they themselves Litangpa *drokpas*, would venture an assault on such caravans.

The philosophy of the nomads was kill or be killed. Many in Tibet believe these easterners were animistic, with abilities to converse with the spirits. People we had encountered on our own trek still had the view that the nomads of Kham were beyond pain and suffering. To this day, many speak in awe and fear of these spellbinding warriors and their abilities to withstand injury in battle. Before going into battle, following a long tradition, high Lamas bless articles of clothing belonging to nomadic warriors to protect them from bullets, knives, and injury. With such rituals, the belief in the blessing is paramount, and these people believed.

After drinking our tea, we continued on our way. Gradually, valleys narrowed into lush gateways, a signal that the great vastness was behind us.

Over meals, Tenzin reminisced about an uncle, Dziwa Anjen, who had been one of the rare inspirations for him. The word *Dziwa* denoted the region from which this uncle came; it was and still is typical for nomads' names to reference their birthplace.

Ambitious and tough, Anjen left his community in his early twenties without telling anyone where he was going. Anjen had a dream of life beyond the tents and yaks. People assumed he had died and mourned his passing with ceremonies. But he hadn't died; rather, he had made his way hundreds of kilometres south into Yunnan, where he trained as a lado, learning the skills to one day become a tsompun and lead his own caravan.

On Anjen's eventual return to this community, he brought with him precious brown sugar, corals, and *pomden*—the aprons from central Tibet. He started recruiting and training local men for a life along the trade routes. He also had the foresight to encourage the high mountain communities to concentrate their efforts on harvesting the caterpillar fungus and the medicinal *do*, commodities their lands had in abundance and the prices for which were constantly rising in the market towns.

Thanks to Anjen, the nomads became more unified and organized among themselves. They realized that they could continue to live their lives in the sanctity of the mountains while thriving on their local expertise. In this way, nomads were known *of*, rather than known, and talked *of* rather than *to*. Their reputations grew in a way that allowed them to live their lives untouched.

Tsompun Dziwa Anjen became well known not only for his bravery and wealth but also because of that always important quality among Tibetans, generosity. Tenzin had inherited much from his uncle by way of his features and personality—but his Nescafé habit was all his own.

Approaching the Yangtze watershed, we knew we were getting close to Batang. The temperature rose into the high twenties Celsius. We were above four thousand metres, and as our little caravan started descending, I noticed that the trees were becoming smaller and increasing in number. Batang, "BaBa" to locals, was a town loaded with fighters and fruit, and both were reputed to be the best in the land. Many of Batang's young men had found employment as body-guards in Lhasa, gaining notoriety for their fists. The fruit in the town was sumptuous. Our own Midju had been ordered by her mother to bring back some of the famous Batang plums. The golf-ball-sized mauve marvels were considered treats by many elders.

Batang, like Litang, was a market-based community that the Khampa nomads could easily access. It was the last stop in western Sichuan before Markham and only thirty kilometres east of the Yangtze River. Tea caravans from Sichuan treaded through on their way toward Tibet's higher and dryer landscapes.

When I had arrived in Lhasa with Sonam, Nomè, and Norbu, we had entered anonymously, barely noticed in the swirl of life and activity. Entering Batang, a town of twelve thousand, was a different affair altogether. The tempo of life in the town was sluggish in the nauseating heat, and mid-afternoon *tsapo* or tea time was the equiva-lent of a siesta. Almost two weeks of heat, dust, and sun had turned us into a rough-looking bunch, and so our eclectic crew of nomads, a woman, and a dirty white guy created a stir, conversations dipping into silence as we strode into Batang.

Onshu and cousin Tenzin strutted (Onshu's was a limping strut, for he hadn't yet recovered from the kick his horse had given him) down the centre of the main road. They walked proudly; this strut was a way of saying "Be cautious." Tenzin told me that all nomads with caravans did this upon entering towns, and was a perfect example of the different approaches of the valley folk and the nomads. The assertiveness was a warning to any prospective ill-wishers or brigands that conflict would come at a heavy price.

Cousin Tenzin, with his brooding good looks, was getting a lot of attention from the local girls. Onshu had what I would come to call the Nomad Stare—a steady glare that seemed to look right through things and people. Midju simply smiled, keeping tight to our group, while I did what I could with my hitched-up pants and lank hair.

Heat, plums, fighters, and telephone shacks summed up Batang. After resting for three days, and consuming plums by the dozen, I knew the time had come to use the *kaba*—the telephone—to call Daba at the base in Shangri-La to see how plans were shaping up for the next segment of my journey.

"Come quickly; you don't have time for plums in the sun," Daba said when I reached him.

Midju, Tenzin, and I arranged to take the five-hour bus ride back to Litang, where I would then make my way south to Shangri-La. Onshu and Cousin Tenzin packed up their horses and prepared to head back the way we had come, back into the land of the mountain gods.

The incorrigible Dorje.

5

Litang to Yong Jr: Dorje

Part horse, part goat, and a tiny bit human.

—DAKPA, DESCRIBING DORJE

MIDJU'S MOTHER, who had few teeth and limited culinary pleasures, accepted the Batang plums we had brought her with a huge, gaping smile. Cool mountain air had greeted us in Litang, after an eight-hour bus ride of stops, starts, and jolting gearshifts as we made our way higher into the famed treeless landscapes. I was overcome with a wonderful and slightly disorienting feeling of arriving somewhere that isn't home but somehow is intimately familiar, and I knew I would enjoy the two days I'd be spending in Litang.

The main tea-growing area of southern Yunnan and that particular corner of Yunnan that marked the beginning of the Tea Horse Road beckoned me. Following the sections of the tea route out of sequence as I had, I had come to appreciate the deeper effects of tea and its relationships with the isolated peoples of the mountains—by starting my journey in the Tibetan regions, where the tea was destined for, I had a first-hand taste of how little tea's influence has diminished. I was able to see how crucial tea was to so many, and gain an understanding of the reasons for its valued longevity in lands far removed from the green leaf's origin. Now it was time to head to the misty birthplace of tea.

And so I returned to Shangri-La, where Dakpa and I cocooned our-selves once again among maps of Yunnan's subtropical south in preparation for our excursion into the land of Puer—steamy forests, indigenous tribes, a land dedicated to every aspect of tea. Even Dakpa was excited about our pending departure.

And then the telephone rang.

It was Dorje, irrepressible, energetic Dorje. "You must come to Yong Jr," he said eagerly, referring to his small hometown in the mountains. The village lay deep in the valleys outside Deqin and was known for both its mushrooms and its pilgrim routes—the many dirt tracks and pathways converged here into a couple of main paths that would take the worshippers on the grand circumambulation of the greater Kawa Karpo range. His voice dropped to a dramatic whisper, and I had to ask him to repeat his words. "Part of the old trade route still exists—yes, the Tea Horse trade route."

Some of the elders in his community had remembered trade cara-vans using the smaller local trails to access the main routes. While the main trunk of the Yunnan–Tibet Tea Horse Road was now largely cov-ered with highway, vestiges of trails—often no more than tiny stria-tions—still existed. Untouched by tourism or by government, they didn't warrant interest—except, of course, mine.

Dorje then spoke with Dakpa, and as he repeated what he had told me, Dakpa almost dropped the phone, so surprised was he by how passionate Dorje sounded. "Are you sure?" Dakpa asked. My body was humming with excitement. Discoveries like these were not made through any research but, like many of the sublime moments we had experienced on our excursions, passed on by locals. So many of our risky pleasures and unpredictable rewards had come out of nowhere, appearing when we least expected them. These diversions often led in turn to more discoveries, to more truths that lay dormant in the fogs.

Two days later I was on a bus alone, heading back to the lands in the shadows of Kawa Karpo Mountain that sat tucked into the north-eastern corner of Yunnan. When Dakpa heard of the treks and climbs involved, he refrained from joining me. I don't think his body was ready for another onslaught of the mountains. Dakpa and the tea plantations would have to wait. Apart from the anticipation this new-found segment of the trade route brought, an added bonus was, of course, that I would see where Dorje Kandro came from. I would get a look at his lair.

Dorje met me at Deqin. He hadn't changed since I last saw him. He had the same ruggedness—his moustache was restored to its former glory—and he was still chain-smoking, still prone to laughter, and still wore inch-thick long underwear despite the heat. I was glad to be with him and his slightly lunatic world again.

He looked down at my now darkened *bagu* band, the bamboo bracelet he had given me just before we had started the first leg of our journey, and his mouth lifted into a smile. "Oh yaa," he said, using a expression as common to Tibetans as it is to English speakers—though Dorje drew out his "Oh yaa" for long seconds, until it dropped off into nothingness.

Staying the night at the home of an old friend of Dorje's, I felt reassured listening to his tales of the hidden tracks that weaved through the bamboo forests. These were legitimate trails and their location made sense, as the area was a natural confluence point. Other trade routes coming from Weixi and Gongshan along the Burmese border to the south of us united with the route from Shangri-La, once again converging into one main trail, before heading west into the Himalayas. The export of bamboo, essential as waterproof wrapping for cargo, particularly tea and mushrooms (and yes, our fungus friend too), would have needed routes accessing points south into Yunnan and west into Tibet. Local timber was also exported by caravans to be used for building material, as this commodity was scarce farther west in Tibet. Dorje's birthplace and these valued routes were south of Deqin, tucked in between the Mekong and Salween rivers, and what Dorje termed the *romba*—valley country.

One aspect of the Tea Horse Road's importance was that it acted as a receptacle to so many tributaries; it was a main axis with which small caravans carrying specialized local items could link up to join the flow onward to the Himalayan markets in the difficult-to-access hinterlands. Like the nearby Mekong and Salween watersheds, it drew nearby resources into its ever-moving folds.

Our breakfast the next day was a local Tibetan tradition, an unimaginably sweet, sticky treat. The woman of the house (who, I was informed by a winking Dorje, had been *zeemundoo*—beautiful—when she was young) presented me with a hunk of *palè* and a bowl of *djon*—honey—that had been boiled together with a slab of butter. The rich mixture stirred my taste buds and generated groans from deep inside of me. Dorje proudly informed me that the honey was from Yong Jr and I could bathe in the stuff if I wanted to when we arrived at his home.

Dorje's village, accessible only by foot, was forty minutes off a main road that ran south from Deqin. Crossing the swollen Mekong, we made our way past an old cable that straddled the river, itself part of the old transport system, and headed west into a sliver of valley. I was more than curious to meet Dorje's wife, the woman behind this live wire of energy and life, imagining an equally powerful force who could efficiently harness this restless man.

Dorje's house was like most in the area. The first floor was home to a mix of snorting pigs, ranging chickens that ran between the legs of horses, and the odd goat. Disinterested dogs wandered about like drunks, looking fearful of having to assert themselves. Sonam had once told me that Dorje's son was a replica of his father, with one important distinction: "Brains ... the son has some." This harsh assessment was at least half-correct. The handsome son had his father's wide shoulders and lightness of spirit.

Dorje's wife was clearly the firm foundation of the home. Thin and tough, she balanced her non-stop motion with warmth and a desire to see people content, and she made clear one important rule: no one, at any time, was to serve himself, not anything. The "kitchen," which took up the main floor, was effectively off limits to us. Her authority in her domain was unquestioned, and her glare directed at Dorje reinforced this. A demure teenaged daughter, who struck me as a perfect blend of Dorje and his wife, appeared with tea. There was a sense of ease among the family, and I could see that they found joy in being together. It stirred me to be so casually adopted into this clan, with so little fuss and pretension. Dorje's powerful arms swung wide as if to encompass his home as he said, "Treat it as your own." I sat down, satisfied with the world, and, of course, with the tea. Dorje's son had a perpetual smile on his face and treated his father as though he was a delightful but slightly deranged burden, while the daughter raced from one task to another.

"The bright one of the bunch but prone to ferocious bouts of car-sickness," Dorje said. He gleamed with paternal pride, then added, as if to remind me that he hadn't become totally soft, "If she doesn't puke herself to death, she might go to school somewhere away from here." As in many of the rural mountain towns, education was a great conundrum. Children were the future, literally and figuratively, needed at home to help with the work and with caring for elders, while at the same time being the object of great expectations if they had the smarts to continue with school. Dorje's family modelled those of the lados of the past, with the man of the house travelling distances to find employment or his "place in life" and returning to find changes at home. Women, who maintained virtually everything in the men's absence, had to have great faith that the men would return, and knew that with every return there would inevitably be another departure. Like many of the lados, Dorje's edgy curiosity would force him to move, to seek, to drift again and again.

"Being away, one can always return," Dorje once explained to me. Such men had a quality about them that allowed them to sample life without becoming exhausted. Here in his home, Dorje was the most calm I had ever seen him. I basked in this temporary resting place with my surrogate family. The warmth enveloped me, the warmth of silently and effortlessly belonging to something, however fleeting. It was these unassuming pleasures that could feed and re-energize like no others, strengthening relations with friends and fortifying the body and the will. So often in the past months my exhaustion had simply been pushed to the side as I reacted to wonder and risk. There was no time for pondering or reflection—everything was in the now. I felt in need of nourishment, even if only brief moments of humanity or camaraderie.

My thoughts journeyed briefly to my own family, leagues away, and I recalled my gypsy father's words long ago: "One must live standing up." These words emphasized the unparalleled worth of first-hand knowledge and of being immersed in life. Being the son of immigrants, my father had probably understood this as a necessity. So far, my own journey had stressed not only the necessity of doing and seeing but also of partaking. It was in that partaking and struggling that real experience seeped into me, creating vibrant memories. Wafts of Dorje's cigarette smoke filled the room and as I sat collapsed in a gracefully disintegrating couch, the past month's exertions, words, and joys passed through my mind. I wished the rest of our team could be here for this moment. Before me in the room I imagined Sonam berating Dorje, Norbu tucked into a corner of the couch munching on a snack, Nomè silently helping with the food preparation, and Dakpa entertaining us with some tale. I pictured the "ancients" we had encountered—Dawa, Drolma, Neema, Dandee—sitting together sharing tales of the road for one last time, bringing to life the sounds and smells of their trials, reminiscing about unrequited and indulged loves. At that moment, nothing would have given me more satisfaction than to see that picture played out in real life in Dorje's kitchen.

Dorje's father-in-law—who said little, drank heaps of "firewater," and lived in an upstairs room—nodded gravely at the mention of the trade routes. He and Dorje rarely spoke and barely made eye contact. Years ago, an incident had occurred that marred their relationship, but Dorje refused to comment on the long-ago episode. Although his father-in-law had not journeyed along the old trails, he knew of them. "They and the worshipping trails are the same," he muttered. Dorje himself had travelled along the portions without knowing their significance. The worshipping trails were part of a network of routes that Tibetan pilgrims had used for centuries to circumambulate the greater Kawa Karpo range. Running on a northwest–southeast axis, the paths took worshippers on a two-week journey around the range, leading eventually to that never-ending wanderer, the Tsa Yu Chu, or Tsa Yu River, which had led us up into Tibet almost three months earlier. Pilgrim routes doubled as trade routes and vice versa, and it was these routes that Dorje and I would explore.

PASSING THROUGH CORNFIELDS and under ledges of bright flowers, I could make out the unmistakable deep drone of bees. Dorje explained that these particular types of flowers provided lots of nectar for the ambitious bees; the resulting honey was known for its light and fragrant sweetness. "The best in Deqin," he quipped, and what followed was one of those rare and magical Dorje performances. Here on a hill, alone in the mountains, Dorje did a "show" that demonstrated his undying love for the succulent honey. Gyrating his hips, moaning to the distant bees, he writhed and twisted in a frightening display of flexibility and psychosis. Long before he had finished his solo act, I continued on. This was what Dorje brought into the world—a necessary bit of insane joy.

Moving south along narrow stone paths and carrying a minimum of provisions, we covered distances rapidly and soon came upon a giant, murky swell of trees. With Dorje's pace and power, I felt in my element, unafraid to wander from the path, as I tended to do. As much as I had needed the day of rest with Dorje's family, my muscles stretched again in pleasure at being released. Periods of rest only served to allow the body time to realize how fatigued it was.

Our path widened threefold and I could make out a deteriorating ledge alongside the now-broadened route. Clearing leaves and debris away, I could see that the path had definitely been broadened by human hands to allow for significant loads to pass. Rough stones had been fitted together in a coarse patchwork, evening out the surface for ease of travel. This would have been unnecessary for pilgrims. As I slurped my tea and Dorje madly sucked on a cigarette, we tore at vines and mouldy foliage to reveal more and more lonely flagstones. Before long, we had uncovered an antique road. Without a doubt, it was a caravan trail.

The trail, if taken north, would have provided access to both Deqin and the pilgrims' routes heading northwest to Kawa Karpo and beyond into Tibet. To the south it would have provided access to minority areas along the Yunnan-Burma border. Of all our journeying to date, this was the first time I had seen a part of the old trade route so intact, so physical. Through the mountain portions, our paths had been nothing but dirt. This winding road was different. It had been altered specifically to aid traffic. The physical traces were by their very existence gifts, linking me concretely with the trade routes of old. Remnants such as this decrepit path were probably unknown to anyone other than the pilgrims, locals, and yaks. It felt as though the path had been held in a guarded vacuum, in some kind of a secret trust. This part of the route was special for two reasons: first, because the lonely flagstone strip was not on any map, and second, because it was a collector route that wound like a worm, converging with other dark routes into the main Tea Horse Road before spilling out into the various destinations. Activity along here would have been hectic. With so many smaller routes diverging from or merging into the main route, the Tea Horse Road could at times be called the Tea Horse *Roads*.

This tiny chunk of land, once so prosperous, so trodden upon, now sat still, its decaying stones shaded by branches. I wondered aloud if all the traffic and vast exposure to peoples, cargo, and movement had kept the locals in this area so open to and accepting of the outside. Giving me a smile and taking a drag on his cigarette, Dorje said, "Buddhism keeps us open." This simple statement took me by surprise, coming as it did from a man of impulsive exploits. For all his dalliances with women and spontaneous eruptions, there was, in fact, a Dorje of introspection. These moods, however, never lasted long.

Looking at me with his mad smile, Dorje earnestly suggested we start a mushroom export business and use mules to transport the prized cargo along the traditional routes, as in the olden days. He started walking, leading the way, continuing the discussion with himself. His restless character was probably closer to that of the old men of the caravan route than anyone else I had met. Dorje's slow, meandering Khampa dialect was regional and different from the hard Litang or melodic Lhasan. He was prone to long-winded discourses of any and all topics that came to mind. While both of us could function in Mandarin, we generally spoke in a mix of languages. I was making slow but steady progress toward some semblance of fluid speech in my halting, not-yet-grammatical Khampa. Conversations between us took on a comedic aspect, with Dorje often tilting his head, trying to pick out enough intelligible words to put together an idea of what I was saying. Never mind the mountains and their risks—our hand-sign interactions were adventures in themselves.

We climbed into the cold wet of the clouds and onto a wondrous plateau that ran along a path of slick stones prone to sliding into the valley below. Dorje smiled and lit another cigarette; these lands he had known since he was a child. Now he, too, looked on them with a new wisdom of what had passed long ago.

We climbed still higher, through various layers of heat, until we finally met again with bearable freshness. Heat could unravel me quickly, and its waning was welcome. But climbing at a fair speed, an incident, though only a second in duration, served to remind me of the constant vigilance necessary in any venture in the mountains.

A portion of our trail had been wiped clean by a landslide, so Dorje and I were forced to take a higher line through a pinched valley, which we did on all fours, then hop from one minuscule outcropping of dirt and stone to another. With Dorje in the lead, we each leapt from one foot to land on the other, immediately springing to the next foothold so that no ledge would endure too much weight at any one time. As I landed on a ten-centimetre-wide shelf I felt it disintegrate beneath me, leaving precious little to get traction on. Fuelled by panic, I shot forward awkwardly, feeling the last scraps of earth beneath my feet spraying down sixty metres into a rock-bed with a *whoosh*. In the mountains, the reactive senses often needed to be quicker than the mind, and if they weren't, your time would be cut short.

I had known of Dorje long before I had met him, for his reputation had preceded him. A local guide had told me an anecdote, one that helped explain the phenomenon that was Dorje Kandro. Taking some particularly well-heeled Asian clients on a hard climb virtually straight up, Dorje climbed not only with a huge supply pack but while chain-smoking. The clients had prepared for the trip by sleeping in oxygen tents, and had brought with them oxygen, nose strips, pills, liniments, vitamins, and the latest in gadgets and gear. On the way up, two of the six people began getting headaches, so Dorje obligingly slung their packs onto his back as well. By the time he reached the summit, Dorje was hidden under three packs, with only a trail of cigarette smoke hinting at his presence beneath them. He then proceeded to take a swig of *arra,* barley whisky, while the clients gasped and gaped. Assuming that Dorje was taking the caterpillar fungus to "enhance" himself, they asked how many he consumed a day. He told them he didn't use the fungus. They didn't believe him, though—how else could he drink and smoke so much without being fatigued? He explained that he rubbed a yak-dung compress mixed with whisky on his chest every night. That was Dorje.

As we approached a wooden hut that hugged the mountainside, a hulking dog roared its warning. The fearsome Do Khyi mastiffs had been bred to defend, to hunt, and to bring down. Pound for pound, few creatures could match them. But this was the first time on the trip I had seen one with a temperament to match its looks. Gorgeous and absolutely furious, it wanted off its chain. Black eyes and a handsome muzzle radiated menace. It launched itself at us repeatedly from its wide, flat paws. Dorje looked mildly uncomfortable as he wondered aloud why they needed such big dogs up here and, then quickly answered his own question: bears.

The dog's owner could not have been more different from the raging animal. Whispering a little sound to silence the dog—though a throaty rage continued to rumble from it—the man welcomed us quietly into his home. He seemed ageless and almost transparent, and totally neutral—not tall, not short, not strong, not weak ... just very calm. His home was nothing but pieces of wood nailed together and a sunken fire pit, but as with all Tibetan homes I had visited, it comforted.

Six such huts made up the little community. They were summer homes for shepherds, who lived alone for months tending to yak herds and their prime grazing spots. In this tiny paradise I once again felt the diversity that the Tea Horse Road encompassed. Although their families might come once a month to see them, usually the only company the men had was their five mountaintop neighbours. A part of me longed to just sling off my bags, fix up a hut, get a mastiff, and start herding. After peeking into the lives of others for so long, I wanted to experience it myself.

The sacred mountain of Reno Maya—known to Westerners as Peacock Mountain—rested above the cloud line. It was considered an auspicious location for grazing, and Yong Jr shepherds had used the high pastures as long as anyone could remember. It has also been a pass crossed by caravans, and still the odd caravan destined for Deqin straggled in for supplies.

The fire warmed us as our serene host prepared a yak stew. The garlic he chopped in the palm of his hand, and then with the same knife he cut chopsticks for us from a fresh stock of bamboo, placing them neatly in front of us. Large green leaves served as potholders. As we ate, he and Dorje talked of the outside world, about what Dorje had seen, about his relationship with me. Our host was curious and attentive.

His life on this mountain was one of patient repetition, each day being as predictable as the last. When I asked him if he ever wanted to leave the place, he hesitated, carefully forming his answer, before saying that here he knew exactly his place and his purpose, and that he had what he needed. I envied his straightforward thinking and insight, and I realized that as much as I longed to be a part of the land, I, like Dorje, was a ranger, a restless wanderer. It was not enough to belong to a place; I had to search and stretch my version of belonging. All the lados had spoken of this "plight," and now I, too, felt it.

Our host had heard from his elders that caravans had long ago ventured through the valley, often to collect the prized *dènè*, a type of evergreen, found in abundance here. He then produced a tiny wedge of the wood and placed it at the edge of the fire, where it crackled to life and released its camphoric aroma. Used for religious ceremonies and as incense in homes, it was another item that would make the long journey along the ancient highway, to be appreciated by someone faraway.

After eating, we piled into our sleeping bags. Lightning from a distant storm rifled through the night air. Since we were at an altitude of close to four thousand metres, it seemed close and immediate. As the embers in the fire pit smouldered, I laughed myself to sleep to Dorje's made-up songs about lonely men on tops of mountains with only their mules to love. Although I was unfortunately reintroduced to Dorje's reeking feet that night, I wouldn't have traded places for anything.

WE HAD LEFT BEHIND the dry winds of Litang and the Tibetan interior, but although the wind's force had diminished, icy clouds of fog and their accompanying damp gusts numbed my joints. A cold, wet clamp gripped the mountains, freezing the tiny lakes scooped into north-facing pockets of the mountainside, just as the winds had commanded the nomadic abodes farther north. Mornings required a rehabilitation for any limbs unfortunate enough to have become uncovered during the night. For the next two weeks, we wouldn't experience any warmth, only degrees of cold. Our nightly fires were our only refuge. Snaking along pilgrim and caravan trails and traipsing along any path that interested us, we travelled over rain-lashed peaks and into wet, silent valleys. All the routes had in their time played host to caravans, and every step provided a little more insight into the abilities of the paths to access any land, however remote.

When we returned to Yong Jr for a night to pick up more supplies, we refuelled with a meal that I would remember for the rest of my life. We watched the man of the house, a friend of Dorje, prepare it from scratch. A chicken was dispatched and then another. One of the wonderful contradictions I've observed in Tibetans is that although many are capable of explosive violence and have enviable reputations as fighters, they deplore killing any animal. Indeed, most Tibetans pay to have their animals slaughtered by outsiders. Dorje muttered prayers and blanched noticeably as our host quickly ended the hens' lives.

Dorje referred to the lean and muscular birds as "Himalayan chickens." The recipe for the formidable dish we were to be served had been passed down from one generation to the next and had been a favourite among muleteers. Known as *sharra*—whisky chicken—it fuelled and restored the weary bones of traders, as it would mine that night. The chicken was plucked, drained, and cut up, then slowly boiled, along with its organs (considered a specialty and often offered to guests as a sign of welcome and respect), in litres of *arra,* and with a sprinkling of salt and some gingerroot. The concoction cooked slowly for hours while we warmed our gullets with nips of our own *arra.* As the whisky reduced in the pot, more was added. When it finally came time to eat it, the lean meat, saturated with the heady booze, fell off the bones. We gobbled bowl after bowl as its warmth spread to our extremities. We made "reservations" to return for another dinner and then headed for home—though we spent far longer looking for Dorje's house than we should have.

Dorje's cousin Ashi joined us early the next morning, and the three of us headed west. Dorje explained how he and Ashi were related, but I couldn't follow the "my wife's ... sister's ... cousin's ..." Once again, everyone seemed to be related, and again my view of the mountain people's isolation had to be qualified. In the uncompromising mountains, you might be isolated, but you were never alone.

The locals were softer-spoken than the nomads. Their language was more formal, and came out in rapid, bubbling sentences. Throughout Kham—eastern Tibet—the delicate Deqin dialect of Jo gè was admired because it retained its original character and pronunciation. Ashi spoke quietly and his words were often lost the moment they were uttered.

Wearing trousers that ended ten centimetres above his ankles, a T-shirt, and an oversized blazer, Ashi led the triad, carrying the cooking gear in a bamboo basket tied high around his forehead. Fistfuls of the orange, red, and yellow currants whose shrubs lined the paths ended up in our mouths, despite Dorje's warning that eating too many would bring on a headache. Walls of bamboo took over where the berries left off. Upon hearing greetings from above, we looked up to see a dozen or so pilgrims, mostly women and children, descending a nearby path. They wore cheap running shoes and carried bamboo walking sticks and little packs of food; their other belongings they carried on their backs in simple bamboo baskets similar to Ashi's. On their *kora* of Kawa Karpo, they, like the lados, would find shelter with *netsang*, families who had hosted travellers for hundreds of years. For every outer *kora* done, a bamboo walking stick was taken home and kept as a reminder of the pilgrimage, and every notch in the cane had significance. Dorje's belief was that each second notch was the equivalent of a "She loves me," which meant that an even number of notches was better. This, not surprisingly, was never confirmed by anyone.

Whenever we happened upon mushroom pickers on the path, we would drop our loads in order to share a few words and ask about the trail conditions, and inevitably a specimen or two would be offered to us. The hard-to-locate mushrooms commanded exorbitant prices, and most were exported overseas or transported to city centres for cooking or to be used in medicines. Of course, during these encounters, tea was always made, using water collected from nearby streams. Ashi, being conservative, collected only a minimal amount of fuel. We used a piece of *dènè* for the base of the fire. The high sap content of *dènè* made it a long-burning wood, one that could dry out and eventually light even the dampest of other woods.

Sitting around the smoky fires sharing tea was part of the mountain peoples' social fabric. Some days, we would have such encounters every twenty or thirty minutes—sometimes we had just barely packed up and resumed our journey when we met another group of mushroom pickers with whom to sit down and share tea. At first I had to wonder how much new news and information could be gained at each successive sitting. But soon I realized that that didn't matter—news, trivia, love stories, and laughs were all shared, and the point was about taking time to take time. I came to appreciate the manner in which the informal gatherings kept people bound to one another in the often lonely environment. We rarely exchanged our own names but, instead, those of hometowns, fathers, and mothers—those provided clear links to a person's identity. These people were the sum of their ancestors and their geography. Occasionally, a personality trait had bearing too: everyone, of course, knew Dorje.

Food aficionados might call our meals slow-food masterpieces, consisting as they did of fresh pickings untouched by pesticides and herbicides. Leaves, vines, and roots found their way into the cooking pot. Vegetables with bitter, sweet, and sour flavours eliminated the need for spices. Bulbs were occasionally dug up, and berries were sometimes also added to the mix. Dorje often disappeared into the woods to examine the underside of a log, dig through a pile of dirt, or investigate a growth on a tree. Sometimes he returned covered in dirt and vines, with an armful of orange fungus, the famed *moo er*—the Chinese name for wood ear fungus—or a huge morel dangling out of his pocket. Ashi, meanwhile, was the greens expert and provided a mesmerizing description of the health benefits of each green, from antioxidants to intestinal cleansers. Each meal energized and stimulated us in short order.

One afternoon, an hour-long debate ensued that stopped our progress completely, despite a wet, freezing wind. Dorje paced around a tree, cigarette jammed into his mouth and eyes downward, peering at the topic of dispute. A cluster of perfectly round mushrooms sat at the base of an old tree. Ashi calmly sat back, telling Dorje in his whisperlike voice, "That is not edible, and never has been edible ... you don't know what you are talking about." Dorje fumed, heaved, and grunted his disagreement, finally threatening to eat the little mushrooms raw just to prove that they were edible. Ashi told him he was welcome to, except that his corpse would not be taken back with us but be buried right under the tree. Dorje's bluff had been called, and we carried on, but Dorje gave me a wink to signal he had not yet accepted defeat.

"We will see bears," said Dorje a few days later. Sodden and cold, we had been plodding through vicious rains. Most of our gear had been drenched. A white onslaught of rain silenced everything, including Dorje—a rare bout of stillness for him. Reaching a shepherd settlement, we agreed to stop for a couple of days in an attempt to dry ourselves and our belongings. Whereas winds could inspire, steady frigid drizzle or, worse, heavy rains, pummelled our spirits.

The locals we were gathered with around a fire nodded in agreement: without a doubt, we would see bears. Bears had long roamed the mountains, having come to peaceful cohabitation terms with the perennial human and yak populations.

The old settlement was a series of winterized stone dwellings dug into the slopes. We were guests of Dorje's brother-in-law, who for the past two decades had spent four months of each year here with his herds of yak and *dzo,* an animal that is half-yak and half-cow. He seemed to carefully weigh his words before he spoke. One of the quirks of the locals was their stylized communication: headshakes and nods, pursed lips, bulging cheeks, and a distinctive tongue cluck accompanied all discussions. The cluck seemed particularly effective in emphasizing a negative or conflicting opinion. I kept my own tongue still, aware that a mis-cluck or an off-pitch one could severely alter the discussion.

Caravans passing through the lands would link up with the Tsa Yu Chu, one of the Salween River's biggest tributaries, and head directly into the Tsarong area of southeastern Tibet that Dorje and I had navigated so long ago. Grandfathers and elders who had in their time tended herds here had often bought and traded supplies with the caravans. *Arra* was supplied to traders, as well as reports of the weather conditions to be encountered along the way.

Just as we were finishing our meal that evening, we heard the yells of a young boy. *"Dong ... Dong ..."*—"Bear, bear." Dorje ran outside and the rest followed. Scanning the mountainside, we spotted a smidgen of black in the failing light, way up. Dorje and I raced up the mountain through the grey mist, our lungs burning, our breath coming out in tiny blasts in the cold air. We weaved up to a spot where we could see the black form moving nimbly across a landslide. Dorje was adamant that we get a good look at the bear so that I could compare it with its western counterpart. This bear was surprisingly big and making its way toward our side of the mountain, although it was still quite a way above us on the slope. We moved slowly, getting smacked by the underbrush and stopping every now and then to peek through the wet foliage. Then nothing—the bear had disappeared.

Dorje decided it was time for a cigarette, although his fervent attempts to light it in the rain were futile. The cigarette, however, remained limply standing guard at the corner of his mouth.

Crawling out onto the landslide clearing, we still saw no sign of movement. Then, from off to the left where we had just been, came the sound of cracking underbrush as something moved through the woods. Down below, the men were hollering, but their words were lost in the rain. Clinging to the steep slope, we stayed where we were, getting soaked. The clearing was surrounded on all sides by dense woodland, and as the light ebbed away, we lost more and more of the details of the landscape. To my right there was movement—or I thought there was—but then nothing, and after a while we slid down the slick rocks and continued to wait. Again, a vague movement up to the right and then a small rockslide, and then nothing. Dorje's expression was intense as he scanned the woods.

The slanting rain was numbing us and we decided to ski, slide, and grapple our way down before the last bits of weak light disappeared altogether. On making it down the slope, we were told that there had been not one but two bears: the one we had seen up and off to our left, and another coming from the right. Those vague movements I had noticed were, in fact, made by a bear not even twenty metres from us. Dorje rather predictably sat down for a drink and a well-deserved cigarette.

This was one of the few bear hotspots on the route into Tibet, and so dogs became highly valued by the muleteers during their negotiation of the passes. In the past, the locals might have killed the odd bear, but these days the danger for the bears from hunters is much more acute: areas along the Yunnan-Myanmar border, just south of where we were, are prime locations for hunters seeking bear organs to sell for use in Chinese medicines and as aphrodisiacs.

"RENAKO," said Dorje over the churning wind, to announce the old nomadic settlement we were coming upon. Dorje was suffering from what he called "damp lungs," from our recent bear expedition. While there was no noticeable decrease in his cigarette consumption, he had increased his dose of *arra* to five nips a day to counter his mild discomfiture, beginning first thing in the morning.

We had just powered through an area Ashi called Dongtang, meaning "bear plain," and were in no hurry to meet up with the great foragers. Dorje, however, often stopped to examine bear scat, telling us in spectacular detail what the bears had been indulging in. Squatting down with a stick, he poked through it, remarking how the bears that year were in great shape. He even went so far as to tell us that he recognized one particularly fresh pile and its owner because of its particular seed content. At one time he had hunted in these mountains, but not any more. "Not good for my soul," he chirped, "but I miss it."

Ashi offered a quiet contrast to our bear-dung authority and was in many ways a leaner version of Nomè. I wondered what it was about these travelling chefs and their constitutions that made them such calm arbitrators of the world.

Our destination was a remote (even by locals' standards) canyon that housed three nomadic dwellings. The tiny community marked the start of an alternative route back to Yong Jr by which strong caravans with relatively light loads could make up time. Our own route from Yong Jr had come around the main mountain range, taking days. It was the standard trail most took, since it offered the most shelter, but there was a more stunning—and riskier—route. The alternative path we would now take to return to Yong Jr cut directly over the mountains. Looking at it from where we stood, it appeared to be nothing more than a thread, a thin line that mounted a distant ridge and disappeared into a narrow wedge.

As we left the tree line behind, the path narrowed to just centimetres. The mountain sloped off to our right. Glacial streams spanned out in the distance, white striations criss-crossing the mountainside and draining into the canyon. Above us, impervious to the heights, yaks stood on minuscule ledges peering down at us. Munching on cud, they seemed disdainful of our labours, and I felt humbled. Their massive bodies—hunched oversized shoulders supported by nimble legs and wonderfully delicate hooves and covered with long hair— seemed in complete opposition to their skills: they could casually perch on outcrops, seemingly without the slightest concern, enjoying some particular delicacy. During an epic Dorje monologue about the lives and loves of the great yak, I was informed of how even this crea- ture suffered *la du*—altitude sickness—above sixty-three hundred metres, and how the more independently inclined beasts left their herd and simply disappeared into the mountains, to live out their days grazing. Known as *drong,* the wild yaks are not threatened by anything in the wild, and meeting one alone might be considered both auspi- cious and a death knell, as these huge creatures could stomp or gore you in a flash.

Unlike in the Nyanqen Tanglha range, where stunning glacial slopes hid risk in the purity of white, risks here were masked by the emerald greenery. Aesthetically, nothing suggested the peril that lay just centimetres to our right, where slopes, made slick by sleet, were just as steep and deadly, plunging a thousand metres into valleys that from our vantage point seemed carved in miniature. Death here would come just as swiftly as on an icy cliff.

A milky layer of clouds spread out before us. We had reached the pass and were ready to begin our descent. A brown trail staggered into the community below: Renako, population three. Renako sat a quarter of the way down the hollowed-out mountain—it looked like a volcano, except that the basin was filled by grass and a lake. While the art of the ascent is largely one of stamina, pace, and a good pair of lungs, it is the descent that is really the great danger of mountaineering. Knees and spines grind and creak, sending throbs into every part of the body, and one roll of the ankle or one misstep can potentially bring the whole business to an end. We scaled down into Renako unscathed but in need of a forceful dose of tea.

A curly haired teenager wearing an old suit and what I came to know as the six-layer system of clothing, subscribed to by many Tibetans, welcomed us and promptly made us the much-needed tea. The wild-eyed young man was his own boss and clearly thrived on the isolation, making his way around his little home to clear a space where we could sleep. Happy to have visitors, he dusted off places for us to sit, fretted over our bags, and cleaned out cups. In less than five minutes he had wordlessly offered us all he had. I still hadn't gotten used to such offerings. The unquestioning generosity to travellers was part of life here. To me, it spoke of a different time, a time when people needed each other and were not self-conscious. The simple act of giving to strangers served to maintain a wordless cohesion among people far more than any doctrine could. Self-reliant and hardened as this boy was, his generosity was genuine and unhesitating.

For half the year, the young man tended a herd of seventeen yak and lived in his dwelling of wool and wood, occasionally visiting his two "neighbours." Noticing me admiring a large handmade slingshot, he handed it to me, watching me closely. Then he reached into a small bamboo box and extracted four dried little brown nondescript lumps, which he placed carefully in front of us. I recognized a breastbone and two folded wings—a tiny bird corpse laid to rest in a tiny bamboo coffin. He placed two of them over the fire. The other two bodies were wingless and I couldn't make out what they were.

The young man glowed with pride as he told me what the other two lumps were: mice, killed with the slingshot. As he put the two bodies next to the birds on the fire, I hoped that they were related to the nocturnal rodents, the *avra*, we had encountered in Dotok. But his smile put everything into context: they were an offering to us. The morsels of meat were a gift to us, an honour for both him and us, and one we couldn't refuse. The young man watched us intently as he gave us tips on how to extract the meat from between the tiny bones with our tongues. There wasn't enough meat to even taste much, but that wasn't the point. When we were done, his "Oh yaa" summed up the satisfaction we all felt.

The mountain mice were known for their curative powers for stomach disorders and "heating the body," and like most traditions, their use was steeped in a long history. Muleteers often purchased them from men such as our host, to keep as part of their medicinal supplies. It was in this land that Dorje had learned the healing properties of urine.

The next morning as we packed up our gear, the young man beckoned me toward him. From beneath his layers of clothing he pulled out his *tongwa*, an amulet worn around the neck. He meant to indicate that this was how he was protected. This gesture touched on something I've found increasingly rare in the Western world: a belief in something very much outside the self. Declining his offer to stash a couple of mice corpses in our pockets, we left him to his hill. As we departed, I felt restored and revitalized.

As we approached Dorje's village, Dorje became distracted and stopped frequently, looking around the ground, grunting. At last he gave a triumphant yell. He pulled back some grasses to reveal three little *bagu*, the same species of bamboo as my bracelet was made from. Lovingly, Dorje gently cut one of the green stalks with his knife. Smiling, he told me that this one would be a special gift for a woman he knew. Ashi softly shook his head, and I rolled my eyes and moved on, afraid of what he might tell me. Dorje roared in laughter, amused at our reaction. Catching up with me, Dorje reminded me that we had a reservation for another lethal dose of *sharra*, whisky chicken. Later that night, as we made our way to his friend's house, Dorje told me earnestly that I needed to find a wife in his village so that he could pop over whenever he wanted. "Much easier," he said.

It would be a long night.

Stacks of Puer tea cakes lie drying near Xiaguan, Yunnan. For centuries, tea has been steamed and moulded into these shapes for ease of transport, whether on mules' backs or by human hand.

6

Simao to Lijiang:
Sleep Between Slurps

You may laugh at us for having too much tea, but may we not suspect that you of the West have no tea in your constitution?

—OKAKURA KAKUZO, *THE BOOK OF TEA*

A TINY SPOUT OF TINTED WATER arced out of the teapot and into the
two thimble-sized glass cups. It gleamed a reddish brown. Bringing
the steaming cups up to our lips, we took in the earthy liquid with a
loud slurp. The taste was both musty and bitter, but trailing into the
throat, it became sweet. The tea server nodded her appreciation for
our slurp. Dakpa laughed that the cups were so small. "How can we
drink from these? It will take an hour to quench our thirst." Our *cha
sifu's*—tea master's—face clouded for a moment, looking at him with
a hint of disdain. "That is the point. Tea must be consistent in temperature, in strength. Tea is not water." This woman would have fainted
in horror at my Thermos method of preparing tea over the past
months, and my slugging it back in panting gulps.

Returning alone to Shangri-La after my entertaining "Dorje
travels," and significantly more knowledgeable on bears and their
bowel movements, I was joined once again by Dakpa, who was keen
to see the origins of tea. We had made our way south in a slow
winding course, eventually taking a flight into the sleepy city of
Simao, in southern Yunnan Province. It would be just Dakpa and me
for this most southern of expeditions. His subtle charm, as well as his

"tropical training" in India, prepared him well for the venture ahead, and he had gained back most of his scant weight. I couldn't picture Dorje down here nursing tiny splashes of coloured liquid—his sheer force of personality would lay waste to the place. Norbu was unlikely to get any more time off from work in the next decade, though I had heard that he was threatening to quit his job to "pursue a life outside of phones and walls." Sonam and those amazing reedlike legs of his were engaged in another trek farther north, and Nomè's talents would not be needed, as local fare was abundant.

As we slipped down a Simaon tea alley in the tropical heat, a stern teahouse hostess invited us into her shop with a forcible hospitality more common to Tibetans than the Chinese or minority tribes. The alley consisted of neat rows of nearly identical teahouses that opened onto a walkway. We were in the realm of tea purism; such alleys were visited by addicts rather than by tourists. The shop we now found ourselves in was a small tidy room with a tea table that took up a good quarter of the space. The room smelled of dried tea, and every bit of space was occupied by bags of tea, boxes of tea, stacks of dry tea cakes, a shelf of vintage tea, loose leaf tea, bricks of tea, and poorly printed photographs of tea fields. While most teahouse owners engaged themselves with card games or television, this woman appeared to have deemed herself responsible for educating the two foreigners in the ways of Puer, and it was her intensity that drew us in.

In the Simao Prefecture, tea was not only enjoyed but revered, used in ceremonies, and purchased not by the gram but by the kilogram. Here there was a ritualistic aspect to tea, in both its preparation and its consumption, whereas in the Tibetan regions it was a basic ingredient of life, one that nourished and warmed. But we were far from the rough ways of Tibetan tea etiquette. I tried to imagined a tall raw-boned Khampa encased in a *chupa*—a long wool coat—and pleated hair sitting next to us, with these delicate ornaments and discussions of tea-drinking etiquette. Although his meaning of tea might differ, its importance and value would be the same.

Both Dakpa and I were covered in sweat. The temperature outdoors had conspired with the heat of the tea to turn us into soggy messes. My sweat glands had in the past three months been shut down, frozen, and cleansed; now they had been blown wide open. In front of us, several bricks, cakes, and balls of tea sat awaiting our attention. Simao had been a centre of tea cultivation for thousands of years, and Simao's tea had been making its way to Tibet for more than thirteen hundred years. Even in China, tea purists referred to the area as the home of tea.

Simao's climate and altitude is perfect for growing that oddly named and most unusual of teas, Puer. Tea, its production, its culture, and particularly its consumption were all of the utmost importance in Simao. First consumed as a medicine and as a food, tea was originally referred to as *tu*, meaning bitter herb, before becoming known from the eighth century onward as *cha*—tea. It has always been integral to the lives and diets of Yunnan's ancient Tibeto-Burman tribes.

Our *sifu*, a stocky woman with a square jaw and small hands, nodded that it was time to continue our education. "There are two types of Puer: *shou cha* and *sheng cha*." But Dakpa wasn't listening, and I just wanted her to pour another cup. Like a couple of hardcore addicts, we fidgeted.

"The *shou cha* is first fermented—aged—and then formed, whereas the *sheng cha* is simply dried and formed; it then ferments in that form. It is a pure Puer."

A pure Puer, say the experts, must be a variety of broad leaf tea, and be grown, harvested, sun-dried, and produced in Yunnan. The Chinese use the expression *tai yang wei*—"taste of the sun"—to describe properly sun-dried tea. After drying, it is steamed and shaped. "Many pretenders exist, but those are the qualities the tea has in order to be a true Puer," the tea master said.

The *sifu*'s eyes narrowed as she emphasized her next point. "*Sheng cha* is superior because it ages naturally, not artificially." The *shou* type is often called ripe, even though it isn't, and the *sheng* is referred to as raw, even though it isn't. Nomenclature runs riot in any tea discussion, with the same tea often being referred to by different names.

Picking up a round ball of dark, pressed leaves and stems, a *shou cha*, our tea master explained that this shape was known as *tuo* and had been, like all the shaped or formed teas, easiest to transport. I softly suggested we try some. I was becoming restless, as was Dakpa, who was tapping his foot incessantly. Two weeks earlier, I had been breathing in the cold air of the Himalayas with not a building in sight, gulping pungent Puer out of a beat-up Thermos. Now I sat covered in sweat in a tiny teahouse three thousand metres lower in altitude, desperately sipping out of a thimble.

Using a small, beautifully crafted utensil that resembled a letter opener, our *sifu* dug out a small portion of unattractive brown tea from the tea ball. For all its fame in the cultlike tea circles, Puer is perhaps the least attractive of teas. No wondrous curls or tight black symmetry, no rough rusty hues or brilliant greens—Puer is an understated, underwhelming example of a plant that has fifteen thousand varieties. And no poetically descriptive name or mythical title hinting at otherworldly qualities either—it is named after the town that had once been the main distribution and selling point for tea from southern Yunnan. There is a saying about Puer tea that is insightful: "The better it looks, the worse it tastes, and the worse it looks, the better it tastes."

When our *sifu* reiterated this, Dakpa quipped, "We are definitely in for a treat then." Laughing, he told her, "In Tibet, we would call this yak dung tea. Next time I come here, I will bring you many varieties of this tea; we have countless varieties sitting outside in the fields." Unsure whether he was stating a fact or joking, she nodded, not wanting to offend nor appear naive.

Carefully washing out a tiny clay pot with boiling water, she explained that the water must be at a full boil in order to "open up the pores in the clay." She put the small chunk of tea in the pot, poured more hot water over the vessel—the excess water draining into a pan that sat below the bamboo tea tray—and then over the tea itself. Her movements were crisp and quick. After a few seconds, she poured the contents of this first pot of tea over the cups, but stopped Dakpa's attempt to retrieve one. "This is not to drink; this is to eliminate impurities and bitterness." Dakpa looked at her, sceptical, then at me. "What kind of talk is this?" he asked.

Speaking between rapid exhalations of breath, our *sifu* explained that the first infusion, which lasted only a second, opened the leaves, waking them from their slumber and preparing the essential oils for release. "We don't want to steep the leaves, only wake them. The leaves' bitterness will come to the surface and be poured out." She then poured a second dose of water over the now damp mound of tea sitting in the pot. After just ten seconds, the tea was served. My hands were practically shaking as I reached for the little cup of burgundy fluid. The tea was pungent and stimulated my entire mouth with its potency, but, as before, when it hit the back of the mouth, it left a sweet, clean trail.

Things were now speeding up, and the teapot was kept busy with successive infusions. As fast as they were poured, we consumed, being ordered to "drink while it's scalding." A stubby finger suddenly halted everything as it wriggled mid-air. "The third and fourth infusions reveal the true character of the Puer tea," our *sifu* said.

"Why?" asked Dakpa.

"The leaves have unfolded completely, and the proteins have been released into the infusion." The tea master looked close to rapture.

The powerfully flavoured tea left little aftertaste. When I asked about this, the slightest hint of a smile played at the corner of her lips. "An old tea smoothens as it ages—its finish is cleaner, but it fills the mouth with wonderful vapours and aromas. It begins and ends in the mouth. But you should know that this Puer is flawed."

We looked at it and smelled it but didn't notice any flaws.

She continued on with her instruction. "Fermented tea is aged artificially. This process speeds the fermentation process time to months or even weeks. It is not a natural process, and that makes the tea inferior." Her stiff, formal body language told me that black Puer—force-fermented Puer—was a contentious issue in tea circles.

As the theanine, tannins, catechins, minerals, vitamins, and antioxidants roared into our blood streams, Dakpa and I sat back to watch in a state of wired enthusiasm. Tea's long history hadn't complicated the serving process. The tools and supplies involved were simple: clay pot, cups, water, and tea leaves, and, of course, a thirst. Our *sifu*'s hands and tea instruments were now flashing in a dexterous show of proficiency. Another one of the teapots was being readied. Tiny clay pots from Yixing, in Jiangsu Province in eastern China, were used only for Puers or oolongs, teas that could handle the high heats that the pots were designed to maintain. A lighter, unfermented tea would simply cook too fast, destroying the leaves' delicate essences. Hot water swelled the clay of the Yixing pots slightly, letting its pores absorb the essences, and sealing the fate of the pot. The pot, after this "initiation," would know only this type of tea for the extent of its life, or that of its owner.

Cross-brewing—mixing types of teas brewed in any one clay pot—is considered a great crime among tea traditionalists.

"The beauty of Puer is its ability to sustain repeated infusions. I can make up to fifteen pots using the same leaves," the *sifu* said. She paused to make sure we were paying attention. The thought of an afternoon of non-stop shots of tea and the ensuing feelings of bliss gave me no end of pleasure.

"The better the tea, the more infusions it can bear. No other tea can make such a claim." Puer tea continues to age and improve even after it has been steamed into a cake or ball shape, whether in its green unfermented form or in its dark brown fermented form.

"These leaves"—she took off the tiny teapot lid to reveal the shiny unfurled leaves—"can be used tomorrow." No other tea, we were assured, could be conserved this way, as it would begin to rot.

"So many lie about tea: about its age, about where it comes from, about the manner in which it is fermented," our tea master sighed, and I was concerned that this was a signal that our supply of tea had come to an end. Thankfully, she began to prepare our next pot, and while pouring took another swipe at *shou cha,* telling us that at one time, tea always fermented naturally. The black Puer in its forced-fermented form started being produced only in the 1970s. In her mind, it was an intruder in the world of tea.

Our attention was directed to a round tea cake—a form known as *qizibing*—of *sheng,* unfermented Puer. Our hostess noticeably softened as she handled the light green and dark green buds. "This is Puer in its original form," she purred. "It will ferment or age naturally in this form with no artificial means, no speeding up, no disturbances." Each time she said the word *artificial,* her face darkened, and it occurred to me that beneath her rigid discipline and unsmiling seriousness, she was more than just a tea drinker: she was someone who appreciated and savoured each stage of development of the green leaf, from the snipping off at the stem by a pair of fingernails to its eventual infusion in hot water.

She gently handed us the tea cake to smell, but only after demonstrating the proper technique: pressing her nose onto the leaves, she took two long inhalations and then, surprising us both, released her breath onto the dried leaves and took a third long sniff. The humidity of her breath released the tea's essential oils, revealing its character. Dakpa laughed, until he, after breathing on it, discovered that the fragrance has revitalized in the process. He had, I could see, become a convert. Our *sifu* looked pleased with herself.

It was this type of tea that was first transported in bulk into Tibet, although Princess Wencheng probably transported the small-leaf *Sinensis sinensis* variety, a small-leaf tea plant from which most green teas, though not Puer, come. During the Tang Dynasty (618 to 907), Yunnan green tea was exported in various compacted forms, as well as in smaller quantities as loose tea, and it was only during its months-long three- to four-thousand-kilometre journey that the effects of natural fermentation were realized. With its increased strength, aroma, and medicinal properties, the tea became the favourite of the early Tibetans and remains so to this day.

Deftly manipulating the pot, the *sifu* gave it a twist before pouring the yellowish liquid to splash clean the second set of cups in front of us. Dakpa remembered the lesson and left his cup alone, but his eyes gleamed with a slight madness, the dizzying effects of the multiple cups of tea taking hold. My own head was buzzing pleasantly and my limbs felt airy and light. Soon, we would be in a tea-induced rapture. The powerful amino acid theanine, found only in tea (and a single species of mushroom), was at least partially responsible for our bliss. Making up fifty percent of the amino acid content of tea, it is one of the primary influences on the way a tea tastes and on its kick, and it is unaffected by multiple infusions.

Our next few cups were bitter, the lighter, unfermented *sheng cha* having a more stimulant effect. The appeal of the bitterness was that there was no great appeal at first. Dakpa drew an analogy to sum up Puer's attraction: "In Tibet, we believe that a good heart is the most important quality for a woman to have, rather than great beauty." Seeing that Puer (and I suspect she thought herself) was being appreciated for its essential qualities, our *sifu* seemed gratified. We had crossed a line now and the *sifu*'s demeanour changed completely. Losing her professional hardness, she softened her tone and became more friendly with us, perhaps even slightly flirtatious. Dakpa and I, former tea novices, were now tea graduates who had shown enough understanding to warrant a more personal approach.

She then asked us which tea we preferred to drink daily. Dakpa mentioned the traditional yak butter tea of Tibet that he consumed every morning at home (while still somehow maintaining his svelte figure). I said oolong was my preference. Having no slabs of yak butter around, she took down some rolled oolong (jet-black dragon) leaves from the shelf and prepared a pot for us. I tasted the lightly smoked oolong, but my tongue felt somehow flat, as though something were missing; I felt as if I had been taken somewhere halfway and then abruptly dropped off.

When asked how the oolong compared with the Puer, Dakpa was quick to respond. "It's nothing but water."

"Ah, you have experienced something today," she replied. "Once you have tasted a genuine Puer served properly, you will not be able to drink others."

I remembered an old Tibetan man we had met on our journey to Lhasa telling us that some of the teas he had tried tasted of dust, that they were nothing but tinted water. The only tea he could drink was one "that bites the tongue." The only tea he ever chose to drink? Puer.

Hours later, having downed litres of tea, Dakpa and I staggered out of the shop in a tea climax of sorts, with an open invitation from our hostess to return. There is a legend that the great teacher Dharma, who introduced Zen Buddhism to China, sliced off his eyelids to stop himself from dozing off, and from his eyelids tea plants grew. Whatever truth there was to the story, there would be no sleep for us. We would even light a candle of thanks to the ancient martyr. The humid night heat swam with the scents of exotic flowers, smoke, and cut grass, while the day's odours drifted away. This was the first time in months I had been out of the Tibetan areas, and everything seemed subdued and smaller, less intense. The streets were spotless, the Chinese character for tea—*cha*—ubiquitous. At all hours, on every day of the week, the teahouses remain open, for in this stronghold of green, there is always a moment, an hour, or an afternoon for tea.

Lively voices around us carried softly in the hot air. We were in one of the most culturally diverse areas of Asia. "So different from us, but they drink tea, too, so they are linked to us," Dakpa said. The big-boned Khampas, indestructible nomads, and giant open landscapes that we had recently travelled from seemed far away. The fine, delicate faces and small-boned statures of the locals were those of another people, another culture along the Tea Horse Road. In the streets, there was a sense of unhurried efficiency and a lightness of movement—perhaps because of the heat or perhaps the locals were happily high on tea. Dakpa ranted about the sweltering conditions, saying that if he had to live here, he would be near comatose. I suggested that a better option would be to live in a teahouse, contentedly slurping yourself into tea oblivion.

Days later, we were travelling once again, first by bus, then by Jeep, and finally on foot, reaching farther into the heart of tea cultivation, which cut a giant counter-clockwise swath around Simao. It was important for us to see not only the tea centres but also the tea sources—the fields and the people who spent their lives harvesting the fragrant leaves. Heading west across the Mekong River and watershed and then south, with the Burmese border to our right, we entered the wet tropical lands that were home to some of the world's oldest native tea trees. Worshipped by local indigenous tribes, the trees had been growing for some two thousand years.

None of the mighty Khampa lados we had spoken to on our journey had ventured into this southern fortress of green and heat. Their impressions of this distant land were summed up by one lado as "a green magical inferno"—it was a place where their precious tea grew, but other than that, they knew little about it.

Until the Mongol invasions in the thirteenth century, western Yunnan was an independent territory. Its people were ethnically and linguistically linked to those of Vietnam, Thailand, Laos, and Burma. An important part of Yunnan's economy involved the precious green leaf. During the sixth and seventh centuries, well-established trade routes were busy with caravans travelling south, east, and west, exporting silks, silver, and tea to India and beyond via Burma, but as early as the fifth century, tea had made its way to Turkey and the Middle East.

It's not known exactly when tea first made it to Tibet, but it is known that during the seventh and eighth centuries, the Nanzhao Kingdom, which ruled Yunnan's volatile western lands, had close relations with the Tubo Kingdom of Tibet. Whether it came by way of Princess Wencheng, as legend has it, or in even earlier trade exchanges between the Tibetans and the minority groups of southern Yunnan, tea would prove to be in perpetual demand. Tea has been cultivated by the Dai people of southern Yunnan for close to two thousand years. It probably made its way along the ancient corridors into Tibet, as both the Dai and Tibetans of the time traded extensively. The tea was packaged in bamboo stalks and aged. Once the casing was broken open, the solid tube of tea inside was ready for consumption or travel. Perhaps no one item of trade or tribute in all of Asia can lay claim to have travelled so widely. Tea was commonly given as a tribute to help maintain friendly political ties with both neighbouring and distant kingdoms. Many kingdoms used the Yunnan-Guizhou Plateau, linking Yunnan with the Tibetan Plateau, as a convenient corridor for migration, trade, and military intrigue. It was this route that would come to be known as the Yunnan–Tibet Tea Horse Road.

One thing that the Nanzhao Kingdom learned early on was that the Tibetans were not to be ignored. The ancient Tibetans showed the requisite amounts of daring force and business acumen needed for successful trade. They built bridges to span the many rivers throughout western Yunnan for military use and to encourage trade between the kingdoms. Indeed, it was the Tibetans who established a precedent for long-distance travel and trade; they, before any other minority group of the area, ranged far and wide for trade and expansion.

The Bai, Naxi, and Tibetan peoples also shared a long history of healthy trade and cultural exchange. The now-peaceful Bai were once the undisputed rulers of the Nanzhao Kingdom, and a Tang emperor designated a Bai leader as king and ruler of all of Yunnan. The Bai were also known for being very sharp in business. The agricultural Naxi populate central and northern Yunnan. The Naxi have peacefully cohabitated with their powerful Tibetan neighbours for centuries, and were considered to be sensitive intermediaries. An ancient pillar excavated in western Yunnan depicts the Tibetan horse, the Naxi lion, and the dragon of the Bai people—early animal representations of each tribe—configured in a symbol of unity that suggests that cooperation and trade among the three peoples was alive and well long before the "Tea Horse Road" moniker was adopted for their routes of trade.

The Dai and Bai, the former traditionally populating southern Yunnan, the latter southern and middle Yunnan, harvested the tea and transported it to the Naxi, who dealt with the Khampas. The Naxi, although their language differed completely from Tibetan dialects, were able to converse and negotiate with the Khampas thanks to their homeland's proximity to Kham, and they were accustomed with the Khampa way of doing business: straightforward, with no patience for underhandedness nor word games.

Many Naxi and Tibetans, however, point to another link between their two cultures, an archaic link that might at least in part explain their abilities to work alongside one another. This link takes the form of a fable and stretches back to the time of the Chinese Princess Wencheng. The fable tells of Songtsen Gambo, king and unifier of Tibet during the Tubo period (629 to 846), who sent his most trusted general, Lumbo Gara, to escort Princess Wencheng back to Lhasa to join the king in matrimony. This much of the fable seems to be unquestioned. The handsome general and princess, as the story goes, had an affair and, more problematically, a child, which they were forced to hide among the silks, seeds, tea, and mules. The child's birth was kept secret, and the baby was soon put into a painted wooden box and set afloat on a river, to be eventually found by the Naxi. The baby would in time become supreme ruler of all the Naxi people and be known rather modestly as the Wood Sky King. Lumbo Gara, so the legend goes, had his eyes taken out by Songtsen Gambo for his intimacy with the princess. Both Khampa and Naxi elders hold the story to be true.

AFTER ABOUT A WEEK we arrived in the far reaches of southwestern China, a region prone to rain and magnified heat, and a world where water touched everything. Rows of tea trees extended along the hillsides for kilometres, and Hani and Lahu tribeswomen moved slowly from branch to branch, stem to stem. In ancient times, tea making its way north through the stifling humidity was wrapped in something known to the Tibetan lados as *towa*, a tight waterproof bamboo covering usually made of the pliant "skin," or bark, of the bamboo, to protect the tea from moisture. Farther north, where it became available, a layer of boiled birch bark was added for extra protection, fitted either inside or outside the bamboo wrap. This system is still used in some remote areas for trade among villages. But for markets that had become even more distant, although the tea fields have changed little over time, the methods of harvesting and transporting the tea have modernized—pesticides are used on the crops; more and more, machines mass-harvest the tea, and transport trucks and airplanes have replaced the mules. Most of the tea harvested in southern Yunnan becomes Puer or unfermented green tea, but little these days makes it into Tibet.

We continued to make our way southeast, passing through Menglian County near the Yunnan-Burma border, and through villages of the Dai peoples, the nomadic Yi, the powerful Lahu, and the curious and shy Wa. The Wa's ancestors were headhunters, with a penchant for beheading anyone with whiskers. Dakpa, whose face was perpetually covered in a heavy beard, took this news well, but developed a habit of covering his mouth. When I asked him about it, he said, "I don't want to show disrespect, nor do I want them to remember what they used to do."

Even in the plush rolling hills just kilometres from the Burmese border, tiny plots of tea grew next to rice. Like all the indigenous peoples in the region, the Wa consumed tea and had their own centuries-old method of preparing it. First they packed the tea leaves into a small hotpot and roasted them over embers, often adding rice. Smoky and mildly narcotic, the tea refreshed and apparently decreased body heat, though Dakpa seemed immune to these effects. As much as the mountains had taken a toll on our energy, the feverish heat we were now encountering was merciless, depleting our energy and leaving us with an uninspired lethargy. The only effective cure was an increase in our dosage of Puer, of which we had ample supply.

Although the tea leaf and the process of producing it for consumption might be identical, the methods of serving the tea had many variations among the ethnic tribes. The Lahu depended on their heavily roasted teas, while the Yao make a potent concoction of honey and garlic tea. The Dai still cook tea inside hollowed-out bamboo canes, which sweetens the tea slightly while giving it a roasted flavour; the Pulan have a mouth-churning sour tea, the result of the addition of dried local plants; the Kucong a replenishing salty tea; and the Yi are known for their "fire tea," made by shaking the tea leaves in a small hotpot and adding black pepper for an extra boost. Whereas Tibetan tea comforted, with an addition of yak butter that gave the tea weight and calories, tea in the southwestern region of China was spiced and sweetened to expel heat and cure maladies. But whatever the cosmetic qualities and taste, tea was still the base.

MENGHAI IS BOTH a city and a county, and also an unmatched bastion of tea. It is also one of the important starting points of an ancient trade route that led west right into the belly of Burma. Today, only a small plaque beside a monastery serves as a reminder.

Rain welcomed us, and a hint of coolness was present in the murky skies. And, for the first time in days, there was wind—real wind, not just a murmuring of air. Dakpa and I laughed in joy—we wouldn't languish to death in the heat after all. It was not much more than a gust, but it was enough to energize us and keep us going until our next cup of tea. We didn't have long to wait.

In Menghai, we were to fall under the spell of Napu, of the Lahu tribe. A friend had told us in no uncertain terms that this was the woman to talk to. A passionate tea-grower and tea-lover, she would be our educator in all matters tea for the next few days. The Lahu trace their roots back to the sub-Himalayan plateau, where they once roamed, before migrating south. Napu's sculpted beauty and unpretentiousness reminded me of the mountains' beauty.

Taking us for dinner in a rundown shack where indigenous fare was served, she quickly showed herself a person with a huge respect for the local ways. I knew that the meal would provide difficulties when, passing by the kitchen, I caught sight of the chef emptying a container of green insects into one of the huge pans. When the dishes arrived at the table, I looked at them intently. There were mounds of green leaves, stems, tubers, roots, and wild chicken, but no green insects. Then I saw the plate piled with what appeared to be white beans with flecks of green. Upon closer inspection, I saw small black heads on the beans. In fact, with the rings encircling their thick circumference, the beans looked not unlike the caterpillar fungi that had occupied so much of my interest in the Tibetan regions. I realized that they were actually plump grubs or worms. Knowing Dakpa as I did, my concern was not for me but for his queasy stomach.

Seeing me eyeing them, Napu told us that they were bamboo worms. The creatures lived inside bamboo trees, growing fat and sweet from their diet of bamboo husk. Dakpa's head slumped involuntarily toward his chest. Just as tea in ancient times had been "nourished" by its time within the bamboo casings, so the worms had benefited from their bamboo diets. These hefty specimens had been stir-fried with tea leaves and a smattering of chili peppers. Dakpa muttered something about his "Buddhist diet." He stared at the plate, unable to take his eyes off the worms, while I dug in. Their sweetness had been balanced by the slightly bitter tea leaves and the chili, and the result was stunning.

Our conversation turned to tea. Napu told us how tea was used in foods, as pillow stuffing to ease headaches, as an odour eater (a mesh bag containing raw or dried leaves was often kept in cold-storage areas to absorb smells), and as a compress for wounds. When she mentioned the detoxifying and antiseptic properties of tea, I mentioned our friend Dorje's assortment of uses for urine.

Growing up surrounded by tea—generations of her clan had grown tea in nearby Pulanshan (Pulan Mountain)—Napu understood every stage of tea production. Her latest project was opening a multi-ethnic teahouse in Menghai that served tea in several local styles. "It is in this way that we can keep traditions alive. It isn't enough to simply pass on [ownership of] teashops and tea products. You need to understand the tea itself. It is alive."

If tea was to be understood and appreciated, it surely could not have a more charismatic advocate than this force in front of us. She leaned forward toward the table in her enthusiasm, and her dark eyes danced as she spoke of her beloved *cha*.

"You must see them," she said. The "them" she referred to were the tea trees in the nearby mountains. I had long heard of the legendary trees. Tea picked and sold from the "millennium" trees was rare, highly sought-after, and therefore prohibitively expensive. Rather than being referred to as "aged," the tea leaves were described as being from "ancient tea plants." The indigenous peoples regarded the gigantic trees as testaments to the enduring relationships between tea and people. The trees' longevity was viewed as a sign of their contentment and happiness.

Some of the finest Puers in the world came from Nanoshan (Nano Mountain), home to some of the oldest tea trees. They had been watched over by an adoring community every year of their lives, each generation passing on the responsibility to care for them. A mist that gave into rain welcomed us to the mountain. Everything was enveloped in a wet, grey gloom.

For me, the trees represented not just tea but the old lados we had spoken to: giant monuments to giant people. These living monuments had outlived generations of lados, but were, in my mind, inextricably linked. The old traders, their dependable mules, and these stimulant-bearing trees were connected in the complex weave of the ancient trade. Tea was a cultural bond between people, bridging mountains, languages, and strife. I hadn't expected to find myself here, at the source of some of those teas that had made their way along the Tea Horse Road. What a contrast this mountain was to the trade route, with its choking, dry trails perched on riverbanks or fitted into rock, and the chafed mules and leathery men who carried the bitter, green cargo up and away. I wished that all those who had transported the tea could be here to breathe in the steamy air and experience the grey gloom where the tea was grown.

Nearly all the inhabitants around Nanoshan were indigenous; they and their ancestors had been caretakers of the forests for more than a thousand years. Their ancestors were the first to cultivate tea and to understand its economic significance. They knew the cycles of plucking, knew good years from bad, and most crucially, knew the nature of the trees they protected.

A dark, damp path led us into the forest, where we were quickly swallowed up by a cool blue haze. Vague monstrous shapes obscured the sky above us, and nothing was clearly visible until we were right beside it. It was a ghostly world of shadowy forms.

"Here," said Napu, pointing at some green bushes. "These are the children." In stark contrast to the organized planted rows we had seen earlier, the tea trees on Nanoshan had been left to spread, to go where their crooked desires took them, and in return, their large spade-shaped leaves thrived. Delicate light green buds grew among larger siblings. These were the tea buds, all important in any final product. The supple, slightly curled leaves demanded a gentle touch when clipped with a nimble fingernail. Excessive pressure on the stem or epithelium and the leaf would begin fermenting, its quality diminishing by the minute.

"The only tea made from these leaves is *sheng cha* [unfermented green Puer]," said Napu. "To artificially speed up the leaves' fermentation would be to waste them, as the leaves contain proteins and essential oils that are lost during fermentation. Instead, the emphasis is on purity of purpose, practice, and product. Fermentation—or lack of— is the most crucial stage in tea production. Tea's taste is affected by its environment and the nutrients that its roots can access." Plucking a fat green leaf, Napu sliced it open with her nail, then sniffed it.

"Tea needs mists and mountains. High altitudes moderate the temperature, and mists diffuse the sun and rain. Direct sun is the great enemy of growing tea leaves. Nanoshan is perfect for growing tea." Napu's huge smile told us that she was in her element.

Another advantage Nanoshan had was its forests. "Forests protect the plants from the elements, until the tea itself becomes the forest." Tea was itself a thing of the grey middle ground, needing neither blazing sun nor massive rainfalls to grow, but rather a balance of both; it was a thing not of extremes but of the very essence of moderation, and I wondered if it was this that had kept it eternal, giving it its timeless appeal. "The rows of tea that you have seen in other plantations will make an average tea for people. The tea growing in the mountains and forests is a tea for those who have been spoiled, those who know how the tea was harvested." Then she repeated what I had heard so many times about Puer: "Once you drink this, you will never go back to the others." Dakpa and I were already devout believers; we didn't need further proof.

We fell silent as we moved deeper into the forest, past giant bamboo that glittered in the muted light and enormous banyan trees that climbed boldly skyward, until Napu stopped and looked up at the warped tea trees. "Here," she said. The squat, strong tea trees were not beautiful in any way. Branches arched up and then curved down as if in an effort to return to the earth from which they had come, and their dark leaves perspired in the heat.

Napu nimbly climbed up into a crook of one of the trees, then made her way out to the end of a branch and began plucking. "Come here and see." She passed down two light green shoots. The curled leaf looked barely mature, and its texture was still rubbery from having been asleep—the leaves in their curled state are often referred to as "resting" in Chinese. "Taste it," she ordered, and we did as we were told. "The buds must be clipped with fingernails, not fingers, and certainly not machines. A perfectly shaped, round bush has been cut by machine." The word *machine* came out as a growl.

Tart and fragrant at once, the leaves were the kind you looked for when buying *sheng cha,* and it was these leaves that, once dried, appeared as white tea leaves in a tea cake—the young, white leaves adding both taste value and expense to the cake. Dakpa reached up to a tea-tree branch to grab a handful and shoved them into his mouth.

Napu gently admonished Dakpa, explaining that in his coarse handling he had inadvertently ruined the leaves. Bruised leaves or stems were considered inferior and would be used in lesser quality teas. The Tibetans we had met would gladly accept bruised and battered leaves, buds, and stems, as long as there was flavour and strength to wring out. Tibet, considered a "frontier" region, received the roughest grades of tea, though these were not necessarily inferior. But Tibetans were never exposed to a wide variety of tea and only knew what was sent along the Tea Horse Road. The Tibetans preferred strong tea and didn't judge a tea by its appearance but, rather, by the force of its taste and colour.

Napu told us that the tree she was shimmying along was almost a thousand years old. I wondered aloud what the old traders and muleteers would say of this spectacle, a beautiful woman balanced on a tree branch, carefully picking tea buds. Dakpa responded that Dorje would probably swoon, move here permanently, and never be heard from again. As for the lados, they would appreciate the vital link the people of the area have with the earth. They understood the relationship, as they themselves had their own intimate relationship with the land.

Back in town, as we were about to depart, Napu presented us with two huge tea cakes from her own tea garden, telling Dakpa and me that we, too, were now linked to the land through her gift. Our tea stash having growing so magnificently on account of Napu immortalized her in our minds as a tea deity.

IN THE NOT SO DISTANT PAST, elders of many tribes believed that only tea grown south of the Mekong River bend in southern Yunnan could be considered genuine tea. Even today, tea is still partly legend and mystique. No two leaves, trees, or cups of tea are ever completely alike, something that helps to maintain tea's unpredictability and preciousness.

Rounding south and cutting east from Menghai, we sliced through what Dakpa and I simply called "hot country," where Yunnan borders the countries of Southeast Asia. We were moving through the Xishuangbanna Prefecture, the brown, coiling mass that was the Mekong running beside us on our right until it was swallowed up by the perspiring forests. This southern tropical strip is home to thirteen officially recognized minority tribes, all maintaining their traditional methods of tea preparation. In the days since we had left Menghai, the sun hadn't made any attempts to appear, and the prevalent smell was the dank smell of wet.

Like Nanoshan, Yiwu was a mountain long believed to harbour some of the most exquisite teas under the heavens. It provided tea not only to horse caravans for trade in Tibet and Southeast Asia but also prized tribute teas to emperors. Tribute tea would scarcely have been recognized by the nomadic tribes as tea. Whereas solid square bricks and cakes of tea headed northwest into Tibet and elsewhere, the teas destined for imperial abodes were formed into ornate dragon shapes, the more complicated and exquisite, the better. Creating moulds to shape tribute teas was a craft in itself, one that involved its own class of tradesmen. The famous *jingua*—gold melon—was an exception to the trend of flamboyant shapes. Gold melon tea was steamed and then worked into the form of a melon or squash and bound with silk ribbon.

The landscapes around Yiwu and much of Yunnan's deep south retained faint remnants of the Tea Horse Road. Dakpa and I, although suffering the simultaneous assaults of sweats and shivers brought on by the damp heat and repeated rainfalls that were with us every day, tried to trace by foot the vague threads of the tea caravan route. Here and there the odd flagstone glistened, but the wet greenery that folded in on the paths reclaimed most of them before too long.

Dakpa and I had by now given up all pretensions of being in control of our tea addiction and would frequently detour into nameless towns with nothing unusual to see, just so we could visit a teahouse to stop the withdrawal. Like the old monk Zhaozhou of the Tang Dynasty, who answered most queries on life and meditation with the wise words "First, go and have tea," Dakpa and I needed tea to motivate or relax us, conquer our chills, cool us down when we were overheated, take the edge off our hunger, and indulge our gluttonous addiction. Soaking wet in tattered clothes, we inevitably drew questioning looks but by now barely acknowledged anything outside the arena of tea. Outside one town, we were to witness the brutal efficiency with which tea was treated, with none of the passion and love the indigenous peoples had shown for the plants.

We had already learned that after the leaves are picked and sorted, they are thrown into hot pans to stop the natural oxidization process of fermentation. All teas must go through this stage. The moment a tea leaf is plucked, it begins to oxidize, so the speed with which the plucked leaf reaches a heating source is key. In the past, practical tea growers erected simple sheds in the tea fields so that the process could begin immediately after picking. The next crucial stage was the sun drying, to remove any remaining moisture from the leaves. If the tea was to be formed, the leaves would then be steamed and compressed into moulds and stored to age—or, at one time, tied onto mules for their journey to distant kingdoms.

Now, looking for a tea fix, Dakpa and I inadvertently walked into a miniature tea-processing plant. A sweating stone one-room house whose mustiness was just barely kept in check by the earthy tang of tea provided the backdrop. At the rear of the room, a small entrance led to a covered outdoor area where a young Chinese woman, in a blur of motion, was frying freshly snipped tea leaves in a pan about a metre in diameter. A funnellike stove conducted the fire's heat up through a simple flute, and the flames crackled as they engulfed the open pan. The woman's deft hands turned the leaves over with a large wooden spoon, the leaves gradually shrivelling as they expelled their moisture. Not looking up, the woman said in a steady voice, "There must be continuous motion"—and there was. The turbinelike spoon turned the leaves non-stop, with none escaping the pan.

After the woman finished frying the leaves, her husband wrung them out, removing still more moisture. The scrunched and twisted leaves were then spread on racks to dry. Steaming and forming would come later. Very little in this process had changed over the centuries, yet here it was almost clinical, the tea treated as a product rather than respected as a living thing.

IT HAD COME TIME for Dakpa to leave for Shangri-La and his other life with his wife and child; I would continue to slowly traipse northward on my own. He left after a shared dinner in which every dish had either tea essences, leaves, or oil as a prime ingredient. Finishing the meal with two glasses of gripping black Puer, we clasped hands and then my fellow addict and friend was off.

I went back to Simao via Jingdong, where I hooked up with a man I came to call Little Rabbit. Of the Yi tribe, this hyperactive man was a veritable knowledge bank of teas and indigenous cultures. His appetite for tea matched my own, so there was a complicity in our stops. We worked our way up to Puer, the place that gave the tea that fascinated so many, including me, its name. A week's caravan travel from Simao, Puer had the distinction of being the most southerly point Khampa lados had ventured. But now, it functioned as less of a tea metropolis and more of a collection and distribution point for tea.

To reach Puer, Little Rabbit and I travelled by foot on old portions of the trade route, and people along the way happily took us in. Thick, hot forests encroached on the ancient paths, whether to protect them from future witnesses or in an attempt to swallow them up, I didn't know. All things forgotten will be reclaimed, the forest seemed to say. Violet clouds and black skies were interrupted intermittently by sun and warmth, and with the warmth came insects—biting insects. Slowly, a dry, sun-inspired heat took over from the humid heat.

Sweating feet made for pains and smells, though thankfully falling short of the possibly unattainable mark Dorje had set.

Two weeks into our trek, Little Rabbit and I sat resting on a bridge that had once marked the fork of the Tea Horse Road. One route headed northeast to Kunming and Beijing, the other northwest into Tibet. "This Tea Horse Road is about tea, mules, and trade, but mostly it's about people, isn't it?" Little Rabbit commented. I nodded. That was exactly what it was about. Held together by trade and tea, it was a route linking people.

Little Rabbit's own people had been acquainted with the Tea Horse Road. The Yi ethnic group had been nomadic, ranging throughout western Yunnan. They would settle in an area, use the resources at hand, then often move on, disassembling their homes and taking everything with them. Their easygoing natures and nomadic temperament made them well suited for work as muleteers.

At Puer, as Little Rabbit and I said our goodbyes, he shoved a one-kilogram *qizibing*—a round tea cake—into my bag, saying simply, "Drink well."

The Yunnan–Tibet Tea Horse Road continued to make its way north on to Zhenyuan and Jingdong, passing through winding valleys and through the gentle Wuliang Mountain Range. My own slow ascent would follow this path, but my destination was the tea-growing region of Nanjian, which sat along the Yuan River. Known for its rice and that other leaf that had its own alluring tale, tobacco, Nanjian was at the southern extremity of the larger region known to the old traders as Xiaguan, the second great tea reserve of Yunnan.

In Nanjian I was joined by fellow tea enthusiast and tea historian, teashop owner, and friend to the tea gods, Neddy Luo. He knew the growers, the harvesters, the factory owners, the smugglers, and the suppliers—everyone there was to know in the tea world. Having studied tea at a famous agricultural university, he also could claim, like few others could, to know the tea itself.

Neddy met me in Nanjian and we drove into the mountains southwest of the city, to the Xin Feng Huang Cha Chang, the Phoenix Tea Company. The modern-day tea business is big business: every producer has its own trade secrets, procedures, and histories.

Methods of leaf selection, fermentation and production among the larger tea producers are closely guarded secrets, so getting access to the company's factory and particularly its storerooms, sorting rooms, and other workrooms was a minor miracle. Neddy had explained to a local tea "headman," an old friend of Neddy's, that I suffered *cha ying*, or tea addiction. He was delighted that a foreigner was a fellow tea worshipper; as tea devotees, we immediately had an unspoken understanding.

During a two-hour lunch, the headman made one brief phone call, then two more in rapid succession. Neither Neddy nor I knew what had been communicated, but lunch concluded with our headman making a toast and telling Neddy and I that the factory manager and his factory were waiting for us. Provided with a Jeep and a driver, Neddy and I were sent off with the recommendation that we drink as much as we possibly could of the free offerings, for we might come across a vintage of extraordinary character.

At the entrance to the factory, the security guard peeked into our vehicle and smiled, then opened the automatic security gate for us. We were in.

Neddy had warned me that watching how bacteria and fungi were introduced to Puer to artificially ferment it, producing *shou cha,* would not be possible—"That is a secret science," he said—but we were free to walk through the warehouses and tea assembly rooms. But first, the requisite almighty cup of tea. At any time, tea with Neddy was a wonderful affair, but even more so when he tasted a tea for the first time. His face scrunched up and he squinted and winced while his senses, having been honed over years of sniffing, eating, drinking, and studying tea, became focused.

We entered a huge warehouse, a room of almost unearthly stillness. Pathways ran between mounds of fermenting tea leaves, their aroma overwhelming. My aches and blisters from the heat were instantly forgotten in this enchanting room. In fact, I would have been quite content to drop into one of the large piles in front of me and take my last breaths inhaling Puer tea leaves.

Behind me I heard Neddy sigh "Ah, *fa shiao* [fermentation]." To speed up fermentation, microbes and bacteria such as *Aspergillus niger* and *Penicillium* are introduced during manufacturing, creating in months teas that had the smoothness of years-old teas. A black market for black Puer had sprung up in recent years, thanks to the abilities of skilled forgers to create teas that looked authentic, smelled authentic, and sometimes even tasted authentic. I thought of Napu unhappily discovering a fake Puer. The earth would quake with her outrage.

This factory was special in that it owned the tea fields where the tea it sold grew. This meant it could control every element of the tea's growth and production. The 215 hectares produced three thousand tonnes of tea annually, and the company was regarded as one of Yunnan's best producers.

The dark brown tea in front of us was in mid-ferment. The fragrant heaps of drying tea had already gone through what Neddy called the science stage, when bacteria are introduced to the tea. The russet-coloured piles were carefully turned once a week so that the leaves aired out equally. Water was sprayed sporadically onto the piles to aid in the fermentation process, which took fifty days, in a carefully monitored temperature of 15.5 degrees Celsius. After that, the tea was steamed and formed into shapes, then left to air out for weeks, months, sometimes years. One of the special aspects of tea is that, with aging, any has the potential to be a classic. A Yunnan saying summed up the patience required: "Puer is made by the grandparents to be enjoyed by the grandchildren."

We left the room of heavenly scents and proceeded to a huge, well-lit sorting room. Masked women sat behind long tables piled high with brown tea, sorting the grades of the various dried leaves. Some leaves would be used in cheaper teas, others for finer grades. Just as with the ancient teas, those of mediocre quality or appearance were exported to the Tibetans and the tribes along China's frontiers or sold in local markets, where people knew that how a tea looked had no bearing on its taste. Speaking in hushed tones, Neddy gently derided anyone who would judge a tea solely on the way it looked. "The Tibetans never got caught up in the pretensions of tea culture. They liked what they liked." Neddy often spoke bluntly about tea. To him, tea was "good," "not good," or "better in a few years."

Next, we visited the airing room, a room the size of an airplane hangar. It was insulated by tea, arranged according to age, quality, fermentation status, weight, and shape. Mushroom-shaped balls, cakes, and oblong bricks of unfermented teas, fermented teas, tribute teas, and teas with inscriptions on them, made by forming the tea in moulds, lined countless wooden racks, waiting patiently for the day they would be released into the world. I longed to expedite that process but controlled myself. Neddy walked around, picking up various teas to smell, look at, and then smell again. Pointing at one, he said, "Good tea—it smells of the sun."

AFTER VISITING THE TEA FACTORY, Neddy returned to Xiaguan, to wait for me there. He took with him a fifteen-kilogram sack of local green tea for his own soon-to-be-open teashop. I would head back north to Weishan, driven by a need to further explore the quiet city that virtually every caravan had passed through on its journey northwest into the Himalayas. The city sat in between the two major centres of Puer production. It also was once considered a stronghold of the then great Nanzhao Kingdom, which had held close ties with the Tubo Kingdom of Tibet. Weishan had been home to some of Yunnan's most disciplined caravan teams, considered elite because of their prompt deliveries and said discipline. The Muslim traders, as well as many present-day Hui people—*Hui* being the Mandarin term for Muslim people—of the area, were descended from members of Kublai Khan's Mongol armies that had raced through and conquered much of western Yunnan in the mid-1200s. (Indeed, the huge, dark, thickly lashed eyes and noble noses of the Hui hinted at their origins.) The aggressive Mongols had brought the Nanzhao Kingdom into the Chinese fold; on returning to their distant yurts, the Mongols took with them that indefatigable traveller, tea in brick form.

Weishan can unhesitatingly claim to be the capital of all things pickled. No food stuff seemed exempt, though thankfully I didn't spy any pickled tea. What I did manage to track down was a smoky and lethal *cao cha*, a roasted tea that had my palms in a sweat. To prepare the tea, the leaves were put into a pot and roasted over heat, and hot water then added. The roasted taste was fresh and slightly different every time, depending on how long the tea had been roasted.

Sixty kilometres north of Weishan, in Xiaguan, near the ancient city of Dali, Neddy's teashop and companionship awaited me, as did the northern Yunnan version of Puer tea. Tibetans had always referred to Yunnan's tea areas as *jaiyul*—tea country—and viewed the tea as superior. Although the northern Yunnan big-leaf variety was the same as that in southern Yunnan, the higher elevation and colder temperatures of Xiaguan meant the natural fermentation process took longer. And that, said Neddy, made Xiaguan Puer the finest Puer in the world.

By the time the ancient caravans had reached Dali and Lijiang, heading north into Tibet, the muleteers and mule teams were almost exclusively Tibetan Khampas. About as physically different from the Khampas as one could get were the gentle Bai people, who have been traditionally based in the Xiaguan-Dali area. But in Xiaguan and nearby Dali, all traces of the Tea Horse Road, and most traces of the old Nanzhao Kingdom, have been wiped out. Located between the Cangshan (the Cang Mountains) and Erhai (Ear Lake), the area is now a prime destination for the dedicated tea drinker.

The Bai had what was known as "three-course tea," prepared by the Bai women for special occasions such as marriages, festivals, and ceremonies. The three courses linked the fragile realm of humans to that of tea by way of three primary aspects of life: struggle, joy, and acceptance. Each had a complementary taste in tea: struggle/bitterness, joy/sweetness, and acceptance/smoothness. One ceremony I witnessed lasted about forty minutes and was accompanied by a small bit of theatre, though theatre is not always involved. The Khampas, with their no-nonsense approach to tea, must have withered while waiting for these romantic tea rituals to be concluded.

NEDDY'S LITTLE TEASHOP in Xiaguan was a barely controlled mess. Although new shelving stood tall and clean, bearing spotless jars of dried specimens, the neatness proved an illusion. As the eyes shifted downward, disorder reigned—every available centimetre of space was littered with boxes, bags, containers, and spills of tea. Beyond the smell of fresh wood shavings, tea was already starting to exert the power of its aroma in the week-old shop.

"Tonight, someone is coming in with an old Puer, and he wants me to try it and tell him what I think," Neddy told me in a rapturous tone. For Neddy, his excitement had nothing to do with his being consulted but, rather, that he had been asked to share in the drinking of a rare tea. With so many fakes on the market, genuinely old teas were hard to find, and consultations were important in determining a true vintage. With *shou cha*, there was only so long the tea could develop taste-wise, so it was misleading to claim that a thirty-year-old tea was more developed or smoother than its twenty-year-old counterpart, though the price might certainly reflect the difference in age.

Neddy's excitement was contagious. Such opportunities to try old teas, especially genuine old teas, were uncommon. Neddy spoke about the man who was bringing the tea in a manner that suggested he was either a god or an evil creature. Until we knew the tea, he seemed to imply, we couldn't know the man. "My friend knows someone who knows this person, and he is apparently believable. He kept the tea in a storeroom and forgot about it. At least that is what he says." Neddy's eyebrows arched in suspicion. "My worry is that it might have been exposed to odours." Neddy pondered this potential catastrophe as he poured us some tea.

Before long, four of Neddy's close friends and tea samplers showed up. They were there for the tea. Neddy's shop was now effectively closed to the public, and should a customer saunter in, Neddy would immediate switch to serving a more mundane tea. The hushed tension that had gripped us was palpable when the man entered the shop, carrying a wrinkled yellow envelope. Inside was an unevenly dark hundred-gram ball of tea. Neddy almost tore the tea out of its owner's hands, jamming his nose up against it and taking four or five good snorts. I was gripping the side of the table, fixated, along with the others, on the tea and Neddy's dilated nostrils.

With an imperceptible nod, Neddy carefully pinched off a small chunk. As he prepared the tea in a white porcelain *gai bei*, a flared, handleless cup with a lid, in order to see the colour, the tea ball was passed around. The men sniffed, inhaled, and prodded. I had seen such attention to detail before, the thorough studying of every aspect of an object. The nomads and lados I had encountered on my travels had the same intensity and love for their four-legged mates that these tea lovers had for their tea.

I was the last to examine the tea. It looked unexceptional. But I knew that the older the tea, the less symmetrical the shape usually was, thanks to the older moulds, and the more imperfect ... the more perfect.

We were quiet as Neddy washed the tiny white cups, then watched as he poured the first pot of drinkable tea into the cups, serving himself last. We sat at the edge of our chairs, intent on the almond-coloured liquid that sat steaming in the cups before us, though we tried to act casually in an attempt to hide our excitement.

It was time. A series of loud inhalations, a gulp or two, another set of inhalations, then silence. The scorching tea cut into my mouth, bringing with it surges of flavour. All of us were silent, unwilling to risk misspeaking, as we waited for master Neddy to pass judgment on the tea. Neddy studied the wet leaves, smelled them, separated them, and picked them apart with a pair of steel tongs, discerning the character of the mossy, steaming mess of tea that had been unravelled after so many years. Neddy's eyes took on a slight shine, then hardened so as to give nothing away. Adding more hot water to the *gai bei*, he poured two more times. At last he sat back and smiled.

"Yes, very good, and genuine," he said. We all visibly relaxed in our chairs and let out loud exhalations. We congratulated the owner, as though he had handcrafted the little ball himself. Some of the good wishes were meant to encourage him not to depart with his vintage tea just yet. But he was content knowing it was genuine and had little interest in its economic worth; sharing it with other tea lovers was enough, and we quickly got down to the business of drinking the rest of it. It would be a business that took us deep into the morning hours.

For two days after the tea sampling, I felt as though a veil of exhaustion had dropped over me. The past few weeks had finally caught up with me. Everything in my body felt out of equilibrium. The south and its humidity and unrelenting rains, and the massive doses of tea, had brought my senses to a point where I couldn't properly take anything in any more. After a febrile sleep that lasted more than a day, my fever broke, leaving me weak and in need of a dose of my fluid partner, tea. A few cups brewed from my stash brought me round.

The mountains awaited. Jutting up north and west of Xiaguan, the Cangshan range continues north to the Hengduan range, in northwestern Yunnan, which in turn leads onto the Tibetan Plateau. Sodden pine-needle-laden paths along the Tea Horse Road continued to carry traffic through the dark coniferous forests, while locals combed the mountainsides for prized pine nuts under dense canopies and fogs.

My journey through the stillness reinforced for me tea's status as the great bonder. Days into the trek, as my body slowly reconnected to itself, I was interrupted by a wind that brought freezing sheets of rain as it coursed through the trees, soaking and moulding my clothes to my body in moments. Seeking shelter, I joined two pine-nut collectors under the cover of a stone ridge. We sat around a smoking fire: two old men, their three donkeys, and me with my pack. Unwrapping a chunk of Puer, I offered it up, and we sat for hours in the dull light, a wet mist rising from the ground, talking of the old trade routes, the weather, and tea.

"We can still walk everywhere we want to go on the paths—some of us still know how," said the eldest of the two. How refreshing his words were to me, as was the thought that not all the dirt paths, with their long histories, were being transformed into hard-surfaced roadways. I asked the men if they knew about the history of the trails, and the younger suggested in a visionary sort of way that "the history of these trails isn't finished yet."

When Burma fell into the hands of the Japanese during the Second World War, the Yunnan–Burma highway, which at the time was China's only international thoroughfare with access to ports, was blockaded. This stimulated traffic on the ancient Tea Horse Road, as it provided access to ports and markets farther west via Lhasa, at which point it turned south into Nepal and India. The period saw an unprecedented surge in activity on the trade route between China's southwest and Tibet, India, and Nepal. Goods destined for China that had previously been transported through Burma now made their way from Calcutta north to the trading towns of Kalimpong in west Bengal and Gangtok in Sikkim, to Lhasa and east into Sichuan and Yunnan.

Before the Second World War, the majority of trade coming out of the south of Yunnan went north along the Tea Horse Road to the town of Shigu, which sits on the first bend of the Yangtze River, and then continued northwest to Judian, Weixi, and Deqin. After the war started, virtually all trade traffic veered northeast to Lijiang, and this Naxi tribe's stronghold became the market town of all market towns. Lijiang was a treasure trove of goodies for the Tibetans: copper and leather items to wear, for the home, or for horses were favourites. The finely crafted bridles, saddles, and cinches were valued above all else.

The town of Lijiang, called Gongben Zhi (Warehouse Fair Street) by the local Naxi people and Sadam by the Tibetans, was known throughout the trading world and, during the Second World War, it was the major source of goods for Allied troops stationed in Kunming. All sorts of items were available, and all of them were transported on the backs of mules, yak, and sheep. The caravans came via Tibet, on routes originating in India, and the trails buzzed day and night with activity.

Present-day Lijiang is overwhelmed with outsiders buying up shops, and the old town has the feel of an out-of-control circus: it draws millions of shoppers and tourists every year, but it has no real essence. The main streets where horse and copper markets once bustled have been overrun by gift shops, restaurants, and teashops staffed by students drinking coffee.

A BAZAAR WAS IN FULL SWING in Shaxi, an ancient town with caravan history in its blood. Bails of tobacco, heaps of sugarcane, leather items, copper kettles, truckloads of pigs, and battery-powered cars all waited for prospective customers to take them away. It was a loud hodgepodge of old and new.

Groups of barefoot mountain women of the Yi tribe smoked cigarettes and chattered as they watched a man run after an escaped piglet. My own interest was in the twenty-kilogram bags of loose tea lying in a squat row, waiting to be handled, smelled, and even sampled—in each bag sat a jar of brewed tea made from those particular leaves. Ragged umbrellas stood guard over the bags, preventing the tea from percolating in the intense sun. Everyone was welcome to take a swig from the jar. I took several, as my need outweighed my fear of catching anything from the communal cup. I stayed near the sacks of tea throughout the afternoon, taking nips every now and then.

To the east, about a day and a half's walk, the famous horse market of Songui had in the past blared with the sounds of a thousand horses gathered for trade, sale, or appraisal. Tea was often used as currency, though some horses were inevitably stolen. Songui still hosts the odd horse fair in honour of those days, but the din of bargaining and muddy chaos had disappeared.

Horses arriving from Tibet via the Tea Horse Road generally fell into two categories. Horses from the Naqu, Gansu, and Qinghai borderland regions of Tibet were as rugged and fearless as those regions' people and landscapes. Restless, hardened creatures, these horses were wanted as warhorses in the burgeoning cavalries. Other horses were presented as tribute and usually—and perhaps strategically— were of little use other than on farms. Those horses travelled along the more northern trade routes into Sichuan, to be delivered directly to the heads of the empire or to government-sanctioned horse markets. Although their physical stature may have been impressive, they lacked the bloodline or endurance of their nomadic brothers. The irony that wasn't lost on any of the parties involved was that the Chinese dynasties required frontier tribes' mounts to keep those same frontier tribes at bay.

Yunnan and its tribes already had horses of renown. Successive waves of ancient migrations from the Central Asian grasslands had brought with them quality horses, the basis for future breeds that were strong and well equipped for travel and war. Apart from Yunnan, China's southern regions of ancient times did not have much access to horses—they were too far from the borderland regions where horses could be bought, traded for, or otherwise acquired—and so were highly susceptible to cavalry invasions from the north.

Now, with the wars and epic caravan journeys things of the past, surfaced roads had eliminated most horse routes, chubby cars and big, belching trucks taking the place of belching mules and horses. Tea alone had made it through the edit of time.

The cover of a tea accountant's record-keeping book.

7
Ya'an to Pomda:
The Mighty

On earth Pomda, in the sky Pomda.

—MULETEER SAYING, REFERRING TO THE INFLUENCE THE
POMDA FAMILY HAD IN ALL MATTERS OF TRADE

BHASKAR'S WICKEDLY DELICIOUS curries beckoned my tea-stained tongue. Shangri-La would once again provide me with an intermission in my journey, and Arro Khampa was my first stop after dumping off my bags of tea and clothes at the hotel. As I entered the restaurant, I could hear Bhaskar yelling in the kitchen, his tirade directed at some poor employee. Fortunately, there weren't any customers in the dining room yet.

I stuck my head into the kitchen.

"Jep!" he cried, welcoming me back with a frown and a handshake. He shook his head as he looked me up and down. "All you do in the south is drink tea," he said, launching into a monologue on how my tea drinking would make me "go toilet too often," thereby eliminating not just waste but also precious vitamins and minerals. "Also you will not sleep and you will lose your potency." He turned away to continue his food preparations, and I left him muttering under his breath. One of the pleasures of returning to Shangri-La was checking up on the unpredictable Bhaskar. His displeasure with my gauntness was like that of a grandmother. He was one of those people who would be content to spend his life watching his good friends become obese on a diet of his own creations, and he was always plotting to fatten up the bunch of us.

Later that evening, Bhaskar served Norbu, Sonam, Dakpa, and me a feast of curries, along with *shapalè,* a favourite fried dumpling of Dakpa's, and roasted yak, to celebrate an all-too-brief sojourn. Dorje was somewhere in his mushroom-abundant mountains happily out of reach of telecommunications, and Nomè was missing from the group as well, but nevertheless, there was a sense of having been reunited. On and on we went into the night, recalling our travails over the passes, and I realized that, for as long as we would know one another, these tales would be part of the fabric of our relationship. Like some long-ago love affair or battle, we would for the remainder of our days be boring others stiff with ceaseless retellings of our adventures on the Tea Horse Road.

Dakpa was pleased to learn that I had brought from the south a few kilograms of tea for us to share. Norbu, though, was, in his own words, "a mess." Every night he was assaulted by dreams of our exploits in the mountains, and now that he was back at work as a local TV cameraman, he was seriously contemplating a career shift. He had that dangerous condition known to those of us who had been intoxicated by the mountains as "the stare"—in the middle of conversation, Norbu would suddenly slip into an intense trance, one that focused him so completely that no spoken word, noise, or even familiar face could get his attention.

Philosophical as usual, Sonam warned Norbu that living in the past was dangerous from a spiritual point of view and that obsessing on anything was injurious to your internal balance. "The trek is finished," Sonam said. "Now you must take the knowledge you learned from it and move on." I disagreed with sage Sonam, but I kept my tongue, for I knew that in many ways the trek would never be done. We would all relive in our minds parts of it until we ourselves were lined and stooped. The blistering white peaks, cracked old faces, and mottled tea leaves were now part of our own daily mental landscapes.

After telling Norbu not to dwell, Sonam himself dwelled on a recent disastrous encounter he had had with clients. In the throes of hallucinations and altitude sickness, they had turned their delusional wrath on him, accusing him of deliberately misleading them over passes, causing them horrible fits of diarrhea, and purposefully camping in the coldest nooks possible. When we asked how he dealt with this, Sonam folded his hands in his resigned manner and solemnly explained that he prayed twice as much and also apologized to the deities for misdeeds in his previous life, which in his mind were clearly the reason for his misfortune.

Norbu's upcoming marriage in his hometown of Batang was a hot topic, and I was disappointed that I would not be able to attend, as I would be occupied with my own continuing romance, treading along further portions of the Tea Horse Road. After five months, thirty-seven hundred kilometres of the route was complete, though I had travelled a great deal more in total. Autumn's winds were starting their annual command performance as I was about to begin my third season on the old trade route. But the image of Norbu speeding down Shar Gong La so long ago was still razor-sharp in my mind. His brief misstep, rapid descent, and close brush with death on that shiny white slope made his upcoming celebration that much more momentous.

When we separated that night, Norbu said something that I would remember for a long time afterward: "You know what I miss the most? The wind, and the noise it makes in my head."

"... YAK'S TAIL," said Jamyan.

"What?" I asked.

"*Ya'an* to many Tibetans means yak's tail, the end of the Tibetan regions and the beginning of the Han Chinese areas. *Ya* in Tibetan means yak, and *nga* means tail. Said quickly together in Tibetan, it sounds like *yaan*," said Jamyan. "Or maybe just the yak's ass." A rare smile split his blunt features. Whatever the origins or legends, in the fifth century, this "place of Ya'an" had been designated the seat of the Ya Prefecture. It would later become "Ya'an of eternal tea fame" in Chinese lore. Southeast of Chengdu, it was a grey, almost invisible place the day we arrived, making it memorable as a place to forget.

After four days on rough roads, we had made it to the most easterly point I would reach on the expedition; more importantly, it was the beginning of the Sichuan–Tibet Tea Horse Road, a tea route that would come to supply tea in quantities equal to the Yunnan–Tibet route. A city where tea was venerated as much as it was in Simao, Ya'an had once been home to horse markets and the dreaded tax officials. Whereas the deep south of Yunnan had been largely in the hands of the ethnic minorities, Ya'an has always been a Chinese stronghold. Simao and Puer in Yunnan were the southern-most points visited by lados; Ya'an was the most easterly.

I had driven with Jamyan—a Tibetan from Shangri-La and my latest guide—into Sichuan, taking three days to reach Ya'an. Jamyan was a gentle man of muscular proportions who charmed and intimidated in equal measure. His soft voice and manner coupled with an imposing physique gave people the impression that he was a man barely in control of himself, a man who, if he were to unleash himself, could bring great destructive power to bear. The truth was, he was a gentleman who didn't need to threaten or even to ask in some cases.

Teas from Ya'an were readily available in Lhasa, sold in their recognizable long woven bamboo containers, though the teas themselves were completely different in shape, colour, and type from the Yunnan Puers. They had been imbibed not only in Tibet but in all the frontier regions for as long as the caravans had been carrying tea. We were in the land that became the largest producer of teas for Tibet, home of the "Celestial" green tea of Mengshan and of the famous *bian cha*, the frontier/borderland tea. It was also an area where the local governments held a monopoly on the export of tea, controlling completely the production and trade of the green.

Sitting in the back of the bouncing Jeep, I realized that we were lost. Somewhere north of Ya'an we had entered the sleepy village of Lushan; whistling past a police car on our way, our driver casually said, "If the police drive too slowly, I pass them, no problem." We were to meet a man acquainted with a tea porter, a man involved in yet another element of tea's journey. Our connection, who went by the name of Zhen, knew of one of these relics who now lived in a secluded area, somewhere in the not too distant mountains. Tea porters were legends in their own time among those who knew of them, but as the need for them waned, so did interest in them. Thus far in my travels, the "ancients" were traceable only in that very Asian way of finding anything: through people. There were no websites, no books or information pamphlets giving addresses or phone numbers; rather, someone knew someone who might have heard of someone.

The porters carried much of the tea, piled high on their backs, treading along the mountain paths that led from the tea towns around Ya'an to the main markets of Kangding (Dartsendo to Tibetans). Many died tumbling off cliffs, tied to their tea. Merciless treks in bamboo sandals, carrying hundred-kilogram loads of tea for weeks on end— the porters' stories were the stuff of legends. And, like the lados, there were fewer and fewer porters still living.

Eventually hooking up in Lushan with Zhen, we had an introductory tea and then followed his van up and down and round the valleys, along narrow black roads, veering around throngs of people on bicycles. Turning onto what amounted to a path, our two vehicles scaled upward into forest, coming out into a glade. The village of Wan Shan Zhui was poor, and in the first moments of arriving, I felt the weight of generations of poverty. It was a village that felt as though it had only ever known poverty. People came over to inspect us. "Why have they come?" asked one woman in the local Sichuan dialect. The village was tidy, but in the eyes of its inhabitants there was the weariness of those who had struggled with too little for too long.

We were greeted by nods once Zhen explained that we had come to visit Shu. One man offered us jars of tea. That for me at least broke some of the tension—or was it sympathy? We couldn't accept the invitation, though, as we had the old porter to meet, and I was always slightly fearful that we wouldn't be in time: so many of the ancients hovered at an age where every day was a welcome surprise.

Jamyan, Zhen, a local, and I walked through stony fields, up through barely fertile terraces of corn, past several simple houses and some curious farmers, over a rise, and onto a small landing. The brown burnt air hinted of the end of harvest, a generation of corn stalks set on fire to clear the fields and make way for next year's crop. Little of value could grow on the stony land. Finally, we reached a house draped in drying tobacco leaves, backing onto a dark patch of woods.

A woman shyly showed us in, brushing aside a child who had come to see the new arrivals. Entering a large inner courtyard, we came upon an old man standing bent over drying tobacco leaves. As he lifted his head, I found myself looking into a pair of the most haunting eyes I have ever seen. The eyes sat in an oversized head, accentuated by a shaved scalp and heavy cheekbones. It was a face that in an instant communicated its pains and great exertions. Hardship had formed and grooved the man's face and pale, undersized, and undernourished body. Oversized hands hung loose at the sides. Hard toil and poverty had been here for a long time.

Off to the right, there was a commotion as the old porter came out of the house to see what was happening. Limping out in slippers that barely fit his exceptionally big feet, Shu gave us a quick glance before collapsing onto a stool. Large ears framed a head covered by a cap; he was an older version of the man with haunting eyes. It was a mystery to me how he had managed to find the strength to stand, let alone move on his bowlegs. Arthritic knees bulged through his light trousers.

He was one of the last of the porters who had lugged tea over the mountains, their backs taking the place of mules. I tried to imagine this figure stooped under the weight of tea bricks and climbing up ravines along slippery paths. Sitting with his elbows leaning on his knees, he looked barely capable of making the journey back into the house.

The man with the haunting eyes approached us slowly and awkwardly as we carried stools from the house outside. Turning from us, he hustled into the house and brought out little glasses and a Thermos of tea. How long had it been since guests had visited? We offered the old porter a cigarette, and his thin lined cheeks seemed to disappear as he inhaled deeply. A sigh passed through him and, after introductions, he slowly began his story. I got the sense that he had been expecting us. Although the men who travelled and worked as transporters weren't arrogant about what they had done, many of them seemed aware that their lives were part of something larger. Shu took his time, waving his cigarette at us, his head obscured by a cloud of cigarette smoke. His story was one not of holy cities and adventure, nor of women and wind-swept lands; rather, it was of the two sharp opposing ends of commerce.

Poverty had pushed him to find work outside his town—one day he had simply packed up the basics and left. Any work would have sufficed, but generally the more punishing the work, the greater the demand for workers, and no more punishing work in that day existed than that of a tea porter.

"The land here is infertile, and our harvests were never great, so a friend told me about the work as a porter, and I took it. I was young and I didn't care what I did. I am now eighty-four, and I began at sixteen." He stopped for a moment to do some mental math. "Yes, eighty-four. I was happy for the work, but it was work that killed many." He blinked a few times at the memory.

Travel by night, ascending and descending cliffs, exhaustion and winter conditions all took their toll. Many of the porters worked year-round, crossing and recrossing three-thousand-metre passes with heavy loads on their backs. "We took our loads over the mountains to Kangding, bought new shoes, ate, and then returned as quickly as possible. Kangding had very good soup stalls," Shu added with a smile, then elaborated on the kinds of soups that had been available.

Round trips to Kangding and back took the porters about forty-five days, including soup stops. Many took only a couple of days' rest before beginning the trek again. Eager to get on with the work and get home, the porters rarely stayed in the bigger towns longer than to buy shoes and nourish themselves with some soup; no romance here, no wanderlust, and certainly no voluntary delays.

Kangding was the main tea distribution centre and market town, and it was here that tea was rewrapped in waterproof leather skins and bamboo for its two-thousand-kilometre, months-long journey to Lhasa. The Tibetans referred to teas from Ya'an as *chalep* (pressed tea cakes) and *chapso* (soft tea), and they could be found throughout the nomadic communities.

The old porter coughed up phlegm, spitting it out in a remarkably youthful gesture. The man with the haunting eyes smiled, exposing stained teeth, as he held out freshly dried tobacco. It was all he had to offer, and I wrapped mine and tucked it into a pocket; to refuse would be the equivalent of telling them how poor they were.

The porter, picking up his story where he had left off, told us that porters were often paid before their journeys. "People were more honest then than they are today. It was a different world. We never cheated or ran off with money. Well, some did, but not me," he said, shaking his head slowly. The porters were paid per kilogram carried, so the heavier a porter's load, the more he made. Many of the young porters, wanting to make more money, took on too heavy a load, which brought on injury or even death. As in the great Himalayas, not all that went up into the mountains came down.

Moving in small groups of seven or eight, porters travelled with their own food and supplies, such as changes of shoes, tied atop their tea packages. "We would often go through two or three pairs of shoes on one journey," the old man said. The porters didn't have the benefit of *netsang* to stay at. It was simple grunt work, brutal labour. They carried carved walking sticks with contoured handles that provided a prop for the buttocks: the men, carrying anywhere from 75 to 140 kilograms of tea, took standing breaks, propping themselves up on the stick handles. "Couldn't get back up if we sat down," Shu told us.

Porters who could carry more than a hundred kilograms were viewed as Goliaths, though size rarely had anything to do with strength. "I could only manage eighty kilograms," the old man purred, "but a friend of mine could carry a hundred kilograms, and he wasn't much bigger than me." Jamyan glanced at me, and I looked again at the massive feet on the old man. "Anyone who needed work could take tea over the mountains."

Each bamboo package, bricks of tea stuffed tightly inside, weighed between six and ten kilograms. Loads of fifteen of these bamboo packs were not an uncommon sight on the backs of porters. An uncomfortable wooden bracket was slung over both shoulders, and the bamboo packages were then piled high on this frame. "We could carry these loads because of the way the frame was designed, but if our momentum started going the wrong way, that would be the end of us," the porter told us. The load was then secured with binding, which meant that if one pack fell, the entire load would fall, and the porter along with it. Many minor stumbles took porters over the edge of cliffs. An ominous saying used by many who worked on the Tea Horse Road perfectly evoked the risks porters faced: "The money earned on this route can be enjoyed by nobody but the parents." Fatalities were high and injuries were seldom slight.

Chuckling, old Shu told us that Kangding was the "town of the big men and women." Tibetans waited there with their mule caravans and horses for the shipments of tea they would transport into Tibet. "The Tibetans were big and fierce, but as long as no one touched their horses and mules, they were fine. Horses and men crowded the streets, and everywhere you looked, deals were being made." One thing that could be counted on was that tea would sell, regardless of the price. Indeed, astute businesspeople and trading companies often bought huge amounts of tea, waiting months or even years until the price went up, as it inevitably did, and then made fortunes selling it.

Kangding had forty-eight major trading families or brokerages, and most of the tea that arrived in Kangding was dropped off at their stalls or warehouses. Porters knew where to take the tea shipments they had carried from Ya'an by matching the embossed stamp on the tea package to the stamp on a market stall in Kangding. "Many of the bosses of the Tibetan trading families were women, and they knew exactly how much tea was coming and when it should arrive. No one scared me more than those women," Shu said, nodding his head to emphasize that he was telling the truth. I had seen these women and didn't doubt that they could be forces of fury if messed with.

Commercially, politically, and healthwise, tea was paramount in people's lives, but seldom had the real legs of the operation, the legs that took tea from the fields into the markets and beyond into the mountains, been mentioned in the teahouses or in the shops. "We were servants, nothing more, and none of us made much money unless we started our own trade businesses," one old lado had told us.

Accepting a couple more cigarettes from Zhen, the old man grew silent, and I asked a question that had been floating around unasked since we had arrived. Who was the man with the haunting eyes? "My son," Shu said. The son looked as though he, too, carried the scars of his father's trade. "He couldn't do what we did," said the old man, interrupting my thought. "None of the young could do it. They don't have the desperation or the stamina to travel in those conditions with so little." He didn't mean to brag, only offer an observation, one I didn't doubt was true. Many of the old men had similar views.

Thanking the old porter for the tobacco, we made our way out. In a hoarse voice, the son offered me more of the drying leaves, while his old father, who remained seated, merrily lit another of his newly acquired cigarettes—perhaps one of his few remaining pleasures.

On our way back to Ya'an, Jamyan turned to me and said, "It's sad, isn't it, seeing them so old and withered after such lives?" It was, I thought, but only if it were forgotten.

YA'AN THE GREY, the Yak's tail, the home of tea was all of these things and more—it was a barrage of phone calls. In my hotel room, the phone began ringing at 8 P.M., the start of a torrent of attempts to provide me with services. Picking up the phone, I heard a young woman ask in a sweet voice if there was anything I would like. "A nice massage, a haircut, a young woman, an old woman, two women ... ?" A slew of services were available, for instant delivery to my room. When I politely refused, saying that I had tea to keep me happy, she told me without hesitation that she could "assist in the acquisition of tea." I politely hung up. The phone rang again. This time it was another female caller detailing for me a more conservative menu of services, including a special "program" to "ease your stressed body." I refused, thanked her, and hung up.

With the third call, I decided to play the ignorant foreigner, which wasn't difficult. Not to be deterred, the voice on the other end told me in broken English that a "sexeee masageee" was available in just moments. I was beginning to picture a room full of girls behind telephones strategizing on how best to break down my defence. Finally, I disconnected the nasty noisemaker and sat down for a quiet cup of tea from Yunnan.

It is said that, sometime during the Western Han Dynasty (206 BC to AD 24), a Chinese monk named Wu Lizhen planted seven exquisite tea trees on small Mengding Mountain in Sichuan, just outside Ya'an. He would in time become known (and envied) as one of tea's founding patron saints, for his wonderful foresight.

From the Tang Dynasty (618 to 907) until late in the Qing Dynasty (1644 to 1911), Chinese monks and officials would climb in an annual pilgrimage to the summit of Mengding Mountain, carefully choose 360 leaves from the seven sacred tea trees, seal them in special silver containers, and send the leaves to the emperor at the imperial court.

This annual event occurred regardless of who was in power, as it was believed to link the people to the Divine.

Our ascent of Mengding Mountain was somewhat less grand, lacking the incense, gongs, colourful flowing brocades, and stuffy officials. Jamyan, a pretty young guide, and I made our way through acres of tea plants on our way up to the "special seven." I felt delirious with all the tea around me. Jamyan's interest in tea history was equal to his interest in tea: zero. But he *was* interested in the woman who was explaining the intricacies of tea to us.

"All the tea around us is small-leaf green tea, and the tea that you now find in Korea and Japan originated with these plants." This wasn't Puer tea, but Celestial. Grown green, picked green, withered green, and unfermented, these teas were slightly bitter, tasting of cut grass.

We were far from the wilds and misty greens of southern Yunnan and the animistic worship of the giant tea trees. Here, statues of attendants serving tea to reclining emperors—figures in poses of deep meditation (with nearby teapots and cups waiting to sate the practitioners)—ornate inscriptions and engravings paid homage and tribute to the mountain and tea in stone. Inscriptions tying and incorporating Taoism, Buddhism, and Confucianism together with the mountain and tea were abundant. This was altogether a different worship of tea than that of the south. But although it was a different kind of worship, and a different species of leaf, the precious green still had the same presence as it did in the south.

The seven sacred tea trees looked slightly anaemic, almost waif-like. They were enclosed in an area called the Imperial Tea Plantation, which amounted to little more than twenty square metres surrounded by a low stone wall—not nearly high enough to prevent me or anyone else from hopping into the enclosure and picking a couple of two-thousand-year-old tea leaves for a treat later on. I felt slightly incredulous as I looked at the delicate prodigies.

Pruned and kept low to the ground, the tea trees did not dominate the enclosure, as I had been expecting; in fact, they lacked vibrancy. According to our guide, the monk Wu Lizhen lived on Mengding Mountain for a time, planting tea and meditating. Tea and its stimulant, addictive character have long been acceptable in the lives of even the most disciplined. The study of texts, accompanied by a cup of tea, was part of every monk's daily and nightly ritual. Indeed, Dakpa had told me how had it not been for tea, he would have been comatose for much of his monkhood in India.

Jamyan, playfully trying to distract the guide, was curious to know what secrets and mysteries the monk had contemplated. "Apart from the tea, what wisdom has he imparted to the world?" Jamyan asked. This jolt of philosophical talk gave us all something to think about.

Our slightly flustered guide responded innocently, "He gave us tea and wished for everyone to be eternally happy. Isn't that enough?" Certainly was for me, I thought, while Jamyan gave some thought to his next verbal diversion.

The nearby "Dragon Well" recalled the obsessive worship of water throughout the ages. Many, particularly in the Tang Dynasty, believed that the quality of water was as crucial to the enjoyment of tea as the tea itself. The preparation and boiling of water was a careful procedure, and the noble classes had their own wells, used specifically for tea and often days away by foot. Caravans of water bearers coursed over many lands searching for or bearing water from auspicious water sources.

Our arrival at the base of the mountain signalled that our tour was finished, and we were subtly ushered into a teashop, where sixty grams of Emperors rolled green tea, picked from the grounds above us, cost the same as five hundred grams of Puer at Neddy's shop in Xiaguan. I feel a nag of regret at not having nicked a few leaves from the Imperial Tea Plantation when I had the chance.

Later in the day, Jamyan told me with a smile how much he enjoyed his day and how he wouldn't mind at all if we headed back to the mountain the next day too. His interest in tea had perked up.

Just as Jamyan's own interest in tea had grown, the Song Dynasty's interest in tea, and its value, would lead to the establishment of the famed and despised *chamasi*, the Tea and Horse Trade Offices, around 1075. Taxes from tea provided a major source of sorely needed funds, and the offices became some of the most hectic places in the land. Traders, accountants, officials, tax books, tea, horses, and dung all came together in one swirling mass in the offices; it was a busy time as twenty thousand horses were brought in annually from the Tibetan regions to consolidate the military aspirations of the kingdom, while half of Sichuan's total tea output was pouring the other way, into Tibet. It was during this time that the Sichuan–Tibet Tea Horse Road became the main tea supply route into Tibet, the volume of tea being exported via the Sichuan–Tibet route equalling that on the Yunnan–Tibet Tea Horse Road. The Sichuan–Tibet route also became the main route for the bulk of horses coming from the Himalayas. Small as many of the Tea and Horse Trade Offices were, they conducted furious sessions, handling the processing of up to two thousand horses a day.

During the severe Ming Dynasty times (1368 to 1644), loose leaf tea became the pre-eminent tea form for drinking in China, in part because the use of teapots had become more common and loose tea was easier to use with them, and to mix with other flavoured ingredients. Puer in its simple brick form was one of the few remaining brick-form teas. There were strict regulations and vicious retributions for those who did not abide by the stringent trade regulations. A certain Emperor Taizu executed his own ambitious son-in-law because he was caught smuggling tea out of the empire. The tea trade was the biggest business of the time, and it is impossible to overestimate its importance and influence. The Chinese's rules around tea were intended to protect a resource that would fund an empire constantly at war.

During the Ming period, gold plates were allotted to the head trading officials. These plates allowed them to pass through checkpoints on an official errand. Anyone who was not officially permitted to deal in tea and was caught trafficking was executed, with no exceptions. Tea flowed and heads rolled. By controlling the export of tea, the governments could effectively secure their own ever-shifting borders. The trade amounted to a mass exchange of green plant matter for equine flesh, with politics and bribery inevitably playing a role. High Lamas in Tibet were provided huge tea allowances in return for keeping the peace, both literally and figuratively. It is recorded that the Qing Dynasty (1644 to 1911) allocated as much as five thousand *jin* (twenty-five hundred kilograms) of tea annually to the Dalai Lama, to do with as he pleased. The Qing rulers themselves graded Puer as tribute tea and demanded an annual tribute of more than thirty thousand kilograms of Puer from certain tea growers and suppliers. Princess Wencheng's long-ago initiative to secure the western hinterlands had put into practice an effective strategy that lasted centuries, keeping the mountains flush with tea.

Caravan leaders and lados viewed the tea tax, like any tax, as an evil, and reserved special scorn for the tax collectors. Tea tax was imposed on caravans travelling through the mountains. Each of the major routes had a tax station. In Tibet, tea taxes were often paid with tea itself; elsewhere, levies were imposed. Until the end of Tibetan independence in the 1950s, an amount, usually ten to twenty-five percent of the total load, was taken as a tax in Tibet. A mule caravan made up of ten mules carrying tea was required to pay one or two mule-loads of tea as tax, depending on the time and the degree of corruption. One neurotic but creative official in the last decade of the Tea Horse Road's heyday took his tax payments in the form of watches—despite the fact that he wasn't able to tell time. He had no apparent interest in learning to decipher it, either. Rather, he ostentatiously adorned himself with seven or eight watches at once. He also had a habit of charging higher tithes to those lados who neglected to bring him a new timepiece to add to his increasingly impressive collection.

An unsanctioned tea and horse trade prospered despite the harsh penalties, as it was such a lucrative market. The quality of the horse, its attributes, or lack thereof dictated the quality of the tea offered in exchange, though undoubtedly there would have been many heated discussions about who was fooling whom in terms of the quality of offerings. Charlatans seeking to capitalize on the tea horse mania of the times would have peddled lame horses and inferior teas.

IN THE TIDY REMNANTS of a former Tea and Horse Trade Office in Mingshan County, outside Ya'an, the bustle of traders and harried voices of the old days have long since disappeared, though a light, tangy horse smell remains. A brown stain of sun added a sad aspect to the place as Jamyan and I wandered in. It would have been invigorating to be confronted by horses' rumps and men in sheepskin breeches screaming at taxmen, but instead, the inner courtyard where most of the horses would have been tethered was empty—there were only a couple of trees, and a well-used broom leaning against the wall.

The main room was similarly clean and barren; nothing remained but some scrawled numbers on the walls. From a back doorway, an old woman with parched lips and stiff hair shuffled in to tell us that we had to pay an admission fee. After all the time that had passed since those murderous taxes were demanded in this very space, the tea horse office was still operating in an economic capacity.

At the rear of the building, three elderly women sat around a fire, chatting, counting fake money used in offerings to the gods, and paying us little heed. What an ironic twist to our visit, I thought, watching fake money burn at this ancient money-collection office. When I asked if many people came by these days, one of the women simply shrugged and looked to her companions, who shrugged as well. The place hadn't even retained a haunted aspect, so blank were its memories. It felt depressed, and I along with it. Although the lados, and others, had viewed the tax offices as an evil, I felt sad that the crush of life had given way to only a few old women who showed up every day to clean up messes that no longer existed.

TOWARD THE END of the Qing Dynasty (1644 to 1911), progressive tea-house proprietors began erecting signs that took an unambiguous stand on the mixing of politics and tea within their establishments. With slogans reading "Talk of politics banned" standing boldly outside tea-drinking hot spots, it was clear that no matter how important clients might be, the enjoyment of tea was a more important consideration than their opinions. Tea was available for all to drink at anytime, anywhere, with no accompanying dress code or restrictions regarding the position you occupied in society, and no judgments on quantities or types of tea imbibed. The Qing Dynasty's view of tea and its enjoyment seemed to be perfectly summed up in the man standing before Jamyan and me, an intense yet unpretentious man who was presenting us with two glasses of shimmering Ya'an tea. With pants hiked up past the knees and a white T-shirt pulled up in the heat to reveal a substantial paunch, he looked at the tea with bright eyes brimming with adoration. Unable to get out of the tenacious grip of Ya'an's tea, Jamyan and I had yet to leave the town of rain, yaks' bottoms, and phone calls.

We sat in an unremarkable parking lot of one of China's two most important exporters of tea to Tibet, the Ya'an Tea Factory. The man of bright eyes and paunch was the manager, the third in his family to enjoy the title. Metal chairs, Thermoses, and glasses at the ready, we were politely but forcefully urged take a sip from the tall glasses of tawny water. The first surprise of the day came when Jamyan, sipping from his glass, moaned a sound of approval—rare for him. I slurped. The tea was fragrant, light, and almost tasteless. I slurped again ... fractionally more flavourful than water.

"Ya'an's best teas are blends of various leaves. The best teas are a combination of semi-fermented leaves, fermented leaves, and unfermented leaves, which give the tea a more rounded flavour, whereas the Puer teas are made from the same type of leaf in the same state. Puer is what we call a pure tea," our host told us.

Pure tea was what I preferred and I quietly said so. Calmly looking me in the eye, our host said, "Yunnan teas have more caffeine and tannins and show their character immediately. Ya'an teas age naturally, showing their character in layers, subtly."

Three categories of tea existed in Sichuan during the Tea Horse Road times. Gong tea was reserved for the nobles and was considered superior, but actually wasn't. Guang tea was sold only in markets that traded it for horses, and it was excellent, even though most people thought that it was too inexpensive to be good. Ma Cha—horse tea— was sold in the frontier regions, including Tibet, and it was this tea, simple and rough, that gave Ya'an a name on the tea map.

Our host took us on an informal tour through the massive factory, where we were free to look, touch, and taste. Our only interruptions were a series of lightning rushes to relieve our near-rupturing bladders, after consuming two litres of tea in a little more than an hour.

The enormous warehouse directly adjoining the parking lot fairly burst with tea. It was here that transport trucks and their drivers came to pick up their loads, a modern version of the lados with their mules. Chocolate-brown bales of dry tea sat rumpled and tied, and off to one side were piled the materials to construct the bamboo containers I had so often seen. "The same methods of wrapping and binding tea are used today that were used hundreds of years ago. It is still the best way," our host told us. Bamboo sheaths just like these had been carried by the porters over the mountains to Kangding and could still be found in nomads' tents and in market towns throughout Tibet. The suppliers of Sichuan tea learned a marketing lesson when they attempted to do away with the simple bamboo packaging in an attempt to modernize: there was an immediate plunge in sales in the Tibetan regions. And so the idea was scrapped, and the bamboo casings reinstated. I recalled seeing on my own recent travels the long woven bamboo containers stuffed into corners of tents and homes, just as they would have been in the past.

In what had become a ritual in the tea centres, our host presented Jamyan and me with three tea cakes each of his "best tea" before we set off, intent on getting to Kangding, roughly two hundred kilometres to the west, by nightfall. Night caught us as we reached Kangding, and a swift cold wind welcomed us back into the Himalayan lands.

FEW TRACES of Kangding's past incarnation as a trade metropolis were in evidence. The old tea and horse trading stalls that we had heard about were no longer standing, nor were the soup stalls. Market areas had been razed and built over, and only the prowling winds contributed to the frontier feeling, ripping into town from all directions. From Ya'an, tea made its way over Er Lan Mountain into Kangding—considered by most people to be the most easterly trade centre linking the Tibetans and Chinese—harnessed onto the bent backs of the valiant porters.

It was in Kangding, too, where the Sichuan Tea Horse Road divided into two main trunks: a northern route, known as the Kangbei Thoroughfare (*bei* meaning north in Mandarin) accessed Chamdo via Kham's cultural capital of Dege, gradually making its way to Lhasa. The main southern route, the Kangnan Thoroughfare (*nan* meaning south), had in its time been active as a migration route, postal route, tribute route, and the main branch of the Sichuan–Tibet Tea Horse Road. The southern route flowed between Ya'an and Kangding, relentlessly pushing westward, and it was this route that we were following. It was now known simply as Highway 318, though the term *highway* needed amending, as even now, travelling it was probably still as comfortable by mule as by vehicle.

Continuing west in our Jeep through the perpetually unfinished town of Yajiang, we entered the Tibetan grasslands, heading back toward the treeless highlands and the nomad centre of Litang. The air had become sharper and our lungs heaved in the thinning mountain air.

Jamyan in his new-found passion for tea had become one of the enlightened, drinking at all hours of the day and promoting the benefits of Ya'an tea to whoever would listen. His restrained bulk had given way to a certain lightness of step, a daintiness almost, motivated in part by successive cups of tea. The interior of the Jeep had become a repository for all things tea.

After an eight-hour drive from Kangding, we arrived in Litang, where we were welcomed by Midju with a *"Samasa ubè?"*—"Have you eaten yet?" An unnecessary question, considering that a yes or no answer would bring about the same results: a plate of freshly made *momos,* or dumplings, and a pot of butter tea that was thick enough to call cream. Midju's straightforwardness reminded us of how much I had missed the mountains and their residents. On being assaulted with tales of our tea-drinking episodes, Midju brought us back into Himalayan reality, her husky voice telling us bluntly, "Tea is for drinking, not talking about."

High in the mountains around Litang, the change in weather had brought a nomadic exodus: slow-moving waves of horses, yaks, tents, and wool—wool tents bound by wool rope, reams of wool, wool clothes—made their way into sheltered valleys for the winter. Our own eventual move, with our stomachs contentedly reacquainted with butter and yak meat, involved continuing west, through Batang, of fruit and fighter fame, and on to Markham, with a stop at Jubee Zhuka—if we could find it. The town was a place where caravans would have waited patiently—and sometimes not so patiently—to cross a moving sixty-three-hundred kilometre-long monster known to the Tibetans as Dri Chu, to the Chinese as Jinsha Jiang, and to Westerners as the Yangtze River.

Jubee Zhuka was one of the crossing points for caravans trying to reach the other side of Asia's largest river, a river that, at some point or other, still carried almost half of China's ocean trade along its racing waters. The ancient caravans used two methods to make the river crossings. Yak-skin boats that looked like square mattresses often conveyed entire caravans across the river, sometimes piece by piece, body by body. These boats were risky in floods but generally safe. Bamboo and rattan cables, on the other hand, counted their victims in the thousands, thanks to lines that chafed and broke from neglect, overuse, or age. Many a life—man's and mule's—and cargo dropped unceremoniously into the river or ravine below, to be swept away by fast-flowing muddy waters. At first, a single cable was strung across gorges and rivers, with another attached to the main cable to act as a pulley, aiding and guiding bulky loads, which included mules. In later years, a safer two-cable system was put into place. Each cable had a high point on opposite sides, using the momentum in the descent to slide along to the lower point on the opposite side. It was when caravans had to wait for broken cables to be repaired that tempers often exploded.

"Sometimes two or three hundred mules would be lined up as caravans waited for the cables to be fixed. There was bound to be trouble, as there was no alternative but to wait, and the repairs could take days," an old lado named Lobsang had told us, adding that it was up to the *tsompun,* the caravan leader, to make sure his lados behaved. "It was difficult, as they were men of movement, men of the outdoors. Keeping them still and quiet during the waits was sometimes impossible. Once the men got that out of their systems, everything went back to normal," Lobsang said, laughing. Payment of wages was dependent on arriving in the trading times within appointed times. Even behind the massive personalities of the Khampas, there was a shadow of economics.

The yak-skin boats gradually fell into disuse as bridges were built at key points to span the river. Little Jubee Zhuka wasn't quite large enough to warrant having a bridge, though it remained a crossing point: in 2005, steel cables were installed there, and what was once an adventure in the currents became a two-minute adventure gliding above the water.

We knew we'd arrived in Jubee Zhuka by the crowd of people and pickups off to the side of the dirt road. Boxes, canvas sacks, and men squatting effortlessly surrounded an elderly man wearing a cap: the unofficial conductor controlling the traffic gliding over the Yangtze.

Standing straddling a steel wire, he bellowed instructions two hundred metres across the river. Villagers responded by sending all manner of goods and bodies humming through the air, attached to the cable by a huge clasp and on the other end to a belt that was secured around the waist or package. The bags and produce arriving at our end were jammed into the backs of waiting Jeeps. The conductor kept traffic moving with a series of yells and dramatic arm movements, in a well-coordinated aerial show that lasted twenty-five minutes, and one that would repeat itself in the late afternoon.

Experienced crossers let their bodies go slack as they zipped through the air. Caravan mules, which made dozens of such crossings attached to the cable with clasps, learned to ride as competently as their keepers.

We, however, decided to make an uninspired crossing by bridge, so we made our way through dry, isolated canyons until we reached the wide span at Markham—in Tibetan, Garthog Dzong. It was a crucial stop for caravans heading to Chamdo or Lhasa. Located between the Yangtze and Mekong rivers and technically in the TAR (Tibetan Autonomous Region), it sits seemingly close to nothing. Places often bear the scars of their past, but it is the people who inevitably carry the memories, and Markham is a place that seems to be losing both the scars and the elders.

There was little in the swollen valley of red earth surrounding Markham to remind us of the trade routes. A series of new buildings had given the town a rather bizarre aesthetic. It was in this massive basin that the two main caravan routes, the Yunnan–Tibet and the Sichuan–Tibet, converged into one for the final surge into Tibet. Grazing lands were plentiful, as the travelling parties came in slow packs, filling the land with life. Old friends and dreaded enemies, bringing with them supplies and news from other parts, came together in what one trader called a "party under the sky."

If Markham has lost its history and memories, the tiny town of Pomda has both its namesake and memories kept alive by the legacy of the most powerful trading family in the history of the Tea Horse Road, the Pomdatsang, or Pomda clan. South of Markham, Pomda rests in a plain of dust and sun, and feels leagues away from the nearby Mekong and Yangtze rivers. Far from the Celestial teas of

Ya'an, eight hundred kilometres to the east, Pomda is a town that still sees more mule traffic than fuelled vehicles, and where a single telephone hut acts as a gathering point on its one dirt thoroughfare. It was the birthplace of men who would in time control almost half of the trade done along the Tea Horse Road, the former home to the family that changed and dominated the entire trade system with will, smarts, and force. Seeing a small mule caravan come into town, and another leave in the span of fifteen minutes, brought the Tea Horse Road into perspective and focus. Pomda had an unsophisticated realness to it, one close to the way things once were.

No one who had travelled, traded, sold, lived, or looted along the Tea Horse Road was unaware of the Pomdatsang. A family-run trading business started by three uneducated brothers, it would become a dominant force in four countries. During the early twentieth century, the thirteenth Dalai Lama escaped Tibet under threat from the British, fleeing, after the Chinese refused to help him, with the help of the loyal Pomda clan. In return for his safe passage home to Lhasa, he granted the clan exclusive rights to trade Tibetan wool, setting in motion their swift rise. In their dealings, the members of the Pomdatsang displayed all the qualities associated with the Khampas they were: decisiveness, unerring bargaining skills, and hard work.

In a time of much trickery and scheming, they built a reputation based on honesty and autonomy and, because they rarely bowed to commercial pressures and always paid their employees and treated them fairly, they quickly gained a following of loyal lados and customers. They also offered a guarantee that was outrageous in that era: accountability for all deliveries, whether they arrived or not.

During the 1930s, they fought and defeated the Tibetan army, which the Regent Reting had ordered to attack them, likely because his own trade firm (humbly called Reting) was enjoying far less success. After the confrontation, the Pomdatsang's base of operations and the family itself moved from Pomda to Kangding in the 1930s and 1940s, where they fought the Chinese republicans. Through fighting, trading, and expanding, the Pomdatsang encompassed an ever-greater portion of the trade that made its way through the Himalayan corridors. Organized, wealthy, and backed by its own fierce army, the clan also had one very Khampa-like advantage: fearlessness. Few organizations of the time could muster the force to compete with or confront the Pomdatsang, instead imitating its successful business model and hoping for a chunk of the business.

For a time, the Pomdatsang was untouchable in both war and trade, having more than two thousand mules carrying on its behalf and hiring the best that money could buy, whether that be traders, warriors, or accountants. The clan's business offices and stations could be found in Nepal, India, Tibet, and China. Those belonging to the Pomdatsang were known, even by their rivals, as people who kept their word. Other trading-family companies, including the Samdutsang from Ganze and the Andutsang from Litang, were powerful, but no other organization commanded the respect and loyalty the Pomdatsang did.

Another practice that put the Pomdatsang in good stead was its non-interference with smaller trade firms and independent caravans. It had no intention of swallowing up the village caravans—the Pomdatsang itself had its roots in a simple village. Although it commanded thousands of mules, had its own army, owned its own banks, and traded throughout Asia, even exporting wool to the West, this apparently didn't lead to abuse and in turn it gained a tremendous amount of respect in the isolated communities. The Pomdatsang's business philosophy stands in stark contrast to today's prevailing business model of profit to the exclusion of all else.

"They traded in everything: herbs, musk, fuel [during the Second World War], caterpillar fungus, wool, tea, cotton, carpets, leather ... there wasn't anything that they couldn't get or wouldn't trade," a lado in Ponzera had told me. "They had their own stationery, with the letterhead in Tibetan and English, and used their own seal for documents. They were like a small nation operating under the old Khampa codes of conduct."

Each of the three Pomdatsang brothers had a focus: one took care of business matters and accounting, one took care of trade in the more remote regions, and the third took care of security and military issues. Nothing summed up their influence like a Tibetan saying popular among the muleteers of the day: *"Sa Pomda, nam Pomda"*—"On earth Pomda, in the sky Pomda."

The deserted home of the Pomda clan still stands. A stout flat-topped dwelling, it is a reminder that such power can have a humble birthplace. The residents are cognizant of the history of the town but don't dwell on it. The pace of commercial activity in the old trading town has since slowed; it has been left alone to dictate its own speed of change. Sitting with the former neighbours to the Pomdas, we nursed our butter tea while we waited for an old Pomdatsang servant to come speak with us.

After an hour, two frail relics limp in, bracing each other. "My body and health are a mess, so it takes me a long time to do anything," said Yeshi, the old servant. The old man who assisted him in whispered to us that Yeshi made this supreme effort because he was so excited to talk about the old days.

Yeshi's face was deeply lined, his mouth loose, his eyes bloodshot, and he wore a traditional *chupa*, a long wool coat. Behind him, members of our host family prepared food at an old stove, a shaft of light beaming down onto their working hands. A handsome young man stood near us, ready to replenish our teacups. Yeshi's laboured breath creased his features as he settled down to spin his prayer wheel.

He clarified his station right away: "I was never a lado, no, no, only a servant and helper." More than sixty years ago, he began to work for the family, starting out "doing everything," eventually keeping accounts and records of moneys, products, and employees. As a neighbour, he had long known the clan, and as the trading family's business expanded, it clung to people it trusted. "They trusted me because they knew me as someone from home. It was important to them, to trust," Yeshi said.

"Tea was the most important commodity, and the family had specific caravan teams transporting tea from Ya'an to Markham via Kangding. These teams knew tea, tea care, the markets for tea, and how best to transport it. At Markham, other caravans would be waiting to transport the tea north to Chamdo but mostly west into Lhasa." Taxes were anything but simple for the big trading families, but, for the Pomdatsang, "special arrangements" were made with local authorities in areas of frequent travel, and no errant watch-collecting tax official would dare try topping up his kitty.

"We had caravans with four hundred mules, primarily carrying tea. Ya'an tea was the most readily accessible and cheap, but it was the *cheril* [tea balls from Yunnan] that were the most prized and could turn the most profit. Trade was always about profit. All the big caravans from Yunnan carried the *norbu meibar* [a flame insignia], and when the Lhasa merchants saw this symbol [often on the mules' saddles or on the lead mule's headdress], they were very happy knowing that Yunnan tea had arrived. People waited in long lines for the tea in the markets."

Gradually, Yeshi's cheeks coloured and his breath settled. "So great was the Pomdatsang's influence in India that although Indians knew nothing about the Tibetan government, they had all heard of the Pomdatsang. Advisors speaking Hindi, Bengali, Nepali, Chinese, English, Lhasa Tibetan, Khampa, and even the Naxi language worked with the Pomdatsang so that business could be done in the language of the locals. Many problems were avoided this way." Yeshi paused for a loud slurp of tea and a few words with the host family. It had been a long time since this fragile man had been the centre of attention.

Dry wind sent sprays of dust through the deep window, and the room darkened as the sun slid its way behind the distant hillside. Jamyan's bulky shoulders were hunched forward to catch Yeshi's words, which faded and rose in the space between us.

"Many were jealous of the influence of the Pomdatsang, but I can tell you that no one worked harder than those three brothers. After they educated themselves, they listened to people, learning from the ground up what was necessary for business. They delegated and understood that each person must do one thing well in order for a company to work. Loyalty was rewarded, as was disloyalty. Travel with the caravans was hard work but so rewarding, so huge, I didn't want to work [in an office] any more," said Yeshi as his gaze drifted to some point in the room. Like Norbu, he, too, had been caught up in the journey.

Glancing out the window, I saw roaming gusts of wind tickling the hay drying on the roof of the Pomda clan's old home but no signs of the business empire that had its origins here in the stark landscape.

THREE DAYS LATER, travelling south past Merishoo toward Shangri-La, I insisted on stopping in on old Dawa. I was worried that he might no longer be with us; seeing him would reassure me. Having heard the tales of how things used to be, having learned so much that so many people have forgotten, and having seen so much change along the Tea Horse Road, I wanted to know that old Dawa was still alive. I wanted to tell him we had made it to Lhasa and over his old nemesis Sho La, and that his counsel had seen us through the white void at the top.

Opening the door to us, he was again gracefully dishevelled—I had caught him in the middle of a siesta. He retrieved his fedora, donning it, as he had five months ago, with a little flick of his hands. The room smelled of cold tea. Thankfully, he was unchanged: the lamenting eyes, long ancient body, and magnificent hands were exactly as I remembered them. I selfishly needed for him to be unchanged and well; I needed him to represent that part of the Tea Horse Road that hadn't changed. I dropped some tea from our journey into his hands as we settled down for a tiny glass of *arra*. "So you have seen it all, have you?" he asked. His eyes bore into me before he dipped his head—he would rather have seen for himself one last time.

All too soon, it was time to leave. Dawa chuckled sadly when I promised to visit again. "Old things don't change, they just disappear," he said. Whether he spoke of himself, the Tea Horse Road, or life in general, I didn't know.

One of the last destinations and resting places for traders on the Tea Horse Road, Gangtok in Sikkim Province long paid tribute to Tibetan empires. Many of the old Tibetan traders settled and remain to this day in this northern Indian Himalayan city.

8

Lhasa to Kalimpong: Down into Heat

There is no time that cannot be recalled.

—FROM A MONGOLIAN FOLK SONG

FLYING DOESN'T ALLOW for a natural transition to a destination. This mode of travel is usually altogether too smooth and sterile to offer an indication of what is to come. I had returned to Lhasa by plane from Shangri-La for what would be the last segment of my journey, the plunge south from Lhasa into Nepal and India, into heat and colour. Months earlier, trekking to Lhasa, I had had a slow and meaningful entry, but now I was expending no effort, and there was no sense of experience. It was as though a switch had been flicked and my mind had to catch up with my senses, which felt as though they were being cheated. My body hunched stiffly in its aisle seat, my yellow, callused hands still bearing the evidence of the route that lay far below.

The flight took us over the spectacular landscape I had trudged along on foot. Did the mountains miss their old friends? I couldn't help but feel that they did, magnificent as they were in their silence. Did they crave the plodding frames of mules and men passing through their empires once more? The massive expanse below had played host to something crucial in the history of the Himalayas. I thought again to Dawa's provocative words, and wondered, Did old things just disappear, or *did* they change?

The plane landed and I disembarked into the dry winds and tree-less mountains of Lhasa.

A rare reunion of Dakpa, Tenzin, Sonam, Yeshi, and me would give us time for plenty of *jia ngamo*—sweet tea—and time to cele-brate, reminisce about, and lament what we had seen in the course of our endeavours along the Tea Horse Road. I was overcome by nostalgia. We had been entranced and humbled by the geography, and moved by the people and their memories. Most difficult for me was accepting that without the passing down and telling of stories of the Tea Horse Road, it would almost be as though the mules and men had never been, that their contributions had been trivia. "But we have seen, we have touched it," Dakpa reminded us solemnly.

Sonam, as lithe and swift as ever, and taking a rare break from his treks, was throwing back the tea in quick gulps. Tenzin's handsome looks had been weakened by a cold, which lent just a hint of vulnera-bility to his rugged features. The masses of people of Lhasa had both refreshed and worn out his energy; Dakpa suggested that it was Tenzin's manic shopping sprees that had contributed to his illness. Tenzin's bargaining, he explained, generally consisted of a tiring twofold approach. First he laid on his thick charm, which unsurpris-ingly did not work with the well-versed shopkeepers. Then he took a brooding approach that, considering Tenzin's features, was without a doubt his stronger suit. As for Dakpa, he seemed in his prime, having finally gained the weight back that Shar Gong La had taken from him. My own features had been shorn into hard angles of skin and bone, and Dakpa suggested I shave as often as possible to avoid the "demented look," which he indicated I now had in spades.

Dry sun, dust, and sweet tea were to be found in abundance in Lhasa: we were in the land of plenty. The "tea of sweet," as the Lhasans called the concoction they drank in such large quantities, was not a recipe that had originated in Tibet but had been introduced from India and Nepal. Dark tea leaves were combined with sugar and milk, then boiled down to a syruplike consistency; the Lhasans' resultant bulging waistlines had long been a point of ridicule in Kham. Tibet's southern neighbours had influenced much of Tibetan life. After many *katser*—traders and business people of mixed Tibetan Nepali parentage who were living and working in the Tibetan lands, and in

Lhasa particularly—were granted Tibetan citizenship in the 1950s, they kept their ties and trading relations with their homeland, importing not only articles of trade but also their ways of life. Statues, silks, jewels, as well as expressions and intonations, continue to make their way from Nepal and India to Tibet, along with the sweetest of teas.

As present-day Lhasa becomes ever more tamed and modern, there will come a time in the not-too-distant future when the rough signs of the days of trade will disappear. Sanitized shops selling wares that would scarcely make sense to an old trader, roads of near impossible straightness and width, and a valley of unimagined hugeness containing not one mule or horse used for trade will rule.

In the surrounding mountains, the monasteries still sit, seeming to be part of both the mountain and the sky. These solemn, sometimes defiant, monasteries were in many ways dependent on the Tea Horse Road. Novice monks from the east and north, all wanting to make the journey to Lhasa at least once, either to visit the sacred Jokhang Temple or join one of the monasteries, travelled with the caravans—accompanying a caravan provided safety in numbers.

But many monks believed that the sufferings experienced by man and beast along the road contaminated the tea the caravans carried and that therefore it was unhealthy and immoral to drink and enjoy the tea. The tea was considered to be stained with suffering and loss, and was often initially rejected by the monasteries. This reaction was met with contempt by the lados, who insisted that their sufferings and that of their mules would be entirely in vain if the tea wasn't consumed by those very monks to whom the tea was offered. According to an oft-repeated story, one fearless lado threatened to beat a good number of the monks at a particular monastery if they didn't change their minds. The monks apparently were inspired to rethink their ways and accept the tea. They may have remembered that the Khampas always stood behind their words.

Today's Lhasa of religion, worship, and pilgrims had not always been a place of good intentions. Many Khampa lados we met heaped scorn on the Lhasans for their corruption and selfishness. One hulking old lado told us in no uncertain terms how he viewed them: "They thought of nothing but their pockets, and they weren't capable of giving a yes or no answer. The black marketeers were as honest as anyone, and the taxes levied were changed daily according to how corrupt the officials were. None of that money ever went back into helping society or the needs of people. There was no honour in Lhasa, no codes. They were a different people from us Khampas."

It was a little bit of justice for the Khampas, then, that they dominated business along the trade routes, even business that extended into Nepal and India. Of course, the Lhasans had their own views of the Khampas, seeing them as rough but adept businesspeople, with "risk in their blood." One Lhasa trader described the Khampas as "being born with an ability to take huge risks in life and in business ... they would constantly reinvest their profits." Many a fortune was lost because of this all-or-nothing philosophy. It was also this view that was in part responsible for the success of the most important mountain trade route on Earth.

On my journey south into Nepal and India, the witty Yeshi Gyetsa, a well-versed source of customs and history, would join me. Yeshi's family history—he belonged to a successful Khampa family involved in trade along the Tea Horse Road—made his participation in my journey indispensable. His intrepid grandfather had tried unsuccessfully to plant tea in the Himalayan valleys to get around the long transportation times to the Tibetan market towns. But his family also had the unfortunate reputation for the odd bit of profiteering and negligence. One trembling lado had told us of the family's tendency to not pay their lados. I kept silent on this point, not wanting to upset Yeshi and jeopardize losing the necessary skill set he brought to the journey. Yeshi was the sort of man who could say one thing while meaning another, all the while keeping a smile on his face. Together, Yeshi and I would go to the end of the route, to what many referred to as the lados' "place of rest," in part because of its comforts for the aging and worn muleteers, in part because many Tibetan muleteers, unable or unwilling to return to their homeland after the Chinese took over, did eventually die there.

Yeshi had first-hand knowledge of our final destination, Kalimpong, in northern India. One other interesting attribute was his linguistic ability, which included fluent Nepali, Bengali, and Hindi, as well as a few other languages we would never need. Having been raised and schooled in the very place we were headed to, our arrival there would be a homecoming of sorts for him. Since it was the last leg of the journey, I wanted to take it slow and really take in what remained.

The morning we left Lhasa, the kind of cold that encourages late starts rushed through town. Sonam, Tenzin, and Dakpa dragged their sleepy bodies from bed to see us off. Although Dakpa and I would certainly see one another again soon, I wasn't sure how long it would be until I next saw Tenzin and Sonam. In the clear brittle morning, we hugged and murmured our goodbyes. Dakpa, as he often did, warned me off crazy climbs and unnecessary risks, and once again urged me to shave regularly. I knew that the moment we left, they would jump back into bed—with the possible exception of Sonam, who might busy himself with morning prayers and apologies to the deities for deeds not yet committed.

The ancient caravans had followed a southerly route from Lhasa, first moving along the Lhasa River tributary, then the main Yarlung Tsangpo River to cut due south to Nagarze and Gyantze. From there they headed south to Pagri and Yadong, and into India. One trail crossed the Nathu La (Nathu Pass) destined for Gangtok in Sikkim, while the other path crossed the Jelep La (Jelep Pass) into Kalimpong, in west Bengal. From these two towns the caravans could access goods at the port of Calcutta.

Pagri and Yadong are, according to both the Indian and Chinese governments, open for trade and commerce, though not (at the time of writing) to travellers. And although I had enough tea on me to start my own import-export company and therefore qualify for a trade and commerce exemption, we would not be allowed over the border on the commercial routes. Sensitive both politically and economically, the border region has been the site of disputes and boundary changes for a thousand years and is still in a state of flux. The strategic importance of the area is accentuated by the fact that the trade routes of the past provided a natural blueprint for travel in the motor age. In this case, at least, the old hadn't yet disappeared; it had just changed. The dependable mules had given way to undependable, wild-coloured transport trucks that broke down with far more regularity than their flea-ravaged predecessors.

Yeshi and I planned to travel by Jeep southwest toward the border-lands—a journey interrupted, of course, by my insistence to explore and detour at will. The southern frontier of Tibet, an incredible peak-pierced geography, touched the northern frontiers of Nepal, India, and Bhutan, all within a hundred-kilometre stretch.

As if in a farewell send-off, Lhasa granted one of my remaining wishes as I left. Lados had often spoken of the yak-skin boats and how gradually they were falling into disuse as bridges were constructed. Buoyant, wide, and agile, the crafts were able to skim over vicious waters fully loaded. The old muleteers, who rarely praised anyone or anything, gushed about the boatmen and their mastery on the fierce rivers. They also rated the swimming skills of various species: mules and horses got an "okay," while dogs and pigs were "superior."

Slowly passing through the stonemasons' town of Saga, southwest of Lhasa, I caught sight of a beetlelike object racing over a tributary; there were dark figures aboard rowing madly through a rushing green froth. The square craft moved quickly, as though pulled by a force from the opposite side. It was what I prayed it would be. Waiting at the shoreline, I watched the yak-skin boat approach. A broad man in multiple layers of clothes manoeuvred the boxy craft with strength and a calm knowledge of the currents, tugging the oars and steering in a series of lightning-fast jolts. As the boat glided in to shore, I could see that the boat held an alarming number of children, nuns, packs, and crates.

The boatman, one in a long line of navigators, knew that soon his maritime contributions would no longer be needed. Pointing at his craft, he spoke in the deliberate tone of someone who knows his skills and limitations. "I have two boats, identically made," he said. "One boat costs me 200 RMB [about CAD$28] for all the materials. It takes six yak skins to make one boat, and it never leaks." The boat's con-struction and simple but efficient design spoke of another time, a time when most river crossings were not nearly so easy. Modernization had put an expiry date on many of these artifacts, and on the people who operate them. This man and his craft had lasted longer than most from the old trade era, but time has no conscience.

GYANTZE HAD ALWAYS BEEN one of the heartlands of Tibetan wool production and agriculture. Raw wool moved northeast to Lhasa and south into India along the Tea Horse Route. Influences of the south reached even here: for a time in the 1930s and 1940s, the Indian rupee was the currency of choice. To this day, herds of thousands of sheep colour the valley floors white. Yeshi one morning turned to me, his eyes gleaming mischievously, and told me of a local saying: "In Gyantze, the wool is great, but in Benang [a nearby town] the women are great, so there is no time to lose." I wasn't sure if the ending was a suggestion or part of the quote, and I didn't know whether we should get into wool business, then run off with a couple of locals into the hills. Yeshi's ability to conjure up quotes and tales about towns and districts we passed through had me wondering if his clever mind wasn't just making them up on the spot, but upon testing them out on elders, his words always held true.

South of Kangmar, we neared the Bhutanese and Indian borders, which were surrounded by a hostile beauty of shorn rock. I had always thought of borders and boundaries in a literal sense, as though an actual line would be visible, and it would be clear that I was entering into a different place. The mountains quashed the notion that any other than they could mark out territories dividing spaces and peoples. The mountains dictated everything. Successful traders and travellers had understood this and accepted it without question, not attempting to bend nature to the will of man.

It was here that we met a man who as a boy had watched in awe as the caravans entered his town. He invited us to take refuge in his daughter's home from debris that was being flung around by the wind. Once inside, we were served peculiar butter tea. Yeshi wore one of his patent smiles but his eyes told me that he was disturbed. Under his breath he told me that our hosts had likely used goat butter instead of yak butter, because they were so poor.

The old man's rough voice came out steadily, "Oh yes, tea, wool, and butter went to India, and textiles, sugar, and canvas back to Lhasa. Those men and their mules and yaks could carry anything. The Khampas would winter in India, returning in the summer. They were strange people. Strong and wild, they could all speak many languages—they could speak with the Bhutanese, with the Nepalese and Indians as well—but they were wild."

It seemed that the farther west we were, the more we heard of the lados' wildness. This was in contrast to the lados of the open plains of eastern Tibet, who, apart from the odd incident, were surprisingly disciplined. Perhaps their exaltation as they approached the end of their journey, having survived the heat and the exhaustion, led them to reveal more of their carefree fearlessness.

In the later years of trade, there was a strictly enforced rule when approaching the Indian area of the Tea Horse Road: all lados and travellers had to surrender their beloved guns in Yadong, at the tax and permit offices. The guns would be returned when the person passed through on his or her way back. Still, this vigilance couldn't prevent bouts of brutality. Knife fights and beatings were far from uncommon along the stretch, almost every incident involving *dala walas*, the name given to the foot-powered porters who carried enormous loads and travelled in large groups—and often took the law into their own hands. Most were Tibetans from central Tibet, and they became as renowned for their confrontations as for their endurance and strength.

Dala walas took part in mass movements of goods between Tibet and India. "Everything could be taken along the route," a lado named Tupten told us. "We took disassembled cars over for the wealthy of Lhasa, piece by piece on the backs of men and on the backs of mules." Whether suffering inferiority complexes about not having mules or feeling brave in their large numbers, *dala walas* often ignored long-established rules of the road, forcing oncoming caravans off the trail. In one often-repeated story, a large group of *dala walas* badly beat up a group of Khampa lados on the trail over a disagreement of right of way. The Khampa lados promptly returned to the gun checkpoint, collected their arms, and waited. Eventually, the *dala walas* passed through again and were ambushed, every one of them shot dead.

Not surprisingly, there is a simple but revealing saying of the Khampa lados: "I have come and measured all of this distance—I have nothing to lose. I have come and counted all of the clouds—I have nothing to lose." Far away from home and guided by their own codes of conduct, they were men of action who believed they had nothing to lose. I understood this view more clearly as time passed:

punishing travel gives insight into yourself and how you relate to the surrounding space.

"More tea?" the daughter of the old man asked. Yeshi's hand shot out to cover his untouched cup.

Travelling with Yeshi, I learned that he had many different personalities, often depending on the state of his stomach. A hungry Yeshi was a Yeshi devoid of life, a man on the verge of a breakdown, whereas a sated Yeshi was a vibrant man content with the world. A good meal or treat brought sounds of delight from him and spurred him on, while an unsatisfactory culinary experience left him downcast, his mood dire. It was this morose Yeshi who now sat before me, his weak smile communicating his lack of satisfaction.

OUR JOURNEY CONTINUED WEST through vast high-altitude deserts. They were places of infinite beauty and fierce desolation. Dust storms whipped through the huge valleys, the only disturbances in an otherwise blue sky. During the storms, it was impossible to determine the scale of anything: mountainous slabs of ice, which seemed "just over there," might in fact be eighty kilometres off. Dirt tracts hectares wide often disappeared in blurred attacks of golden sand. Only the nomads, encased in scarves, braved the storms, puttering up and down steep inclines and across the caked earth. I felt dwarfed in the emptiness. Coming within sight of the strangely uninspiring mass of Everest huddled in the heavens, we stopped for the night outside a town called Old Tingri, while the nearby Cho Oyu—at 8153 metres, almost 700 metres shy of Everest's summit—awash in a fading, angled sunlight, took our breath away.

Yeshi's nose led us to a tiny home, where we were welcomed with a steaming pot of stew to settle our stomachs and raise Yeshi's blood-sugar level. A cup of tea, a shack of bare plank walls that a restaurant owner had lent us, and we all but passed out for the night.

Morning began in the twilight with a diagonally driving blizzard that ploughed into the side of the shack, driving us deeper into our clothes. Yeshi was silent and sullen in the onslaught, while I paced in an attempt to warm my feet in my boots, which had become long, solid blocks. November had arrived overnight, and with it all of winter's hardness. In conditions like these, whether you were travelling by foot, wheel, or hoof, it was critical to keep moving, no matter how poor the visibility. The other option was anaesthetizing cold.

The road was a smooth white hump that disappeared five metres ahead of us in a snow squall. Our Jeep crept forward slowly, cutting the first trails through snow twenty-five centimetres deep. I was thankful that we had hired a local to do the driving. The beam from the headlights hinted at how much we couldn't see, and we were forced to keep the windows down to prevent the windshield from icing up with our breath, since the heater was broken. My eyes strained as I stared at the road ahead, hoping that we were in fact *on* a road. I felt dazed by the storm's unrelenting wind and snow.

Hours later, a dark, grey dawn arrived, and the lashing snow eased to floating wet flakes. Our groaning engine and crunching tires provided the only soundtrack for hours as we drove through a frozen white pack. It took us two hours to travel twenty kilometers, and our faces had frozen stiff thanks to the open windows. As much as the malevolent storms had fought against us during the mountain segments of the journey, I admired their strength and will.

Slowly, as visibility increased and the temperature—which for us was barely registering through our numbness—rose, we began the long, looping final descent toward Tibet's southern frontier. Although our route had taken us off the main Tea Horse Road extension, we were still travelling on an ageless trade route that linked Nepal with Tibet. Over thirteen hundred years ago, Princess Wencheng's competition for Tibetan king Songtsen Gambo's bed, the sultry Nepali princess Chizun, along with traders, would have made her way with her massive caravan into Tibet by the same route.

By the time Yeshi and I reached the border crossing of Dram we had almost thawed out, and our limbs were slowly unknotting. The steaming breath of subtropical forests rushed in on us, and thick, stifling air reawakened our sweat glands, offering us the first warmth in our recent memory. Traders, prostitutes, smugglers, moneychangers, drivers, and soldiers of every shade of skin populated the streets of Dram, perusing, chatting, and recovering from their nocturnal activities. The vibrant, sleazy town, not to mention the heat, was a stark contrast to the barren beauty we had just passed through. Dram was one of those towns where nothing at all would seem out of place; every sort of creature and character drifted through the streets. Nevertheless, I sensed a muted threat in its exoticism and casual attentiveness. No one arrived unnoticed.

It was in this cunning border town that Yeshi's ability to fulfill many roles proved crucial. He began with what I would in retrospect refer to as his command performance. Our first priority was to get money changed, since exchange rates in Dram were far more agreeable than in the cities—that is, if one knew the game. As I was to find out, Yeshi knew the game intimately. He revealed his flair for negotiating—something passed on through his trading family bloodline, no doubt—as we sat in a teashop, small cups of steaming, sugared tea before us. A series of silent women of indeterminate nationality (identically made up and each wearing tidy shoes, a cheap suit, and a large frilly sunhat, and carrying a huge bulging purse) approached the table one by one. Yeshi had strategically chosen the chair with its back to the wall: he was holding court. Each woman waited until the previous one had left before sitting down with us, and each looked to be a veteran in these affairs.

Yeshi's eyes had narrowed to slits, and his good-natured expression disappeared under a brow of haughty boredom (his game face, he would later tell me), in order to dispense with niceties. The transformation to master negotiator was complete. His sole purpose was to find the moneychanger who would give us an acceptable rate of exchange.

In turn, each woman sat primly at the table and reached into her purse to pull out a giant calculator, on which she punched in a rate of exchange. Expressionless, Yeshi looked out the window, then shook his head slowly as he took the calculator and punched in the rate he wanted. No words were uttered, only the odd sigh from Yeshi to indicate it was all so unnecessary. An informed audience had assembled to witness the proceedings; they had seen this a hundred times before. On this ancient border, a bit of theatre was being played out.

After about twenty minutes, one of the women punched in the magic number and Yeshi gave her a weak smile. Wads of money appeared from her purse, bound neatly with fat elastic bands. Yeshi retrieved his own equally neat stack, putting it down on the table: it was time for the counting to begin. The bills became a blur in their adept hands, proficient in the art of money handling. Occasionally, Yeshi grunted and recounted, but still no one spoke. Piles of Nepali rupees and Chinese yuan, tea, and a massive calculator cluttered the table. No passports or permits shown here. Yeshi counted twice, I counted once (taking more than twice the time it had taken Yeshi), the teashop owner got in on the act and counted once, and, finally, the moneychanger counted all the piles twice. Sitting back, Yeshi had the happily exhausted look of a conductor being applauded. The money exchange had been successful.

At each destination of my journey, my senses had taken in new stimulants, emphasizing the great variety of life along the route. But in Dram, they hit a high point. The heat and smells had multiplied exponentially. To cross the Tibetan–Nepali border at Dram, we had to walk across a pedestrian bridge bustling with human traffic. Moustached men in skirts, women in saris, boxes balanced on heads, bags secured around shoulders—it was the most abrupt transition I'd encountered thus far on my journey. Vehicles waited at the other side, their drivers calm with the certainty of business. The fast-paced negotiations involved minutes of head wagging—no discussion was complete without a requisite amount of nodding and tilting of the head—as crucial to communication as the vocal chords.

Yeshi spoke to one of the drivers in aggressive Nepali, continuing to impress me with his ability to alter tactics depending on the goal. His head nodding was new to me, as was his choppy speech. Crowding the driver and forcing him backwards toward his truck into a position of submissive retreat, Yeshi relentlessly drove the price down, until once again the right number was reached, bringing an end to the negotiations. The driver, at first confident, had been beaten down in his price. Yeshi was peerless at this; I had never encountered anyone like him before, and I realized that I was in the hands of a slick operator. We could have used him in our trek section, I thought, as his skills in negotiating might have saved poor Sonam a lot of anguish.

Starting his truck, our driver casually warned us that if armed Maoists happened to stop us, we were to politely tell them that we had already contributed to their cause and were extremely sympathetic but unable in the present circumstances to contribute. His second warning was that under no circumstances was Yeshi to acknowledge that he understood the local dialect.

Maoists had recently begun a campaign of "cleanup weeks," when masked legions of them roamed about, armed with brooms to sweep spotless any offending districts. Fortunately, ours was to be an uneventful drive, and we only stopped once for lunch and several times for the driver to pay bribes to police officers. Given our driver's verbal outbursts after every payoff, I began to suspect that Maoists might have been preferred to the authorities.

Foggy Kathmandu, when we arrived, was surprisingly clean. Wooden brooms had, for the moment, taken the place of guns. From Kathmandu, Yeshi and I would access the Tibetan trading strongholds of Gangtok and Kalimpong, squished into an area of India that was tucked between Nepal's eastern border and Bhutan's western line and the end of the line, so to speak: it was the end of that branch of the Tea Horse Road, and the eventual settling point for many of the Tibetan muleteers who travelled the trade route. Meanwhile, Kathmandu offered me a long dreamed-of pleasure, one that had taken on an almost mythic status in my mind: a Western-style toilet.

Many Tibetans had settled in Kathmandu, and a large community had developed just east of the remarkable Boudhanath stupa. Worshipped by both Nepali Hindus and Tibetan Buddhists and rebuilt sometime in the fourteenth century after being ravaged by Mongol invaders, it is the most sacred stupa outside Tibet. Its thirty-six metres are composed of nine levels, representing the mythical Mount Meru, the supposed centre of the cosmos. Thirteen concentric rings from the base to the summit of the stupa symbolize the difficult path to enlightenment. The original seventh-century stupa had been a first destination for traders coming from Lhasa along trading routes to Kathmandu (known to many Tibetans as Charimando). Just as lados and traders, upon arriving in Lhasa, would head first to the Jokhang Temple to pay homage, muleteers arriving in Kathmandu headed to Boudhanath.

These hardened men never forgot to acknowledge the spirits that aided their safe passage through the staggering landscape. Although business was a secular affair, and toughness was a matter of the will, the muleteers undoubtedly felt the soft touch of Providence at having arrived at their destination intact. As much of a test of endurance as travel through the mountains was, many who had done so spoke in an endearing way of the perilous excursions. In the end, if you were delivered safely, with your cargo intact, all was well. One elder told me long before I began my own journey, "As much as the mountains can take from you, they can also hold and protect you. A successful trip is as easy as surviving."

In the gentle outlandishness of Kathmandu, I briefly forget that the end of my journey was near, as there was so little to identify or remind me of the Tea Horse Road. I hoped, as we boarded our flight from Kathmandu to Biratnagar, in eastern Nepal, from where we would continue on to Kalimpong, that I would be able to see from the air a dark line of mules weaving along the mountain ridges—a bit of fantasy on my part.

Humid heat that had been born in tropical jungles engulfed us as we landed, sucking us out of the plane and onto the hot plains of Nepal known as the Tarai. Driving toward the eastern border that Nepal shares with India, we passed close to the tranquil tea gardens of Ilam. Our very own Bhaskar, in whose restaurant in Shangri-La we had spent many nights planning the whole journey, was from a small village not twenty minutes from there—a bit of coincidence bringing the journey full circle, I mused.

Nothing in the sleepy, hot border town of Raniganj moved beyond an unhurried crawl—a stark contrast to the dangerously animated town of Dram. Although the border might have been sleepy, the officer on duty at the tiny, ramshackle hut was correct, crisp, and, I suspect, high on tea. I recognized his alert eyes and the furtive attention to detail, reflected in his immaculate uniform, as signs of a tea junkie. He stared dutifully at the single-entry visa stamp in my passport and furrowed his brow. I had a searing moment of panic that, after all the kilometres I had travelled, all the treacherous mountains and brutal winds I had faced, the journey would be cut short by some official ripped on tea, just as I was arriving at the conclusion. "Why only single entry? You should get double, triple, or quadruple entry. There is much to see in India." He nodded at me in pity as I drooped in relief.

Reinvigorated, I ask about the tea fields that surrounded us. His head jerked upward and he pinned me with his jumpy eyes. "Yes, the Darjeeling is good, but for real tea"—he tapped an empty cup holding black dregs—"you must drink Assam." The last word was drawn out—"Asssaaam"—and barely whispered, as if he were confiding a secret. Farther east, the mountain kingdom of Assam was home to what Indians called strong tea, the same big-leafed variety that makes Puer. Assam was also one of the only areas outside southern Yunnan with native tea trees. "Where will you be going?" asked the tea-savvy officer. Upon telling him we were heading to Kalimpong, he nodded, "Ah, yes, the old trade town. Next time come for longer."

India, land of unpredictable charm and irrepressible chaos, of casual fervency and undisputed pride, a place where the senses happily overloaded, and the physical end of my journey—a thought I was becoming more and more fixated on. I wasn't at all sure how I felt about it. At times it didn't feel possible that there would be an end to the adventure.

Just crossing the border into India from Nepal, there was a palpable change. Everything seemed more direct, more colourful, and louder. Yeshi selected a driver from the waiting cars for hire, engaging in the same entertaining fare war as before, although he warned me that even his stellar negotiating abilities would be tested—everything was intensified in India. We now had the services of a carefully preened young man, his hair gleaming with brilliantine, whose car was an unsubtle advertisement for Bollywood. Photographs of striking, big-eyed Indian movie stars, beads, and stickers adorned his spotless little vehicle, and I could detect the scent of recently applied fragrant oils. The car made its way through traffic as though choreographed. Our driver's shifting of gears was a performance in itself, and he blew the horn with pomp and vigour.

As we passed by green fields of tea, I was reminded that we were in yet another tea region, one with its own fervency with and history of the green leaf. As always, there was comfort in tea's presence. My own whittled-down clump had marked the passing of my travels; I had little more than a tangerine-sized portion left.

Just as tea was never farther away than my pocket, it was also ever present in the Himalayan regions of India. Its economic and cultural roots had been firmly embedded in the terrain and in the minds of locals for centuries. During the mid-twentieth century, some businessmen in the Darjeeling area of Assam tried to recreate the famed *tuo* (ball) shape of Yunnan tea, hoping to capitalize on its enduring popularity. One such man was Shree Ram, who, using local teas from Darjeeling and Assam, tried to reproduce the *tuo* so worshipped by Tibetans. He even coloured the tea with dye to give it an earthy, aged look. But he underestimated the Tibetans' taste buds. The cheaper varieties didn't sway the Tibetans, whose primary complaint was that it was tasteless. Penny-pinching didn't take precedence over their tea drinking.

In the 1950s, tea from China started arriving by ship in Calcutta, from where it travelled north into the Himalayas: tea from the distant plantations in Xiaguan and Xishuangbanna now made its way in the holds of cargo ships in a fraction of the time it took by mule, which could take up to seven months to reach market centres in Lhasa and beyond. The mountains and their rigours and beauties were bypassed as tea took a more southerly route. Times were changing, and with this new-found mode of transport came more taxes and more monitoring of the tea trade, but it also brought more tea to more people more quickly. Tea wars became common as teas competed for the approval and money of the Tibetans. Tea prices, like most commodities, fluctuated, and when the price of tea from China rose, Nepali and Indian growers deliberately dropped theirs. Most Tibetans, setting store by ritual, stuck to their pungent dark teas of Yunnan, regardless of price. This period in history proved bitter in many ways as the intimate relationship between tea, mules, and lados that had for so long ignored time's attentions began to wane.

Our entry into west Bengal late in the day had Yeshi furtively poking his head out the window in order to give me a running commentary of the sights. Kalimpong extracted a high-pitched squeal from him, worrying the driver that something was amiss. "There, the Novelty Cinema—we used to see films there as children." Yeshi bounced around in the front seat of the car, while I recalled the praise I had heard of this city over the past months.

Yeshi's joy conflicted with my slight sense of dread that this was it—the end of my journey. Kalimpong had been the end point of a six-

or seven-month journey for those lados who transported precious tea from the south of Yunnan to here, and for others who had made their living along the trade route. It was also the final resting place for many. In the early twentieth century, Kalimpong had been nothing more than a small trading town, its main claim to fame being its beauty and the fact that it had a competent postal station. By the 1920s and 1930s, trade from the Himalayas had increased into India to Kalimpong and to Gangtok, eighty kilometres north of Kalimpong in the state of Sikkim. Most caravans could make the trip from Lhasa to Kalimpong in about twenty days, but rarely did they venture farther south. "Horses and mules were susceptible to the heat. It was an unusual place for us Tibetans," a ninety-two-year-old lado told us. Even a Tibetan's mighty intestinal organs could be tested.

In Shangri-La, Litang, Puer, and Ponzera, travellers, pilgrims, muleteers, traders, and even the untravelled had all heard of this distant place of good food, good weather, and easy living. I was here, but it wasn't quite registering; I couldn't possibly have finally arrived.

Built on a ridge backed by lush forest, Kalimpong and its streets followed the natural contours of the land, cresting down on a soft grade. Narrow roads wound into series of S-shapes hidden in trees and shadow. Kalimpong had in its time been occupied by hill tribes, Marwari businessmen, the Bhutanese, the Nepalese, the Tibetans, and the English, and it still carried the marks of each. All the major trading families, including the Pomdatsang, had kept offices in the trade hub. If Lhasa was the spiritual centre for muleteers and traders, then Kalimpong might be considered the spa and retirement centre, a place where many lados and tsompun had lived out their final days in a contentment that their weary bones deserved. It was a town of orchids, pastel-coloured buildings, and gentle breezes, where winter was marked by an insignificant increase in the Himalayan gusts and nothing more.

Before a major flood in 1968, a series of cables were strung along the nearby Tista River, providing a fast, low-maintenance way of transporting goods between the warehouses of Kalimpong and distant rail lines. Trains took cargo deep into the Indian subcontinent. Like much related to the Tea Horse Road, the old cables sagged in disuse along the riverbanks.

Dropping us off in town, our driver had returned to his border post, and we were left to explore Kalimpong on foot, our bags in tow. I followed Yeshi's racing figure past buildings that still bore the names of trading families and firms and the dates of construction. Yeshi's old family house was now a sleepy traffic-police office. Yeshi's speed was motivated in part by his appetite, and we wound through steep alleyways destined for the home of Ashi Penzon—Lady Penzon. Known to muleteers and tsompun as Nemo Penzon—Hostess Penzon—this woman's home and generosity had been for years renowned throughout Himalayan trading circles. Her Somdala Kotee, or Nepali-Orange Cottage, was legendary to Tibetans and Tea Horse Road traders. Lady Penzon and her simple wooden house had played host to countless traders, mules, vagabonds, and travellers, just as now they would play host to us. It was she, in her familiar role as hostess, who would mark the end of my journey.

"She was one of the most beautiful women in northern Yunnan," Yeshi told me as we made our way up the rickety stairs. "She was coveted by all the men." Poor woman, I thought; no wonder so many muleteers and tsompun stayed here.

Her history, like most related to the Tea Horse Road, was full of rich detail. As a young woman, she had been kidnapped by her husband-to-be, who later left her so that he could become a monk. Rather than return home, she eventually made her way to Kalimpong, during the peak years of trade.

I felt as though I was about to meet Tea Horse Road royalty. Fatigue from my travels was wiped away by my giddy nerves as we climbed the stairs. Once again I was entering into the domain of a legend, and my apprehensions about this being the end of the journey were suspended. Although no longer orange, her "cottage" had a comforting lived-in feel, and I sensed it had not yet finished its supporting role as provider.

If Mother Earth had a physical presence, it would be that of Ashi Penzon. Strongly built, she exuded warmth and hospitality. Hers was a force that would soften the harshest of men and settle the most introspective of souls. Her welcome left me feeling as though I had known her all my life. She sat us down her in her "tearoom" and in minutes had tea and homemade biscuits in terrifying quantities on the table in front of us. "This is how it used to be," said Yeshi. "As kids, we would come here for tea and cakes." As Yeshi pointed out later, nursing his stomach, "*Now* the waistlines have increased." I thought of my pint-sized Hungarian grandmother, who would have nodded her approval at Ashi Penzon's priorities: sit, eat, eat again, and then talk, once the stomach's needs had been tended to.

As we ate, I studied Ashi Penzon. She was one of the mountain's born and bred beauties, and had likely outlived most of her admirers. She was still stunning, despite her eighty-seven years, and she knew well that the eyes and bellies of men were their weak points. "*Chu sa*"—"eat" in Lhasa Tibetan—was a phrase I would hear daily during our week-long stay with her. Soft, sympathetic eyes rested on Yeshi and me in welcome, and I was delighted when she self-consciously fixed her wool cap atop her head.

It wasn't long, though, before she was filling Yeshi's ear with the latest gossip and complaints of life in Kalimpong. She was, after all, Khampa. Her silky voice almost purred; it was a voice that would put children to sleep, a voice that intoxicated, a voice I could not imagine angry, though it was hitting some peaks as she unleashed her frustrations. After a lifetime of listening and catering to others, she now needed to unwind. Every few moments, she interrupted herself, cajoling me to eat with a "*Chu sa,*" then picking up where she had left off. I ate, she spoke, and Yeshi nodded. This went on for hours.

I began to relax, my body and mind uncoiling in small bursts. The journey was drawing to a soft closing. After months of travelling, Ashi Penzon's gifts of tea, baking, and warmth were comforting, and I felt quite content to hole up in her house for a while. If this was to be the conclusion, it couldn't have been under a more caring, experienced pair of eyes.

The journey to Kalimpong had taken me just as long as it had the lados, though mine was in a different sequence. Almost seven months, including 117 days of trekking, had given me a taste of the physicality and camaraderie required on the Tea Horse Road, but there was far more to the ancient route. My recollections were a patchwork of land-scapes familiar to few; craggy, animated faces; tea buds; reeking footwear; and mountain names that only old men could recall. By the time I arrived in Kalimpong, I had logged almost twelve thousand kilometres of travel—and three kilograms of Puer tea, hungrily consumed along the way. Nothing of what had been taken in on the journey seemed very far away, though much of it felt like it had happened a long time ago.

THE LADOS I HAD MET had eloquently described how, after making their way south out of the grip of the Himalayas, the sight of Kalimpong's forest-covered hills had a calming influence on their battered bodies and minds. One lado described it this way: "Its name we knew of, we knew of its food, women, and peace, but when we first saw it, we thought, 'It fit in the palm of our hands.'"

Today, the townspeople spoke a mix of languages: a rapid-fire dialect of Bengali, mixed with Hindi, Bihari, and the coarse character of Khampa gè, was softened by singsong Gorkhali (the Nepali language) and the polite monotones of Lhasa gè—Lhasa Tibetan. To this noisy stew was added English, taught at many of the local schools. During my many hours in Ashi Penzon's tearoom, in any given half-hour I was likely to hear three or four languages, and often a single sentence would be peppered with a blend of all of them, enforcing the notion of a coming-together of peoples at this ending point of the trade route.

Gedam was a term known to all who dealt in trade in these parts, but finally in Kalimpong I saw the *gedam* first-hand. The word had spilled out of any trader related to the Lhasa–Kalimpong route. Tibetans, Indians, Nepalese, and English all used the term or its English form, *go down,* to describe the dilapidated warehouses that had once stored the wool, tea, and other items carried by caravans along the Tea Hose Road. The origins of the word *gedam* are unclear, though many people believe it is a derivative of the English term. Sitting on the town's outskirts, many of these immense buildings were in sad disarray, padlocked, their paint peeling—a reminder that their time, too, had come and gone.

I had come to think of my journey along the Tea Horse Road as a reality woven into legends woven back into reality. With each new location, people and things I had heard about but were distant unknowns became intimately familiar, adding, in my mind, to the dimension and history of the Tea Horse Road. Each famed mountain pass, each town and face, once only a vague image in the mind, eventually acquired character.

The shrewd Marwari business class that traced its roots back to Rajasthan encompassed the trading middlemen who had worked alongside the brawny Khampas, and had been spoken of many times by the muleteers. For me, they represented the last element on the four-thousand-kilometre Yunnan–Tibet Tea Horse Road. Any Tibetan lado who had traded in Kalimpong or Gangtok would have at some point worked with or for them.

The Marwari businessmen were respected by the Tibetans as generally being wise and fair, and the relationships between the two were vital to the prosperity of both. Few of the sharp-featured Marwaris remain in Kalimpong, and the ones who did tended neat shops, selling rugs, silks, textiles, and even some suspect "Tibetan" butter. Yeshi, seemingly able to converse with anyone on two legs in any language, found one old Marwari who had been around in the 1940s and 1950s, the golden years of trade in Kalimpong.

Santenin Narai Agarwal awaited us in his orderly but cluttered shop. He sat cross-legged, his neck wrapped in a thick scarf, his sombre eyes watchful. Bowed by age, the intelligence of a hundred generations radiated from him; I had the sense that he had seen much, and what he hadn't seen, he innately understood. His family's shop has survived for more than sixty years since the town's glory days of trade. The darkening sky brought perfumed night air into the shop as the day gently let go. A young female relative served us sweet tea, the aperitif for conversation, relationships, life.

It wasn't likely that Khampas would have done business sitting cross-legged, quietly conversing, but the tea aspect would not have been at all foreign to them. An old woman in Lhasa had once told me that Khampa men "lived, loved, and did business standing up." No, the arrangement here wouldn't work for them, but for Yeshi and me it was fine—though I noticed Yeshi had cut down on his intake of sweet tea. Ashi Penzon's daily refreshments were steadily building up in his system, with both desired and undesired effects.

Looking at Yeshi and me and our meagre belongings—my camera bag and Yeshi's day pack—Santenin asked, "If you have come all this distance, what have you brought to trade?" Sagelike he might be, but none of his business prowess had dissipated over the years. It was this spirit that had kept him going. Deep furrows pulled his long face downward, making him appear submissive to the realities of life, to the tea trade's decline, and to time itself. Like so many, he, too, missed the days of trade, for trade brought life and newness. It brought together the scarred, proud figures of the lados, the booming tsom-puns, scurrying middlemen, excited shopkeepers, and products from leagues away.

Santenin's shop was crammed with rugs, clothes, incense, statues, and all manner of textiles. "In the past, the most popular items of trade were candles, wool, clothing dyes, *shelkara* [rock sugar], precious stones, and, of course, tea. In one afternoon of selling, the shop would be empty of stock." Santenin's eyes glowed with the memory of more exhilarating times.

Busier trade brought money and with it money's inevitable partner: problems. There was no place in the sphere of the Khampas' travels that did not feel the force of the "easterners'" character. Santenin told us of a local Marwari businessman who was known to renege on promises and payments. He made the disastrous mistake of assuming the stern traders of Tibet wouldn't bother to interfere with his brash enterprising. It didn't take long for the locals and the official in question to realize what the repercussions were of messing with Khampas.

Cheating the lados in the central market on one occasion too many, he was publicly threatened with immediate execution by a knife-wielding Khampa, and told in no uncertain terms in front of most of the town's business community that he would be dispatched if he didn't leave town. He did. Santenin grinned at the memory. If you wanted to trade, you had to cooperate with the men of the mountains. Merchants could be replaced, whereas trustworthy men capable of long journeys through the mountains were scarce commodities. Santenin offered one last gem, which summed up the trade route's great, understated role: "How else," he asked, "could we have ever learned so much of others from far off, how could we have known about places we would never see?"

BY NIGHT, Yeshi and I wandered the streets, working off Ashi Penzon's treats. The town, with its old trading houses in muted colours, felt as though it was waiting patiently for the day when the old trade routes would reopen, for a time it could impress yet again.

On a rare break from Ashi Penzon's hospitality, Yeshi and I trekked northeast of Kalimpong to the all-but-forgotten caravan town of Pedong. Standing on a ridge, I could make out a curling, empty road—the old caravan route—as it meandered toward the Tibetan border. Just visible off to my left rose the snow-crowned 8598-metre-high Mount Kanchenjunga, third highest tower of stone on the globe. My gaze took in the two conflicting but iconic views of the Tea Horse Road: a proud, definitive peak and a timid, veiled path.

As my journey drew to an end, I had been feeling the need to check in with my fellow travellers, so one night I called Sonam for an update. He assured me that on my return to Shangri-La a dinner with the team would be set up, under the vigilant eye of Bhaskar. Norbu had married and was still threatening to quit his job, Dorje was bored stiff and complained that no one ever called him, Nomè was not yet finished working on his home, and Tenzin had dropped from sight.

Both Yeshi and I had been content to spend as much time as we had left on our journey with Ashi Penzon. I felt a sense of calm with her, an ability to come to terms with where I was and how I had arrived. She was one of the Earth's givers, one of the great unsung elements of time and space. But eventually, our departure day arrived. We had tea in the tearoom as we had practically every morning. Baking treats and care packages were lined up waiting for us. She had thus occupied herself for years, and it seemed therapeutic for her, a way to diminish a sense of loss. I detested this departure as I detested many leavings along the route. How many before me had she sent off with treats tucked into their satchels; how many men left having been fattened up for yet another trip?

Yeshi and I would return to Kathmandu, promptly get on a plane, and return to Shangri-La, where familiar faces waited for us. Two weeks after that—though too bizarre to contemplate now—I would be leaving Asia. But not before I had made a little side trip—I had made a promise to an old man living beneath Sho La, an old man whose words and face had been entrenched in me for the better part of a year. Dawa.

Departing Kalimpong, it was suddenly clear to me how once again the statistics of the Tea Horse Road were pushed aside by the faces, the trials, and the journeys themselves of the ancients. I reflected on what I believed to be the most important aspect of the Tea Horse Road. It was beyond all else something that had linked people, a great unifying force, a route known by the Tibetans alternatively as Gyalam (Wide Road) or as Drelam (Mule Road), whose name in Chinese, Cha Ma Dao (Tea Horse Road), reflected the components of its parts: a pliant green leaf and the four-legged beast, both crucial and both taking turns to be heroes.

Dakpa, years ago, pointing with his arched finger to the wisp of a trail he had travelled from India, had inspired my own journey on it years later. Unwittingly, he had reanimated a dirt route spanning the grandest mountain range on earth, and fired, if only briefly, the old minds that could still evoke a time of perils and mules, and a time of tea. The world had seen the demise of the tea trade routes, the mule-teers, and the mules as a mode of transport. Ever-practical tea, of course, had retained its allure.

Ashi Penzon waved to us from her little balcony, tears welling in her eyes.

"Some things lead into the realm beyond words," wrote Alexander Solzhenitsyn. Some journeys are best described that way. Beyond paths and distances, they lead us to others, to ourselves ... or, perhaps, to just another teahouse.

Acknowledgments

A huge debt of thanks to Lynn Wang for quiet encouragement from the outset, Neddy Luo for keeping my tea supplies stocked and being a formidable tea instructor, the boys at Khampa Caravan for their incredible logistical work, Dakpa Gedan's compassion and company, Sonam Gelek for unhesitating courage and patience in every situation, Janosz for his passionate reminder never to lose faith, and finally, to those magnificent Himalayas and fearless traders who shared, threatened, and ultimately ushered us throughout an incredible voyage.